UTOPIA METHOD

Ralahine Utopian Studies

Series editors:
Raffaella Baccolini (University of Bologna, at Forlì)
Joachim Fischer (University of Limerick)
Michael J. Griffin (University of Limerick)
Tom Moylan (University of Limerick)

Volume 1

PETER LANG
Oxford · Bern · Berlin · Bruxelles · Frankfurt am Main · New York · Wien

Tom Moylan and Raffaella Baccolini (eds.)

UTOPIA METHOD VISION

THE USE VALUE OF SOCIAL DREAMING

PETER LANG

Oxford · Bern · Berlin · Bruxelles · Frankfurt am Main · New York · Wien

Bibliographic information published by Die Deutsche Nationalbibliothek
Die Deutsche Nationalbibliothek lists this publication in the Deutsche
Nationalbibliografie; detailed bibliographic data is available on the
Internet at http://dnb.d-nb.de.

A catalogue record for this book is available from the British Library.

ISSN 1661-5875
ISBN 978-3-03910-912-8

Third unrevised edition.

© Peter Lang AG, International Academic Publishers, Bern 2007, 2009, 2011
Hochfeldstrasse 32, CH-3012 Bern, Switzerland
info@peterlang.com, www.peterlang.com, www.peterlang.net

Printed in Germany

Dedicated to

Lewis L. Glucksman (1925 – 2006)

Visionary

and

Patron and Friend

of

Irish

Culture and Education

Contents

Acknowledgements

Our first acknowledgement is to our contributors, not only for their essays but also for the seminar presentations and discussions leading up to them and, not least, for their promptness, cooperation, patience, and enthusiasm for this project. More broadly, we thank the community of utopian scholars, in particular the members of the Society for Utopian Studies (North America), the Utopian Studies Society (Europe), the Centro Interdipartimentale di Ricerca sull'Utopia (Italy), and the Ralahine Centre for Utopian Studies (Ireland), for the collective body of work that provides the larger context for this collection. We would also like to thank our undergraduate and post-graduate students who, at several universities in several countries, have shared in and challenged our engagements with utopian thought and practice.

More immediately, we want to thank all those who helped to produce the original series of "Utopia Method Vision" seminars sponsored by the Ralahine Centre for Utopian Studies at the University of Limerick. For funding, we acknowledge and appreciate the support provided by the Irish Research Council for the Humanities and Social Sciences; the Research Office, College of Humanities, and Department of Languages and Cultural Studies of the University of Limerick; the Department of Interdisciplinary Studies on Translation, Language, and Culture (SITLeC) and the Advanced School for Interpreters and Translators (SSLMIT) of the University of Bologna at Forlì; the National University of Ireland, Galway, Centre for Irish Studies; the Queen's University, Belfast, Institute of Irish Studies; the Canadian Fulbright Commission; and Loretta and Lewis Glucksman. For helping to organize and expedite the seminars, we thank Marie Kirwan and Claire L. Ryan at the University of Limerick and Louis de Paor and John Eastlake at the National University of Ireland, Galway. And, we thank all those who joined in the discussion and debate at the seminars held at the University of Limerick and the National University of Ireland, Galway.

We are particularly grateful to the people who worked with us in producing this volume – the first in the Ralahine Utopian Studies book series: in particular our Peter Lang editor, Alexis Kirschbaum; our Ralahine series cover designer, David Lilburn; our *UMV* cover designers, Roberta Baccolini and David Lilburn; our Ralahine series copy-editor, Maureen O'Connor; our production editor, Helena Sedgwick; and our indexer, Letizia Cirillo.

Raffaella would like to thank her colleagues at the University of Bologna: especially, the members of the research group on "national identity," Diana Bianchi, Derek Boothman, Adele D'Arcangelo, Patrick Leech, Simona Sangiorgi, Ira Torresi, Jenny Varney, and Sam Whitsitt for their inspiring discussions; Rita Monticelli and Rosa Maria Bollettieri for stimulating conversations and friendship. She is also grateful to Breda Gray and Sinead McDermott of the University of Limerick for their exchanges on memory. She thanks fellow utopians Lyman Tower Sargent and Hoda Zaki for encouragement and thought-provoking questions, and is grateful to Tom Moylan who did all the traveling during the time it took them to complete this project. Most of all she would like to thank the women in her life who variously contribute to make her work possible: Adua Nesi, Roberta Baccolini, Maria Rosa Appi, Bruna Conconi, and Anna Vitiello all offered support, assistance, food, babysitting, conversations, love, and friendship. Finally, she wants to thank the men in her life for making her existence more difficult and yet more interesting: Giuseppe Lusignani and Giacomo Lusignani who with their negotiations, support, and love continue to help her to redefine perspectives and priorities on life and loving.

Tom would like to thank his colleagues at the University of Limerick: especially, Vice President for Research Vincent Cunnane; College of Humanities Dean Pat O'Connor; COH Dean of Research Eugene O'Brien; COH Humanities Librarian Pattie Punch; Department of Languages and Cultural Studies Head Martin Chappell; and his Ralahine Centre fellow travelers (Joachim Fischer, Associate Director; Luke Ashworth; Liam Bannon; Bríona Nic Dhiarmada; Breda Gray; Michael Griffin, Michael Kelley, Carmen Kuhling; Patricia

Lynch; Serge Riviere; Tina O'Toole; Geraldine Sheridan; Mícheál Ó'Súilleabháin). He thanks Luke Gibbons and Terry Eagleton for their interest in and support for the Ralahine Centre, and he is most grateful to Raffaella Baccolini and Giuseppe Lusignani, and Jack Zipes and Carol Dines for their hospitality in Bologna and Rome. For their long-standing advice and wisdom, he thanks Lyman Tower Sargent, Vince Geoghegan, Ruth Levitas, and Tadhg Foley; and he thanks Raffaella Baccolini for another enriching collaboration. Finally, he thanks Katie Moylan and Sarah Moylan yet again for proving that utopian aspirations are worth it. And, Susan McManus for life and for love.

TOM MOYLAN AND RAFFAELLA BACCOLINI

Introduction: Utopia as Method

Utopia

Since the millennial year of 2000, there has been a growing attention
to Utopia and its uses. In the names given to products and services,
this traditional appeal to a better world is associated with the pursuit
of immediate, material satisfaction and happiness. With a Utopia bank
loan (Ireland), Utopia jewelry line (Italy), Utopia clothing store (Aus-
tralia and New Zealand), Utopia financial service (Ireland), Utopia
adult entertainment shop (Ireland), Utopia fitness and well-being
(U.K.), Utopia trailer park (U.S.), Utopia yarn (U.S.), Utopia security
(Italy), Utopia furniture (U.S.), Utopia night club (U.K.), Utopia as an
acronym for Universal Test and Operations Physical Interface for
ATM (U.S.), and Utopia computer games and toys, such as Dinotopia
and Barbie Fairytopia, we see this once-denigrated notion alive and
well in the commercial imagination. More overtly, we see appeals to a
better world embedded in political initiatives ranging from the George
W. Bush administration's "Project for a New American Century" to
the World Social Forum's claim that "Another world is possible."

This utopian revival in popular and political spheres has, simultaneously, been paralleled by a series of challenges to the legitimacy
and efficacy of utopian anticipations. In both the apocalyptic preach-
ing of religious leaders and the pragmatic planning of policy makers,
the idea of a utopian alternative in this world is condemned as sinful
hubris, useless speculation, or dangerous intervention. On a theoretical
level, utopian thought and practice has been rejected by studies as
diverse as Francis Fukuyama's *The End of History and the Last Man*
and Oliver Bennett's *Cultural Pessimism: Narratives of Decline in the
Postmodern World*.

In a significant development, however, this twinned revival and renunciation of Utopia has been countered at a more substantial level in theoretical works such as David Harvey's *Spaces of Hope*, Zygmunt Bauman's *Community: Seeking Safety in an Insecure World*, and Fredric Jameson's *Archaeologies of the Future: The Desire Called Utopia and Other Science Fictions*; and in creative works such as Ursula K. Le Guin's *The Telling*, Kim Stanley Robinson's *Mars* trilogy and *The Years of Rice and Salt*, and Robert Newman's *The Fountain at the Center of the World*, and films such as Michael Bay's *The Island* and John Sayles's *Limbo*. As it investigates both theory and creative practice, our 2003 collection, *Dark Horizons: Science Fiction and the Dystopian Imagination*, traced this persistence of Utopia in recent dystopian fiction, film, and politics. In a series of essays by scholars from different countries and in different fields, the stubborn presence of utopian hope was examined in a range of works in the new dystopian writings and films of the 1990s as well as in the political practices that came alive in that decade. In what we called the *critical dystopia*, we examined a series of texts in which a militant or utopian stance "not only breaks through the hegemonic enclosure of the text's alternative world but also self-reflexively refuses the anti-utopian temptation that lingers in every dystopian account" (Baccolini and Moylan, "Introduction" 7). Whereas the traditional dystopia maintains hope, if at all, *outside* its pages, the new critical dystopias preserve hope *inside* their pages as they "allow both readers and protagonists to hope" by imagining resistant utopian enclaves within the dystopian world and by proffering – through a strategy of "genre blurring" – ambiguous open endings that resist closure (7).[1] In so doing, we affirmed the importance of utopian critique in scholarly studies of culture and society and in political life.

While this utopian renaissance is relatively recent, the paradigm for scholarly investigations of utopian thought and practice developed

---

1   Examples of critical dystopias include print works such as Le Guin's *The Telling*, Robinson's *Antarctica*, Marge Piercy's *He, She and It*, Margaret Atwood's *The Handmaid's Tale*, and Octavia E. Butler's *Parable of the Sower*, and films such as Gary Ross's *Pleasantville*, James Cameron's *Terminator*, and Andy and Larry Wachowski's *Matrix* trilogy.

in the mid 1960s and has since been elaborated within the field of utopian studies. Organized in professional societies in both Europe and North America, and in Research Centers such as those in Limerick and Bologna, and furthered by publications (book series – Syracuse University Press, Longo, and Peter Lang – bibliographies, monographs, collections, and essays in the journal *Utopian Studies* and elsewhere), international conferences, and an increasing number of taught courses, the scholarly articulation of Utopia has grown in archival, theoretical, and pedagogical sophistication. Working with this current utopian turn, several leading scholars have broken new ground in the field. Among recent studies, Phillip E. Wegner's *Imaginary Communities: Utopia, the Nation, and the Spatial Histories of Modernity* brings the utopian problematic to bear on our understanding of the production of modernity and of nation. In *Living in Utopia: Intentional Communities in New Zealand*, Lucy Sargisson and Lyman Tower Sargent extend the utopian ethnographic gaze beyond traditional western parameters as they study the rich array of utopian communities in this Pacific state. In *Utopian Audiences: How Readers Locate Nowhere*, Kenneth M. Roemer delivers an important new theoretical and methodological approach through the first fully developed analysis of utopian texts by way of reader reception. Finally, Hoda Zaki's *Civil Rights and Politics at Hampton Institute: The Legacy of Alonzo G. Moron* deploys a utopian framework in her study of the U.S. civil rights movement.

Utopia Method Vision

Utopia Method Vision: The Use Value of Social Dreaming grows out of the work of these scholars and others. Between spring 2003 and autumn 2004, the Ralahine Centre for Utopian Studies of the University of Limerick invited twelve international scholars in utopian studies (from Canada, England, Ireland, Italy, Northern Ireland, and the United States) to participate in a two-year research seminar. In

parallel meetings at the Ralahine Centre in Limerick and the Centre
for Irish Studies at the National University of Ireland, Galway, the
participants addressed the ways in which they approached their study
of the objects and practices of utopianism (understood as social
anticipations and visions produced through texts and social experiments) and how, in turn, those objects and practices have shaped their
intellectual work in general and their research perspectives in particular. In so doing, the participants helped to develop a larger, self-
critical look at the limits and potential of the entire paradigm by which
utopianism is known, studied, critiqued, created, and received. Thus,
this collection that grows out of these seminars has a unique focus on
researchers themselves (as intellectuals, as citizens), while it also
concerns itself with the substance and impact of utopianism in its
examination of the object of study, and of the purpose, method, and
impact of that research.

Utopia Method Vision (*UMV*) therefore intervenes in critical and
cultural studies as it encourages a productive self-reflexivity that we
hope will expand the substance of utopian research, critique, and
practice. This focus is informed by feminist, Marxist, ethnographic,
and post-structuralist theories on the standpoint or positionality of
researchers and the impact of that standpoint on the objects and
practices of study (and vice versa); however, the collection does not
stop at the register of self-assessment. Rather, the self-reflexive
moment opens into an interrogation of current research in utopian
studies and an exploration of new research directions on objects and
practices freshly approached in terms of the utopian process.

Method

Coming from different academic disciplines as well as different
national traditions, the *UMV* contributors engage in a shared exploration of their method and vision. In this regard, they enter a
general conversation on research method that is of current concern in

the social sciences and in cultural and literary studies.[2] Beginning with a look backward at the individual contributor's particular standpoint and early engagement with utopianism, each essay moves forward to identify and explore new areas of investigation and intervention.

Focusing on both textual and experiential versions of utopianism and on the question of its political future, the contributors address larger historical and theoretical issues even as they identify further opportunities for textual, ethnographic, and political studies. In the course of this discussion, specific objects analyzed include political phenomena such as the U.S. civil rights movement, the anti-globalization/alter-globalization movement, the intentional community movement, fundamentalist utopianism, the World Conference Against Racism, and the World Social Forum; literary texts such as Thomas More's *Utopia* (Eng.), William Morris's *News from Nowhere* (Eng.), Edward Bellamy's *Looking Backward* (U.S.), Joanna Russ's "When It Changed" (U.S.), Bernadette Mayer's *Utopia* (U.S.), Octavia E. Butler's *Parable of the Sower* (U.S.), Kim Stanley Robinson's *Mars* trilogy and *The Years of Rice and Salt* (U.S.); and films such as John Sayles's *Men with Guns* (U.S.) and Marco Bellocchio's *Buongiorno, notte* (Italy).

The volume opens with Lucy Sargisson's essay, "The Curious Relationship Between Politics and Utopia." Sargisson begins with definitions of both Utopia and politics, and she moves into a theoretical interrogation of the nature and practice of politics. From this, she presents a defense of Utopia by way of her critique of the anti-utopian position as advanced by Karl Popper, Jacob L. Talmon, and others. She then reflects on her ethnographic studies of intentional communities in Britain and New Zealand; and, in particular, she discusses the importance of the processes of decision-making and consensus-building in creating and sustaining such utopian experiments. She ends by emphasizing the deep relationship between utopian theory and politics and asserting their increasingly necessary linkage.

---

2   See, for example, Clifford and Marcus's *Writing Culture*, Jameson's *Brecht and Method*, Greenblatt and Gunn's *Redrawing the Boundaries*, and Heckman's "Truth and Method."

In "The Imaginary Reconstitution of Society: Utopia as Method," Ruth Levitas shifts to a direct focus on Utopia and method as it grew out of the theoretical work of H.G. Wells and the discipline of sociology. After describing her development as a utopian scholar and activist – and her particular engagement with the work of William Morris and the locale of Hammersmith – she introduces her own major methodological contribution: "IROS," or the imaginary reconstitution of society. This analytical and political method involves "the construction or constitution of society as it is, as it might be, as it might not be, as it might be hoped for or feared." In doing so, it offers both "an *archaeological* or analytical mode, and an *architectural* or constructive mode" that can contribute to Utopia's most radical function, that of transformation.

This essay is followed by Vincent Geoghegan's "Political Theory, Utopia, Post-Secularism." Geoghegan begins with a review of the canon of political theory (from Immanuel Kant to John Rawls) as it has developed over the last forty years. He then relates his own study of and critical engagement with political and utopian thought. While he values categories not always privileged in utopian studies – namely, Utopia as a realist mode, or perfection as a legitimate utopian attitude – he also stresses the importance of the ethical stance within the utopian process. Drawing on his own studies of Ernst Bloch's work on religion, he ends his essay with an extended analysis of the contemporary discourse of post-secularism.

Next, Gregory Claeys, in "Rethinking Modern British Utopianism: Community and the Mastery of Desire," explores the eighteenth- and nineteenth-century British utopian imagination by way of a self-critical reflection on his extensive archival and scholarly work. He moves from a personal account of his engagement with Utopia to a discussion of his long-term project on British utopianism, as it has moved from studies of early modern to contemporary utopian writing. He develops a critique of the received thinking on British utopianism and offers his own re-interpretation of how British utopias responded to the changing pressures and needs of modernity. He specifically develops an analysis of the ways in which desire and want were addressed and managed through a "combination of explicit regulation, laws and customs, and an ideology which reinforces and underpins such regulations."

The collection continues with Phillip E. Wegner's "Here or Nowhere: Utopia, Modernity, and Totality," wherein he explores his own development in utopian studies by way of a long-standing engagement with the work of Fredric Jameson. He approaches Utopia as a "problematic": that is, "not a set of propositions about reality, but a set of categories in terms of which reality is analyzed and interrogated" (Jameson, "Science Versus Ideology" 283). With this hermeneutical approach, he addresses the place of utopian figuration as a form of cognitive mapping within textual studies and social critique. He concludes by asserting the deep link "between the figure of utopia, the concept of totality, and the project of revolution."

Kenneth M. Roemer's essay, "More Aliens Transforming Utopia: The Futures of Reader Response and Utopian Studies," opens with an account of his entry into utopian studies by way of American studies. He then describes his teaching of utopian texts and explains how this led him into his work with reception studies. As he summarizes what became a twenty-year project of studying readers' responses to Edward Bellamy's *Looking Backward*, he reminds us of the ways in which diverse readers give meaning and reality to utopian texts. Looking forward from his *Utopian Audiences*, he suggests a range of possible new research projects that could emanate from his approach. He concludes by stressing the importance of what he calls *book power*, "the belief that reading a book can transform readers and their societies."

In "Finding Utopia in Dystopia: Feminism, Memory, Nostalgia, and Hope," Raffaella Baccolini begins her essay with her personal and political encounter with Utopia, and dystopia. She then traces some of the ways in which feminist literary and cultural theory intersects with utopian studies. In so doing, she links questions of location and positionality with issues of desire, memory, and nostalgia in a perspective informed by gender. Bringing this critical matrix to a discussion of the nature of the utopian genre, she especially foregrounds the production of resistance and hope through a "critical nostalgia" and illustrates this in examples taken from contemporary literary and filmic dystopias (see Russ, Sayles, Braghetti/Bellocchio).

Tom Moylan's "Realizing Better Futures, Strong Thought for Hard Times" narrates the place and development of a utopian impulse in his personal, political, and professional lives. In particular, he discusses the activity of reading and its relationship to political activism. Reviewing his studies of science fiction (sf), liberation theology, political theory (Bloch, especially), and dystopias, he stresses the place of the *political* within the utopian project. Ending with a discussion of Utopia's temporal dynamics, he reflects on the pedagogical and political impact of the ephemeral, yet long-lasting quality of Utopia, especially as it produces a "temporal solidarity" across generations.

In "Utopia and the Beloved Community," Naomi Jacobs takes a self-reflexive look at her professional and political practice in the scholarly community of utopian studies. In so doing, she describes "the informal web of relations and the collaborative, sociable approach to intellectual work" that attracted her to the field. Having identified such communal qualities, she then discovers a similar dialogic method in the creative work of Bernadette Mayer and her community of New York poets. She closely examines Mayer's 1984 text, *Utopia*, describing how it grew out of a series of experimental workshops grounded, "like the discipline of utopian studies, in *friendship*, expressing a free exchange of ideas among friends rather than the solitary, potentially obsessive delineation of a private vision."

Peter Fitting, in "Beyond This Horizon: Utopian Visions and Utopian Practice," also discusses Jameson's utopian theory as he examines the link between artistic creation and political activism through studies of sf and the World Social Forum. Mapping his political and professional development, he identifies three moments: a "pre-utopian" moment of sf and Marxism; a "utopian moment" stimulated by 1970s feminist sf; and a moment of "rethinking" utopian optimism, in which he moved from a focus on utopian content (now seen as dangerously reformist) to utopian form (as a radical method). He concludes with a "paradoxical reaffirmation of the need for utopian imagining, even as these visions and descriptions are not meant to be taken literally, but [...] to remind us of all that we lack and are denied by the crushing mechanisms of capital."

In "New Spaces for Utopian Politics: Theorizing About Identity, Community, and the World Conference Against Racism," Hoda Zaki also focuses on Utopia and politics as she examines the concept of community in her analysis of the World Conference Against Racism (WCAR). In a personal trajectory that moves from Egypt to the U.S., she discusses how her early reading of sf and her activism led her to a study of the political value of Utopia through a critical reading of 1970s utopian sf. She then describes her shift to studies of the utopian, political efficacy of communities in two areas: the U.S. civil rights movement and the WCAR. In a detailed analysis of the latter, she identifies this "temporary utopian zone" (esp. its NGO component) as "the site and catalyst for the rebirth of a long-dormant, global, anti-racist civic community."

The collection closes with Lyman Tower Sargent's "Choosing Utopia: Utopianism as an Essential Element in Political Thought and Action." After discussing his first studies of Utopia (centered on "the simple statement that it is easier to get somewhere if you know where you want to go"), he offers an ethical, political meditation on utopian scholarship, texts, and practices based in his extensive bibliographical and theoretical work. Accepting that Utopia can be dangerous, he claims that it is nonetheless essential. After delineating what he uniquely terms "utopian energy" (i.e., "the will/willingness/ability to create new forms"), he argues for the necessity of making a choice for Utopia (with the caveat that this "must be based on educational and persuasive discussion, not coercion"). He concludes by asserting that when "we choose Utopia, we are choosing the possibility of a better life in the future, not necessarily [...] a particular set of institutions. Usually what we accomplish is less than we desired, and, after a rest, we dream again, achieve something, and dream again."

Works Cited

Atwood, Margaret. *The Handmaid's Tale*. Toronto: McClelland, 1985.
Baccolini, Raffaella, and Tom Moylan (eds.). *Dark Horizons: Science Fiction and the Dystopian Imagination*. New York: Routledge, 2003.
Bauman, Zygmunt. *Community: Seeking Safety in an Insecure World*. London: Polity, 2001.
Bellamy, Edward. *Looking Backward, 2000–1887*. 1888. Ed. John Thomas. Cambridge, Massachusetts: Belknap-Harvard University Press, 1967.
Bennett, Oliver. *Cultural Pessimism: Narratives of Decline in the Postmodern World*. Edinburgh: Edinburgh University Press, 2000.
Bloch, Ernst. *The Principle of Hope*. Trans. Neville Plaice, Stephen Plaice, and Paul Knight. 3 Vols. Oxford: Blackwell, 1986.
Buongiorno, notte. Dir. Marco Bellocchio. 2003.
Butler, Octavia E. *Parable of the Sower*. New York: Four Walls Eight Windows, 1993.
Clifford, James, and George Marcus (eds.). *Writing Culture: The Poetics and Politics of Ethnography*. Berkeley: University of California Press, 1986.
Fukuyama, Francis. *The End of History and the Last Man*. New York: Free Press, 1992.
Greenblatt, Stephen, and Giles Gunn (eds.). *Redrawing the Boundaries: The Transformation of English in American Literary Studies*. New York: MLA, 1992.
Harvey, David. *Spaces of Hope*. Edinburgh: Edinburgh University Press, 2000.
Heckman, Susan. "Truth and Method: Feminist Standpoint Theory Revisited." *Signs* 22.2 (1997): 341–402.
Island, The. Dir. Michael Bay. 2005.
Jameson, Fredric. *Archaeologies of the Future: The Desire Called Utopia and Other Science Fictions*. London: Verso, 2005.
—— *Brecht and Method*. London: Verso, 1998.
—— "Science Versus Ideology." *Humanities in Society* 6.2 (1983): 283–302.
Le Guin, Ursula K. *The Telling*. New York: Harcourt, 2000.
Limbo. Dir. John Sayles. 1999.
Matrix, The. Dir. Andy Wachowski and Larry Wachowski, 1999.
Mayer, Bernadette. *Utopia*. New York: United Artists, 1984.
Men with Guns. Dir. John Sayles. 1997.
More, Thomas. *Utopia: A New Translation, Backgrounds, Criticism*. 1516. Ed. and trans. Robert M. Adams. New York: Norton, 1975.
Newman, Robert. *The Fountain at the Center of the World*. Brooklyn: Soft Skull Press, 2004.
Piercy, Marge. *He, She and It*. New York: Knopf, 1991.
Pleasantville. Dir. Gary Ross. 1998.
Robinson, Kim Stanley. *Antarctica*. New York: Harper Collins, 1997.

—— *Blue Mars*. New York: Harper Collins, 1996.

—— *Green Mars*. New York: Harper Collins, 1993.

—— *Red Mars*. New York: Harper Collins, 1992.

—— *The Years of Rice and Salt*. New York: Harper Collins, 2002.

Roemer, Kenneth M. *Utopian Audiences: How Readers Locate Nowhere*. Amherst: University of Massachusetts Press, 2003.

Russ, Joanna. "When It Changed." *Again, Dangerous Visions*. Ed. Harlan Ellison. Garden City: Doubleday, 1972. 233–41.

Sargisson, Lucy, and Lyman Tower Sargent. *Living in Utopia: New Zealand's Intentional Communities*. Aldershot: Ashgate, 2004.

Terminator. Dir. James Cameron, 1984.

Wegner, Phillip E. *Imaginary Communities: Utopia, the Nation, and the Spatial Histories of Modernity*. Berkeley: University of California Press, 2002.

Zaki, Hoda. *Civil Rights and Politics at Hampton Institute: The Legacy of Alonzo G. Moron*. Champaign: University of Illinois Press, 2006.

LUCY SARGISSON

The Curious Relationship Between Politics and Utopia

The relationship between politics and Utopia is curious because politics often rejects utopianism and yet politics is built on utopias. This essay seeks to explore and revive the ambivalent relationship between politics and Utopia and to suggest that whilst utopianism can be a dangerous phenomenon, it is both omnipresent and necessary to the world of politics. My own preferred conception of politics draws on feminist and post-structuralist accounts and methods; and so, for me, politics is about relations of power, which are often deeply embedded in the way that we think about and interact with the world. This includes our personal relationships, our language, and the economies of exchange that we engage in every day. It also includes decision-making, governance, and citizenship. My essay is therefore informed by this approach to the political but refers also to narrower conceptions, suggesting that Utopia speaks also to these. Politics and Utopia, I suggest, exist in a symbiotic relationship and we need to come to terms with this.

Utopias are as old as political thought itself. Plato's *Republic* is the best-known early utopia, although it was not the first.[1] The genre and the word, of course, were invented by Thomas More and entered the vocabulary in 1516, with the publication of *Utopia*. The word "utopia" phonetically conflates an etymological pun on three Greek terms: *eu,* good; *ou,* non or not; and *topos*, place. Utopia is thus the good place that is no place. The study of Utopia is multidisciplinary, traversing such diverse fields as archaeology, philosophy, literary

---

1   For example, Sargent and Claeys begin their *Utopia Reader* with an extract from Hesiod, dated to the eighth century, B.C.

studies, economics, legal studies, architecture, sociology, and politics.[2]
Given this, it is unsurprising that there are many different approaches
to utopianism. However, there is broad agreement amongst specialists
about what the term means and the terrain it covers.[3] The word
"utopia," as used in this essay, adheres to these conventions and is an
umbrella term, encompassing utopianism, utopias, eutopias, and dystopias. Utopianism refers to what Lyman Tower Sargent calls "social
dreaming": "the dreams and nightmares that concern the ways in
which groups of people arrange their lives" ("Three Faces Revisited"
3). Utopias are expressions of this process, articulating, as Ruth
Levitas has established, the desire for a better way of being. They
stem always from discontent with the now and gesture always towards
a better life. Their dreams are expressed in many forms, not just, as
was once thought, fictions, but also in social and political theory, lived
experiments, works of art, music, medicine, and architecture (see
Bloch). My discussion in this essay will be restricted to utopian
fiction, theory, and intentional communities. The eutopia is a vision of
a better place, while the dystopia depicts a nightmare world where
one's worst fears are realized. Many fictional utopias contain both.
Discontented with the now and desiring a better future, utopians
imagine alternative worlds and different ways of being. Utopias tell us
about people's fears concerning the now and desires for tomorrow. As
such, they represent a valuable tool for anyone interested in politics.

   There is no consensus on defining politics. It is variously conceived of as an activity, a set of assumptions, institutions and/or
practices, and a discipline, and there is no consensus about the content
of any of these. Some tie it to specific locations (such as the public
sphere); others insist that it is to be found in all relationships between
people. Even the parameters of the discipline are contested, including
narrow "hard" conceptions of political science, commonly found in

2   See the websites for the Society for Utopian Studies in North America,
    established in 1975 <http://www.toronto.edu.sus>, and her European sister
    organisation, the Utopian Studies Society, established in 1980 <http://www.
    utopianstudiessociety.org>.
3   As defined by Sargent, "Three Faces" and "Three Faces of Utopianism Re-
    visited."

the U.S., to more broadly defined "soft" political studies of some institutions in the U.K. Divisions occur between theorists and empiricists, and also amongst these groupings. When the members of York University's Politics Department decided to write the textbook *What is Politics?*, they little anticipated the difficulties this would cause (see Leftwich). The resulting text is useful; but the process was, it seems, divisive. Within my own sub-discipline of political theory, for example, one encounters methodological and epistemological differences between and amongst analytical Anglo-American political thinkers, normative political theorists, political sociologists, modernists and postmodernists, structuralists and post-structuralists, Marxists, post-Marxists, neo-Marxists, Gramscians, neo-Gramscians, and feminists (including liberal, radical, socialist, black, eco-, French, standpoint, and empiricist), to name but a few. This essay suggests that Utopia is an important aspect of all conceptions of politics. This means that Utopia has something to offer all scholars of politics, and for this reason a variety of competing conceptions of the political are taken at face value in the discussions that follow.

My discussion begins with a refutation of an influential anti-utopian tendency within the discipline of politics which is based on the idea that utopias are dangerous. This stems from a common mistake about the relationship between Utopia and perfectionism. The first section of my essay, then, is concerned with these long-standing debates. I then move on to consider what I call the symbiotic relationship between politics and Utopia, a relationship of mutual benefit and dependence.

Anti-Utopianism Within the Discipline of Politics

Anti-utopians fear that Utopia will lead to the end of history, politics, and change. At the root of this fear is a mistaken association between utopianism and perfection, and between utopianism and fundamentalism. This is complicated. Briefly though, exponents of this view believe that utopianism is at some essential and definitional level, perfection seeking, authoritarian, and intolerant of dissent. In order to explore these fears and beliefs, I will briefly examine the arguments of this view's chief proponent, Karl Popper.

Looking back at Hitler's fascism and Stalin's communism, Popper identified a certain totalitarianism at work in the shadows of utopianism. He believed the utopian project to be inevitably repressive, and his stance has three key aspects. First, there is a commitment to a certain epistemology drawing on liberal individualism: Utopia is supposed to make us all happy, but how could one person know another's interests or desires? Second, stemming from this, there is a fear of repression. One person's dream may be another's nightmare (indeed, feminists have pointed out that men's utopias are often women's dystopias), and yet utopias are supposed to be perfect. If a utopia contains a blueprint for the perfect world, there can be no space for dissent.[4] They must therefore be repressive. Third, there is a conservative view of the possibility of change, which again has its roots in an epistemological claim about the limits of human knowledge. Popper reasons that:

> the Utopian approach can be saved only by the Platonic belief in one absolute and unchanging ideal, together with two further assumptions, namely (a) that there are rational methods to determine once and for all what this ideal is, and (b) what the best means of its realization are (161).

Both of these requirements, he feels, exceed human capacities. Like Edmund Burke and other conservative thinkers, he believes that we cannot have perfect and complete knowledge of the world around us. It is impossible to predict the outcomes of widespread social change and "hardly any social action ever produces precisely the result anticipated" (Popper 164). Further, he believes that the only route to a non-oppressive utopia is to establish one clear, consensual, and universally agreed blueprint. And this is impossible. These claims are based in beliefs about humankind, our nature and our limitations, as well as certain beliefs about the content and function of utopias.

---

4   See, for instance, Baruch; Barr and Smith.

Popper's criticisms have been influential. Other critics, such as Leonard Schapiro and Jacob L. Talmon, have constructed a picture of Utopia as the antithesis of liberalism. Here, the liberal quest for human development through the exercise of toleration, freedom of speech, and a pluralist society, as articulated by John Stuart Mill, is challenged by a utopianism that holds the solutions to all problems.

Scholars of Utopia have long disputed these criticisms, on several counts. Some engage in close readings of Popper. They commonly claim that he (and others) misread the utopias they criticize. For example, Ronald Levinson challenges Popper's interpretation of Plato. Robin Waterfield suggests that Plato's *Republic* is a thought experiment, an investigation into the nature of the individual, and not a blueprint for the ideal polity. Others make bolder claims about utopian method and epistemology. Barbara Goodwin and Keith Taylor challenge "the liberal's trial-and-error political empiricism" and claim that Utopia adds to the study of politics (94). Utopian epistemology and method are valid approaches to political questions:

> in general, utopias enrich our understanding of the world by offering a global, or total, view of ideal social organisation and operation, by contrast with the more partial, schematic views proffered by political theory (207).

For them, the totalizing nature of utopias has positive outcomes. It allows us to imagine ideas in the round, and to consider how innovations in one sphere of life might impact on another. In modern parlance, utopias encourage "joined-up thinking."

I suggest that the *key* flaw in Popper's work lies in a common mistake about the nature of Utopia. He wrongly assumes Utopia to be perfection-seeking. He is far from the first to make this error, for Utopia has long been associated with perfection. Early scholars, like Moritz Kaufmann, made the connection between perfection and Utopia, and it has stuck fast. In 1879, Kaufmann wrote:

> What is a Utopia? Strictly speaking, it means a "nowhere Land," some happy island far away, where perfect social relations prevail, and human beings, living under an immaculate constitution and a faultless government, enjoy a simple and happy existence, free from the turmoil, the harassing cares, and endless worries of actual life (quoted in Levitas 12).

Even today, dictionary definitions and colloquial usages tend to assume perfection as a characteristic feature of Utopia. The 1993 edition of the *New Shorter Oxford English Dictionary*, for instance, defines it as:

> the title of a book by Sir Thomas More (1477–1535). 1) (a) An imaginary or hypothetical place or state of things considered to be perfect; a condition of ideal (esp. social) perfection. (b) An imaginary or distant country. 2) An impossibly ideal scheme, esp. for social improvement.

We can see how the second definition follows from the first – i.e., Utopia is impossible because it seeks perfection – and how the methodological objection to Utopia cited in the introduction follows from this observation about Utopia's content. Politics should not seek Utopia because perfection is unattainable. This is a distraction (see Arendt) and/or dangerous (see Popper).

These assumptions make perfection a crucial factor in anti-utopian critiques. And the fact is that some utopias *are* clearly supposed to be pictures of perfection. Some utopias *are* clearly suggestions for social blueprints. But not all are, and perfection cannot be taken as a defining feature of Utopia, as has long been argued by scholars of Utopia (for examples of this stance, see Wells; Moylan, *Demand*; and Sargent, "Three Faces Revisited"). Perfection is a final condition, it is static and it does not change. However, utopias are rarely static. More's *Utopia*, for example, is not. *Utopia* is, amongst other things, a thought experiment, a polemic, and an exploration of alternatives. Moreover, many utopias are self-consciously flawed. In *Utopia*, More plays and explores; puns and jokes run through the text, undermining it even as the story unfolds: the apparently wise Hytholoday is the "peddlar of nonsense," the river Anyder means "without water," and so on. Some suggest that More wrote a deliberately flawed utopia (see Morton; Logan and Adam). Its very name is a paradox – the good place that is no place – and paradoxes run throughout the text and indeed throughout the genre.

Indeed, utopias of the late-twentieth and early-twenty-first century are often *marked* by incompleteness, offering sometimes just a glimpse of the good life. Many include a dystopia as well as a eutopia.

Often the world depicted stands on the verge of change – Marge Piercy's *Woman on the Edge of Time* is typical of this trend, as is the more recent *Mars* trilogy by Kim Stanley Robinson. In both cases the protagonists find themselves in a crucial position; their actions affect the course of future history, which could be dystopian, eutopian, or both. In both cases, the glimpsed eutopias are dynamic worlds in which change and flux continue, humans are imperfect, and conflict still occurs. These are imaginary "good places," but they are far from perfect. More's original pun writes an essential ambiguity into the very concept of Utopia. It is the good place *and* it is no place. It never arrives.

In what follows, I suggest that utopias are far more than blueprints for a perfect world, and that this has important implications for political studies. The function of Utopia is not its own realization. Once we realize this, we can begin to see what a truly interesting phenomenon this is. We note the warnings discussed above; those who dismiss Popper out of hand are, I think, mistaken. He helps us to see that *if* we identify Utopia with perfection *and* attempt to realize it, the consequences could be terrible. Dreams of perfection informed Hitler's utopia of a pure and noble Germany. He sought to eliminate imperfections, firstly through the (euphemistically named) euthanasia program and then through the mass murder of the Final Solution. Politics and Utopia *could* have a relationship that ends in authoritarianism, totalitarianism, or fundamentalism, with the death of change and progress. Utopia needs, therefore, to be approached with great caution. But approach it we must.

Politics and Utopia

Utopias and politics are clearly different; and yet utopianism is embedded in politics. Utopia lives within politics and utopias are political. First, utopias often tackle political themes. Here, I refer to the view that politics is a process of discussion and debate of contested issues. Second, utopianism has political functions. Here, I draw on a conception of radical or revolutionary politics as a process or activity that subverts and changes our world. In several senses, then, politics and Utopia can both be said to belong to the same "community" of social commentary.

Political Themes

This is an enormous topic, and I can but gesture towards the scope of political issues addressed by utopias. Briefly, utopias (eutopias and dystopias) are a route into the debates of their time. They address political themes critically and creatively, telling us what is wrong with the now and how it might be improved. Historically, for example, More addressed the issues of poverty and punishment, property ownership, the relationship between Church and state, and between counsel and monarch, as well as less obviously political themes, such as town planning, travel, and dress codes. Recent utopias address current preoccupations with issues such as environmental degradation, racial inequalities, gender, and globalization. Octavia E. Butler's critical dystopia *Parable of the Sower* and Kim Stanley Robinson's *Mars* trilogy address all of these themes.

Robinson's trilogy is massive, covering three eight-hundred-page volumes (*Red Mars*, *Green Mars*, and *Blue Mars*). Written towards the end of the last century, the trilogy addresses many contemporary political themes, including those of political economy, environmental politics, party politics, and the politics of self/other relations. Robinson imagines Earth to be in a crisis that develops over the three volumes into total system meltdown. Power and capital have become increasingly concentrated in the hands of a few transnational corporations, some of which even "own" nation states. Global warming has caused climate change to the extent that in the third volume we learn that the ice-caps of the Antarctic have melted, causing the sea level to rise seven meters. Ten percent of the world's population is displaced as low-lying countries become shallow oceans. Robinson has extrapolated from the present concerns about the environment and the globalization of capital, and he imagines them reaching this apocalyptic conclusion.

Against this backdrop the main story occurs on Mars and follows the colonization of that planet. It is rendered inhabitable by the "First Hundred," an international group of scientists, and is humanity's opportunity to begin afresh, to build a better world. However, we soon observe power plays between and amongst nation states, transnational corporations, and the factions that arise within the First Hundred. We can identify a Nietzschean will to power in the maneuvering of some characters, namely Frank Chalmers of the First Hundred and Jackie, one of the Nisei. And we observe Machiavellian manipulations as Frank negotiates with Earth's states, intra-state organizations, and transnationals.

Politics in the classic Arendtian sense (of activity between plural beings) is alive and well in this utopia. Mars has the potential to become many things including a dystopian transnational outpost with wage-slaves stripping the planet of minerals for Earth, a Green or Red eutopia (a pristine planet or a lush artificially created paradise), or a dystopian anarchy of constant civil war. The characters are developed in such a way as to permit plurality to be apparent, both between and within individuals. Even the extra-uterine gestated Nisei, who are the first generation of people to be born on Mars, are deeply individual and diverse people. Advanced technology has not taken the route feared by Aldous Huxley in *Brave New World*; we do not see masses of slave clones on this planet. In addition to plurality, we can observe also the activity of politics as the negotiation of differences. Much of the third volume is dedicated to attempts to manage (not resolve) different wants for the new planet and its social, cultural, political, and economic infrastructures. The trilogy is intriguing, bringing to life many obscure and complex theoretical ideas, and setting them in a context that we can imaginatively inhabit. It offers warnings about the now and places responsibility for the future firmly in our hands.

Butler's critical dystopia, *Parable of the Sower*, imagines a recognizable but nightmare America in the near future. It brings to life some very different aspects of politics and investigates their causes. In this world, governance and civil order have broken down and the worst kind of anarchy means that the police will act only for a fee, ambulance and hospital fees are beyond the reach of most of the population, and violence rules. Gangs prowl the streets and are fierce-ly territorial. Climate change makes water scarce, and food prices are astronomical. Work for wages is rare, and security impossible except at the price of freedom in the form of indentured slavery. This is an extreme gun culture driven by fear. People fear the unknown, and are plagued by a drug-crazed cult, whose dependence on the drug known as "pyro" drives them to light fires which destroy whole townships.

The protagonist, Lauren, is fortunate enough to live in a walled community – her family is poor and black but wealthy compared to people outside the wall, who are vulnerable in the extreme. One scene describes a rare and dangerous trip outside the community to a nearby church. The family ride their bicycles (fuel for cars and other vehicles has long been unavailable) with the adults carrying arms at the perimeter of the group. Outside, they see a naked and bruised woman, a young girl with blood running down the insides of her thighs, corpses, and body parts. Rape, murder, and drug dependencies are commonplace out on the streets.

Parable of the Sower follows a familiar dystopian path as it identifies and extrapolates contemporary problems, stretching them to their limits, and thus holding up a distorted but recognisable mirror for us to see how our own world could progress. Inequality, violence, and fear have created this world. The family is not safe even inside the wall, and their community is decimated by pyros. Lauren is the sole survivor of her family, and she sets off, gathering a small group of stragglers around her as she journeys north in the hope of finding a better place. The larger portion of the book is dedicated to this journey where, alongside violent adventures and misadventures in the material world (fights, theft, attempted rape, and murder), we further explore the ideas of equality and inequality, fear and respect, and relationships between self and other. Fear of difference and the unknown leads to the creation of the stranger as Other, who is treated according to the first-strike mentality of this Hobbesian dystopia. But Lauren and her companions transgress this norm, taking risks with themselves and offering (some) strangers trust, treating people with a cautious respect. Lauren is driven by an internal vision of the way things should be between people, and she calls this "Earthseed." Earthseed is a human-centered belief system described as a new religion with the message that change is inevitable and must be shaped by people. She and her crowd treat others with kindness – rare in this world – and slowly learn together to treat one another better. The book ends on a cautiously hopeful note as the group establishes a precarious community in northern California. As with other critical dystopias of the period, Butler's contains the makings of a eutopia.[5]

Political Functions

Unlike many political texts, utopias attempt to offer solutions. Often, different utopias from different times return to the same problem, exploring different ways of resolving perennial problems. More, for example, identified the private ownership of property as the root of an unjust system of punishment. At the time, a person could be hanged for the theft of a rabbit. As a humanist, More sought to reconcile the expedient with the moral; and this system of punishment, Hythloday tells us, is neither. It is not an effective deterrent, and it is not proportionate to the crime. And so, More's eutopia disposes of private property completely and values of gold and silver are inverted so that only the lowliest objects are made of them. Several centuries later the utopian theorist and experimenter, Robert Owen, returned to the problem of punishment. He believed that it was inappropriate to punish crime. We transgress because of who we are, and we come to be this way because of our experience. Instead of punishment, Owen felt we needed education. In fact, we owed it to the generations who follow us to educate them properly. And so Owen established the community of New Lanark based around his mill, in which workers were subject to a new system of re-education. Children were given schooling, and children and adults alike had a color-coded display next to their workplace, which would indicate whether or not they had behaved appropriately that day. Inappropriate behavior was not punished, and no comment was made, but the shame of having a black card would, Owen hoped, lead the person to take responsibility for her/himself.

5   On the critical dystopia, see Baccolini and Moylan.

Neither More's nor Owen's alternative have been adopted intact –
gold chamber pots never became the norm nor did Owen's system of
education. But this does not matter – both sets of ideas have had
influence on later socialist, communist, and anarchist thought – and
the more important point is that by offering these radical alternatives,
these utopians provoke further thought, debate, and experimentation.

As seen from these textual and lived examples, utopias are
subversive and estranged. These qualities permit them to perform the
political functions long-privileged by feminists: consciousness raising
and critique. They do this by offering radical political commentary in
an accessible imaginary space. Typically, the utopian (writer, pract-
itioner, character, or reader) is a malcontent, a social other, who is
critical of the norms, values, and structures of her/his present. Her/his
estranged viewpoint allows utopianism to subvert these norms and
conventions:

> the classical utopia anticipates and criticises. Its alternative fundamentally inter-
> rogates the present, piercing through existing societies' defensive mechanism –
> common sense realism, positivism, and scientism. Its unabashed and flagrant
> otherness gives it a power which is lacking in other analytical devices. By
> playing fast and loose with time and space, logic and morality, and by thinking
> the unthinkable, a utopia asks the most awkward, most embarrassing questions
> (Geoghegan 1–2).

In fictional utopias, for instance, the reader is distanced from her/his
own world (and that of the author) by use of a common convention,
the visitor, or alien. This allows us to be one step removed from the
utopia and often, we view the eutopia or dystopia through the eyes of
a stranger who sees this world through the prism of their own present,
(usually contemporaneous with the author's). And so, William
Morris's William Guest sleeps and visits the future in *News From
Nowhere*, More's Hytholoday visits and tells us about Utopia, and
Piercy's Connie Ramos mentally visits Mattapoisett. This device ac-
centuates the contrast between the new and the original world. The
visitor is a powerful vehicle for criticism and is part of the estranged-
yet-embedded nature of utopias.

Utopias stem from discontent with the present, and they tell us
what is wrong with the now. They are embedded in what they crit-

icize. This permits them to perform the political function of critique. Tom Moylan writes of this in *Demand the Impossible*, and I have developed this in my own work. Moylan identifies a particular kind of utopia that he calls the critical utopia. These emerged in the 1970s and belong to what he rather optimistically calls a "new historic bloc" of opposition to the status quo. United in their opposition to capitalist hegemony, the utopias of "feminism, ecology, and self-management both at the workplace and of the sphere of daily life," all offered criticisms of the now (27). Moylan had high hopes for these critical utopias, which were, he said, critical in two senses, first in the enlightenment sense of critique, and second, simultaneously, in the nuclear sense of critical mass (10). There is also a third, unarticulated sense of "critical" in Moylan's analysis: he believes these utopias to be necessary. Critical utopias work from the inside of the system, using estrangement as a vehicle for critique, anticipating a radically different tomorrow. In so doing they change their world and them-selves. Moylan's work takes the function of Utopia beyond criticism towards transformation.

The idea of Utopia anticipating a new reality is far from new. After all, this is what Popper was afraid of. But the critical utopias of the 1970s are politically exciting *because they are incomplete.* They were "no places" in two senses: they lie on the horizon, or, as Ernst Bloch puts it, in the "Not Yet"; *and* they are not fully imagined. This is important because it permits a certain pluralism:

> the new movements of liberation insist on a multiplicity of voices, autonomous from each other, but commonly rooted in unfulfilled needs centering around the practice of autonomy. This shared goal of fulfilment of desire for collective humanity informs the utopian impulse at the heart of the historic bloc of op-position. The impulse, however, is one that must resist closure and system-atization both in the steps taken toward it and in the vision that expresses it (Moylan 28).

No one voice can dominate, and no one utopia can become "the" utopia. We are looking here at something very different from Popper's version of the Platonic ideal. These utopias were not perfection-seeking and they do not seek to offer us blueprints. Rather, they provoke what I call paradigm shifts in consciousness, permitting us to glimpse new conceptual spaces from whence to approach the world anew (see Sargisson, *Contemporary Feminist Utopianism*).

According to Moylan, critical utopias are embedded in the present and yet they negate it through their criticisms in temporary coalitions of opposition to hegemony. I have developed this thesis, stressing the transgressive nature of contemporary utopianism, adding that utopias create a new space for the exploration of alternatives (see Sargisson, *Utopian Bodies*). When a boundary is crossed, a space is created – and this is an act of destruction (of old categories and old certainties) as well as an act of creation. In *Utopian Bodies and the Politics of Transgression*, I experimented with these ideas, taking them into the real world of intentional communities, as well as into the theoretical worlds of feminism, green political thought, and historical utopias. I found that rupturing boundaries – whether it be through inter- or cross-disciplinary study, or by contesting oppositional concepts such as mind and body, or public and private – generated the opportunity to look at things afresh, from a new estranged perspective.

For example, members of intentional communities often practice alternative ways of owning property. I have visited some sixty of these groups across the U.K. and New Zealand, conducting participant observation and interviews. Alternative forms of ownership include co-operatives, squats, co-housing, and the establishment of Trusts. Sometimes this stems from a core aspect of a utopian vision. It may, for example, be part of a commitment to a particular ideology. Such communities are places in which it is possible to observe different forms of ownership in practice, to note the pitfalls and gaps between expectations and reality, and to discover effective (and perhaps transferable) systems and processes. More interesting still are corresponding experiments with alternative economies of social and economic exchange. These involve interpersonal relationships, sexual and otherwise, as well as financial transactions. Often, attempts are made at establishing and maintaining non-possessive relationships with partners, children, and others. This is occasionally practised through free-love between adults, but more often as love without ownership or conditions, in which the choices of the other are respected. Or, on a different level, these groups may attempt to devise money-free economies and different systems of exchange. This is usually part of an attempt to devise non-exploitative economic relations. In most cases, these experiments form part of a group's larger project, which seek to re-think the way that we value ourselves and other people and sometimes the environment. In *Utopian Bodies*, I suggested that these experiments represent significant acts of transgression and that they were one way of beginning to change the culture of exchange within which we live.

I have suggested that utopias can help us to think about the world in different ways, to break old patterns and paradigms of thought and approach it anew. By showcasing new ways of being, they can inspire or catalyze change. To take a by-now familiar example, Butler's *Parable of the Sower* depicts a potentially new paradigm of self/other relations. Of course, just treating people with respect and trust will not change the world overnight, if at all, but this simple shift lies behind many current debates on how to negotiate contemporary problems. We can find an emphasis on *respect* in research on non-governmental organizations (NGOs) and aid, in literature on the welfare state (see Fraser), and in theoretical work on self/other relations (see, for example, Levinas). In all of these diverse bodies of thought, a respect for alterity and difference can be found. The other is not to be absorbed into the self, but rather respected as different. Butler's *Parable* goes some ways towards helping us to see how that might feel on a micro-level. In this Hobbesian world of atomized individuals, Lauren and her companions accept other people into the group. They are able to do this because they can co-operate and trust each other. And so they take turns to mount a nightly armed guard in shifts, giving everyone a chance to get some periods of deep sleep. They share food with new and starving members, who have never before received generosity. Working as a team gives the group strength that its many adversaries lack. The pyros may hunt as packs, but they do not co-operate beyond this, and Lauren's group acquire some (albeit limited) sense of happiness and self-fulfillment from the way that they are with one another. By offering spaces for exploration of ideas, utopias offer spaces in which new paradigms can be developed, explored, and inhabited.

On a more material level, intentional communities can be said to showcase alternatives. In recent research, I interviewed people in

some forty intentional communities across New Zealand, eighty percent of whom named consensus decision-making as their most useful
internal system or process (see Sargisson and Sargent). As with all
systems, not everything works smoothly all of the time. Two of the
most difficult problems with face-to-face consensual decision making
in small groups (most communities had between twelve and fifty
members) are being patient and ensuring that everyone's contribution
is fairly heard. These meetings can take hours. The politically or
socially efficacious member can have an advantage over the newcomer. Articulate and confident speakers can dominate debates and
influence discussions in ways that shy or less articulate members
cannot. Men's voices can drown out women's. Language competence
can be a problem. But some groups have devised systems to minimize
this, and members become experts in this difficult process through, for
example, carefully structuring proceedings. Meetings often have a
formal structure that prohibits domination by any one person. Different communities use different tactics for this. Some agree on a time
limit for speaking, some limit contributions, so that a person may
speak only once on an issue, some speak in turn so that everyone
participates. Some prefer informal discussion under the guidance of a
facilitator. Facilitation is usually performed by members in a weekly
or monthly rota. As long as the facilitator remains impartial, this
system functions well and the integrity of the process remains intact.

Consensus decision-making is not majority-based and most of
these groups save the vote as an absolute last resort. Votes, it is said,
create winners and losers and consensus seeks to make everyone a
winner. It is important to note that the object of consensus in these
groups is not to create a conflict-free internal culture.[6] Rather, consensus decision-making aims to enable people to negotiate conflict
over key issues and to live with the outcomes. Consensus, when it
works well, distributes power evenly throughout the group. When it is
done right, nobody is coerced or persuaded into agreement. There is
no exercise of power as domination (see Hobbes) or power as agenda

---

6   "The essence of consensus is the ability to extract something from each opinion
     in a group, and mould it into a statement or plan of action that each member can
     agree with and promote" (James and Roberts, quoted in Swain 13).

setting, or even power as manipulation (see Lukes). Rather, individuals reach a collective view. In theoretical terms, this is probably closest to Jean-Jacques Rousseau's General Will, but there are key differences as well as similarities. The General Will requires a lawgiver, and it requires people to surrender their personal wills to the group. That is not what occurs in consensus decision-making. But consensus, like the General Will, does require high levels of civic virtue and commitment. Of course, consensus is not unique to intentional communities, but they are places where we can observe, and perhaps learn from, people living with consensus decision-making as part of a larger utopian project.

I suggested at the beginning of this essay that the relationship between Utopia and politics is symbiotic. Symbiosis is a biological process that occurs in natural science. It occurs when two entities live connected to one another, sometimes feeding off each other, in a relationship of mutual dependence and mutual benefit. I have, thus far, attempted to show that Utopia is embedded in politics and that utopias are, in many ways, political spaces, forming part of larger political activities and processes. I need now to consider whether the relationship is one of mutual benefit and dependence.

I would suggest, from the discussion so far, that utopias can be seen to be useful to the political process and to scholars of politics. Utopias are hermeneutic texts, they offer us lessons about their present, permitting us access to people's fears and desires. They offer political critique and alternatives – sometimes realizable, sometimes conceptual. And they are spaces in which we can imagine or observe alternative political and economic arrangements. I would like to take this one step further and to suggest that politics actually needs utopianism – and that this is a mutually dependent relationship.

Utopias give the political a sense of direction. They also contain vital lessons for people who are interested in politics. We have established that all utopias and utopianism share certain features. They stem from discontent with the now, and they gesture towards something better. They may do this by depicting another world, where life is radically different and better, or they may offer partial or multiple visions of the good life. As such, they can be said to function negatively and positively. The negative criticizes while the positive creates or imagines something new. This latter aspect of utopianism is intimately connected to political ideologies. Ideologies contain utopias. Utopias inform that portion of a political ideology that maps out the world for us, helping us to plot our aspirations for the future. For example, socialism contains utopias of egalitarianism and liberalism seeks various (economic, social, and political) utopias of freedom. This aspect of utopianism (and this aspect of ideology) brings hope to politics: the hope and desire that things can be different. This is what drives us on and keeps the political world dynamic. Politics without Utopia would be bleak indeed. Utopias (in the sense of visions of a better way of being) give politics a sense of where it wants to be. In this sense, Utopia lies at the heart of politics.

The inverse is equally true. Utopianism needs politics, pragmatically and conceptually. Without politics, Utopia remains on the page. Political movements and institutions help with questions of agency, and political theory clarifies analyses. Practical politics can help us to negotiate the fact that the world's utopias are contingent and manifold. Inclusive political institutions and practices can help us to manage the multiplicity of contemporary utopianism and to construct a pluralism of utopias.

First though, we need to understand their context. Utopias are born of discontent with the now; and, without a working knowledge of the author's and her or his contemporary reader's now, we cannot understand their dreams of a better future. We need knowledge of their world's relations of power, distributions of wealth, belief systems, and culture. We also need to know about debates they engage. This is the case for historical utopias, such as More's *Utopia*, as well as the utopias of today. We cannot understand More, for example, without knowing something about the political and economic times in which he wrote – the end of feudalism and the growth of a new market economy, the relationship between the growing wool trade and the dispossession of the peasantry, the discharge of retainers and consequent mass unemployment. Similarly, to understand his method, we need to know about humanism and its preoccupation with rhetoric, and an examination of the relationship between honor and glory. We can understand More better if we know the work of Niccolò Machiavelli, also a humanist, who took a very different approach to the honor/glory question (see *The Prince*). Also as a humanist, More was familiar with Plato, hence his decision to play with the Platonic method: what is necessary for individual happiness? What are communal goods? What institutions are necessary to secure these? And what form should these components take?

With knowledge and understanding of a given utopia's contexts, politics can help utopianism to move beyond wishful thinking to positive action, off the page, and into lived experience. Politics can help us to address the most difficult and often unanswered problem within utopian studies – that of agency. I noted that most utopias are not intended for realization, but the utopian project itself *is* forward looking and *does* seek change. I have discussed some of the ways that utopias are places of change, transgression, and transformation, but I am concerned here with a more material notion of political change. Not "end state" utopianism, nor the realization of a perfect vision, but rather utopianism as the inspiration for change, or as part of a wider social transformation. Politics can provide some of the vehicles for this. It provides institutions, such as states, political parties, NGOs, pressure groups, and local grass-roots organizations. As a discipline, it studies the ways that power is organized in our world. Politics can thus help utopians to understand and combat or harness power's subtle machinations.

Conclusion

There is a fungus called Amanita muscaria that lives in a symbiotic relationship with the silver birch tree. Alanita live within the roots of these trees, drawing their sap and feeding from it. Fungi do not photosynthesize and Amanita needs the tree as its source of sugars and energy. In return, the tree gains nutrients from the fungus, which, lying deep down in the root, breaks down decaying organic matter to provide the tree with nitrogen and phosphorus.

I began this discussion with the work of anti-utopian critics, who fear or mistrust Utopia because it leads either to primrose paths of dalliance or to the gas chambers of Nazi Germany. These critics suspect utopian epistemology and methods. I have suggested that these suspicions, whilst flawed, have some merit. Utopia *can* be a dangerous political tool. In our time, for example, we are increasingly aware of religious fundamentalism. This is a frightening form of utopianism, so certain of its own rightness, so sure of its vision of perfection, and so unwilling to compromise or contemplate alternatives. Little wonder that we fear utopianism. But the utopian, I have suggested, is endemic to politics, driving and inspiring us to move onwards towards our particular vision of the better world, and it has important and valuable functions. We are right to fear fundamentalism, and its visions of perfection. But the relationship between politics and Utopia is richer than just this, and I have attempted here to sketch something of the exciting potential of a symbiotic relationship between politics and Utopia.

Politics and Utopia have parallel and overlapping concerns, and utopianism lives within politics. Moreover, politics and Utopia can sustain each other. Each gives life to the other and each needs the other. We need political structures and systems to negotiate the multiple utopias of the contemporary world, and we need political studies to help us understand them. We need to learn from the warnings provided by dystopias and from utopian theory and fiction of different ways of approaching the world. And we can learn from intentional communities how it feels to begin to live differently. In return, utopians need to learn from political theory about concepts and ideas, and from political science about questions of method and agency, about how to change the world in sustainable ways, through established as well as unconventional methods. Quite simply, politics needs Utopia and Utopia needs politics.

Works Cited

Arendt, Hanna. *The Human Condition*. Chicago: University of Chicago Press, 1998.

Barr, Marleen S., and Nicholas Smith (eds.). *Women and Utopia: Critical Interpretations*. Lanham: University Press of America, 1983.

Baruch, Emily. "'A Natural and Necessary Monster': Women in Utopia." *Alternative Futures* 2.1 (1978): 49–60.

Bloch, Ernst. *The Principle of Hope*. Trans. Neville Plaice, Stephen Plaice, and Paul Knight. 3 Vols. Oxford: Blackwell, 1986.

Burke, Edmund. *Reflections on the Revolution in France*. 1790. Stanford: Stanford University Press, 2001.

Butler, Octavia E. *Parable of the Sower*. London: Women's Press, 1995.

Claeys, Gregory, and Lyman Tower Sargent (eds.). *The Utopia Reader*. New York: New York University Press, 1999.

Fraser, Nancy, and Linda Gordon. "'Dependency' Demystified: Inscriptions of Power in a Keyword of the Welfare State." *Contemporary Political Philosophy: An Anthology*. Ed. Robert E. Goodin and Philip Pettit. Oxford: Blackwell, 2005. 591–606.

Geoghegan, Vincent. *Utopianism and Marxism*. London: Methuen, 1987.

Goodwin, Barbara, and Keith Taylor. *The Politics of Utopia*. London: Hutchinson, 1982.

Hobbes, Thomas. *Leviathan*. 1651. Harmondsworth: Penguin, 1968.

Leftwich, Adrian. *What Is Politics? The Activity and its Study*. Oxford: Blackwell, 1984.

Levinas, Emmanuel. *Totality and Infinity: An Essay on Exteriority*. Trans. Alphonso Lingis. London: Nijhoff, 1979.

Levinson, Ronald Bartlett. *In Defence of Plato*. Amherst: University of Massachusetts Press, 1953.

Levitas, Ruth. *The Concept of Utopia*. London: Allan, 1990.

Logan, George M., and Robert Adams. "Introduction."' *Thomas More's Utopia*. Cambridge: Cambridge University Press, 1975.

Lukes, Steven Michael. *Power: A Radical View*. London: Macmillan, 1974.

Machiavelli, Niccolò. *The Prince*. 1515. Trans. Russell Price. Cambridge: Cambridge University Press, 1968.

Mill, John Stuart. *On Liberty*. 1869. Cambridge: Cambridge University Press, 1989.

More, Thomas. *Utopia*. 1516. London: Norton, 1992.

Morris, William. *News from Nowhere*. 1891. Oxford: Oxford University Press, 2003.

Morton, A.L. *The English Utopia*. London: Lawrence and Wishart, 1952.

Moylan, Tom. *Demand the Impossible: Science Fiction and the Utopian Imagination*. New York: Methuen, 1986.

Piercy, Marge. *Woman on the Edge of Time*. London: Women's Press; 1979.

Plato. *Republic*. Trans. Robin Waterfield. Oxford: Oxford University Press, 1993.

Popper, Karl. *The Open Society and its Enemies*. New York: Harper and Row, 1962.

Robinson, Kim Stanley. *Blue Mars*. London: Harper Collins, 1996.

—— *Green Mars*. London: Harper Collins, 1993.

—— *Red Mars*. London: Harper Collins, 1992.

Rousseau, Jean-Jacques. *The Social Contract*. 1762. Trans. Maurice Cranston. Harmondsworth: Penguin, 1968.

Sargent, Lyman Tower. "The Three Faces of Utopianism." *minnesota review* 7.3 (1967): 222–30.

—— "Three Faces of Utopianism Revisited." *Utopian Studies* 5.1 (1994): 1–37.

Sargisson, Lucy. *Contemporary Feminist Utopianism*. London: Routledge, 1996.

—— *Utopian Bodies and the Politics of Transgression*. London: Routledge, 2000.

Sargisson, Lucy, and Lyman Tower Sargent. *Living in Utopia: New Zealand's Intentional Communities*. Aldershot: Ashgate, 2004.

Schapiro, Leonard Bertram. *Totalitarianism*. London: Pall Mall, 1972.

Swain, Trystan. *Liberating Meetings: Facilitating Meetings Using Consensus Decision Making*. Waitaha, New Zealand: Vegan, 1996.

Talmon, Jacob Liab. *The Origins of Totalitarian Democracy*. London: Mercury, 1961.

Waterfield, Robin. "Introduction." Plato's *Republic*. Oxford: Oxford University Press, 1993.

Wells, H.G. *A Modern Utopia*. London: Chapman and Hall, 1905.

RUTH LEVITAS

The Imaginary Reconstitution of Society: Utopia as Method

> We shall not cease from exploration
> And the end of all our exploring
> Will be to arrive where we started
> And know the place for the first time.
> T.S. Eliot, "Little Gidding"
>
> I have spread my dreams under your feet.
> Tread softly, because you tread on my dreams.
> W.B. Yeats, "He Wishes for the Cloths of Heaven"

This essay is a reflection on the place of Utopia in my work over the last thirty years or more, and especially on Utopia as method. It has caused me to think about the coherence of my intellectual project, and about the range of applicability of the utopian method. Utopia is about the imaginary reconstitution of society: the construction or constitution of society as it is, as it might be, as it might not be, as it might be hoped for or feared. As a method, this can be called the IROS method, IROS being the imaginary reconstitution of society. It has both an *archaeological* or analytical mode, and an *architectural* or constructive mode. But although it appears in a number of (dis)guises, it does have both a coherence, and a general applicability as a method for critical study of social and cultural processes across the humanities and social sciences. It also has – perhaps more importantly – a relevance beyond the academy to questions of social change and reconstruction.

Like most utopists, my work has sometimes circled round Utopia, rather than always addressing it directly. This is partly because utopian studies crosses institutional and disciplinary boundaries, and partly because utopian studies had only an immanent existence at the start of my academic career. As Tom Moylan documents in *Scraps of the Untainted Sky*, the development of this field of study has been a collective improvisation on a series of overlapping themes – perhaps like a form of jazz. But this indirectness arises also because the core questions of Utopia transgress the boundaries of the "legitimately" academic. Utopia is born out of a conviction and two questions. The conviction is "it doesn't have to be like this." The questions are, "how, then should we live?" and "how can that be?" To study Utopia within the academy is therefore always to be subject to the contrary forces of the overtly dispassionate questions of how others have construed Utopia, and the moral and spiritual quest that is at the core of Utopia itself. How one comes to the question of Utopia is therefore always implicit in one's own riffs, and for that reason this essay is written partly as intellectual autobiography.

The sculptor Barbara Hepworth wrote: "I think what we have to say is formed in childhood, and we spend the rest of our lives trying to say it." In light of that, my interest in Utopia seems to be, if not predestined, at least overdetermined. I was nineteen, and went to University, in 1968: the year of the Prague Spring, the Soviet invasion of Czechoslovakia, of student unrest across Europe, of the slogan "Be Realistic: Demand the Impossible." But the die was cast earlier. I was born into a communist family, brought up with the assumption that a better world was something to be fought for, and that there was a moral requirement to engage in this struggle. My Dublin-born father fought with the Connolly Column in the International Brigades in the Spanish Civil War. The earliest surviving photograph of my mother shows her on a soap box in Hammersmith in 1939 (possibly at one of the sites where William Morris used to speak fifty years earlier) campaigning against conscription in front of a National Youth Campaign banner. Many childhood Sundays were spent on political demonstrations, just as in February 2003 I joined the largest such demonstration ever to take place in Britain, when two million people protested against the impending British and U.S. attack on Iraq. Other Sundays were spent walking by the Thames at Hammersmith, past Kelmscott House which had been William Morris's London home. Here, the young William Butler Yeats (who attended the same school in Hammersmith that I went to in my teens) argued passionately with Morris at meetings of the Hammersmith Socialist Society. And then, in 1966, my mother gave me her copy of Morris's *News from Nowhere*. I blame the parents: but Morris was the original inspiration of my interest in Utopia.

This interest was first and foremost about a place, a *topos*. The attraction of Morris's utopian vision was that it provided a "base outside," from which both the *actual* Hammersmith and the *emergent* Hammersmith could be called into question – important at a time of drastic and unsympathetic urban development. Planners had just driven the Great West Road, later called the M4, through Hammersmith Riverside. Utopia operated as a standpoint of judgment, and at least as a possibility for consideration, if not necessarily a possibility. And Morris's utopia insisted on connection – connection between the aesthetics of the built environment, the nature of work, the quality of human relationships, the fundamental economic and political structures of the whole society. This holism is accompanied in Morris by another kind of connection – the process of transformation, the path from here to there. If my overall intellectual project has any coherence, at its core remains Morris's description of my native Hammersmith transformed, as part of London transformed, dependent on an entire social and economic system which has been radically reconstituted, in which work has ceased to be alienated labor, and in which the process of agency and change is an urgent question.

I read sociology as an undergraduate. It soon became clear to me that sociologists only sought to understand the world, whereas I wanted to change it. By the time I embarked on my Ph.D., in 1972, I was committed to studying Utopia. But I lacked the cultural capital or brass neck to conjure a new sub-discipline out of an inchoate sense that this must be possible. There was no shortage of material. There was far too much, and it was too disparate. I was unable to define the field. Utopianism, broadly construed, seemed to involve literature, including recognizably utopian and dystopian novels, science fiction (sf), not-obviously-utopian novels that conjured up other worlds, poetry, song, politics in both theory and practice, philosophy, theological concepts of the Kingdom of God, images of the Garden of Eden, paintings such as Hieronymus Bosch's *Millennium Triptych* and Stanley Spencer's depictions of the resurrection. I spent eighteen months failing to clarify a thesis topic on Utopia, and eventually focused on the quasi-utopian project of the early English Christian Socialists between 1848 and 1854.

My inability to focus my interest in Utopia at that time, my equal inability to let go of it, and my institutional position as a sociologist, have been formative elements in the different ways Utopia has entered into my work. That work has two strands, one of which deals with overtly utopian themes, and one which addresses contemporary social policy and politics, and which serves to illustrate the power of Utopia as a method beyond utopian studies.

Lay understandings of Utopia are generally either dismissive or hostile, seeing it as at best impractical dreaming. When in 1975 I suggested in a women's meeting that feminism was a utopian project, the response was one of rage and hostility. The term "utopia" itself is, of course, drawn from Thomas More's text, in which the title is a pun on good place/no place – thus the good society which does not exist, and which is therefore transmuted into everyday thought as perfect and impossible. As Roger Fernay put it in Kurt Weill's song *Youkali*, "Mais c'est un reve, une folie, Il n'y a pas de Youkali" (but it is a dream, a foolishness; there is no Youkali). The attribution of foolishness, accompanied by the same wistfulness, is expressed in the opening lines of W.H. Auden's *Atlantis*:

> Being set on the idea
> Of getting to Atlantis
> You have discovered of course
> Only the Ship of Fools is
> Making the voyage this year (86).

A more hostile, intensely political anti-utopian discourse which was at its height around 1989 draws on Karl Popper's position in *The Open Society and its Enemies*. Here utopianism is seen as dangerous, holding that the quest for perfection is contrary to human nature. Utopia can therefore only be implemented by force, so that it is necessarily totalitarian in effect. The equation implicit in public discourse, reproduced more recently in Martin Amis's *Koba the Dread* was Utopia = totalitarianism = fascism = stalinism = communism = socialism. Al-Qaida, too, is designated utopian, and indeed some have blamed Isaac

Asimov's sf novel *Foundation* for inspiring Osama Bin Laden and the attack of 9/11, observing that Al-Qaida translates as "Foundation" (see Foden).

Such an approach defines Utopia in terms of its content (totalitarian) and function (domination). It assumes that imagined utopias are not merely aspirational but didactic, and that they are not merely morally didactic, but politically so, and intended as blueprints ripe for implementation. Both in subject matter and approach, this is very different from the field that was being marked out as utopian studies in the late 1970s and 1980s, which was largely concerned with literary utopias and with intentional communities. And this brings me back to the problems that defeated me as a graduate student – the definition and boundaries of Utopia, and the question of what Utopia is for – which have been at the core of my overtly utopistic work. In the newly-emergent field, there was no consensus about what "Utopia" is, and – with certain notable exceptions – not a great deal of reflexivity about this lack of consensus.[1] In the late 1980s I eventually wrote the book that should have been chapter one of my thesis fifteen years earlier.

The Concept of Utopia is a meta-theoretical reflection on the different ways in which social theorists and sympathetic commentators on Utopia have used the *concept*, just as this volume is a meta-theoretical reflection on Utopia as *method*. But they connect up because many definitions of Utopia concern themselves centrally with its function, and especially with the question of didacticism. And, just to complicate matters, the definition I arrived at raises the problem of holism, and thus about whether we can identify Utopia with "the imaginary reconstitution of society" at all.

Most definitions of Utopia prioritize one of the following: content, form, function, or location. None of these is satisfactory. We cannot define Utopia in terms of content, since utopias vary, and there are right-wing and fascist utopias as well as socialist, feminist, ecological, and indeed liberal ones. Definitions in terms of form are problematic too. It is on this point that I differ most from some other

---

1   The exceptions are Moylan, *Demand the Impossible*; Sargent in a series of pieces (see below Works Cited); and Davis.

scholars in the field, notably Krishan Kumar. Kumar, like Lyman Tower Sargent, sees a *utopia* as essentially a literary fiction, a novel. Both, however, recognize a wider field of *utopianism* or social dreaming. Like many writers, Kumar starts from More (see *Utopianism*). But this raises further problems. More's *Utopia* is not a novel. Part two, the utopian part, is a dialogue, and it is preceded by a rhetorical critique of the state of England. None of the utopian socialists – apart from Étienne Cabet – wrote anything like a novel. And in any case, one of the more positive aspects of post-structuralism and the cultural turn has been the understanding that the distinction between fictional and factual texts is itself fictional. Commentators also disagree markedly about the function of Utopia. Karl Mannheim contrasted "ideology" and "utopia" on the basis of social function. Ideology is that which preserves the status quo, Utopia that which transforms it. For Mannheim, a utopia is a transformative idea, irrespective of form, whereas many pictures of ideal societies are ideological in effect. Karl Marx and Friedrich Engels take the opposite view. Utopia is still defined in terms of function, but it is a negative epithet applied to the so-called utopian socialists (Robert Owen, Charles Fourier, Henri de Saint-Simon, Cabet) for preventing change. Owen and Fourier both accept the distinction between science and Utopia that Engels uses against them, but they place themselves on the side of science, denying that their schemes are utopian at all. And in terms of location, Utopia is only unequivocally located in the future in the nineteenth century, at the epitome of the belief in social progress. Utopia may be located in another place on the globe, in space, in the past or in a parallel world – or in a future whose connection to the present is tenuous and indistinct.

If we want to understand changes in the content, form, function, and location of Utopia, we need a definition that is broad enough to embrace these variations. Enter Bloch. Ernst Bloch was a radical German intellectual of Jewish origin, born in 1885, and closely associated with Georg Lukács, Walter Benjamin, and Gershom Scholem. Bloch's work can be characterized in his own terms as an attempt to reinstate Marx's own intentions within Marxism through the fundamental but neglected *Marxist* concept of Utopia. However, his interest in Utopia preceded his engagement with Marxism, with the key concept of the "Not Yet" running through his work from 1906, and some aspects of the structure of his thought bearing a striking resemblance to the Jewish mystical tradition of the kabbalah. Bloch's major treatise, *The Principle of Hope*, was partly written in exile in the United States in the 1930s, and revised and published in the German Democratic Republic in the 1950s after his return – a return underpinned by his already controversial commitment to communism as a potentially utopian project. The first English translation of *The Principle of Hope*, 1200 pages long, was published in 1986. It argues that the utopian impulse is an anthropological and ontological given, so that humankind constantly longs for a better world. The sense of lack at the core of our existence can be articulated only through the projection of what would meet that lack, the delineation of what is missing. The utopian impulse, the impulse to a better world, is ubiquitous in human culture; but its expression is necessarily historically variable, and often oblique and fragmentary. Among the varied cultural forms that have a utopian content, Bloch discusses not just fairy tales and myths, but the alchemical quest for a process that will transmute base metal to gold; travelers tales, such as St. Brendan's voyage in pursuit of the Promised Isles; and music and architecture. Bloch argues that there is a generic utopian content in these, a vital attempt to grasp the possibility of a radically different human experience, even though it is sometimes embedded in forms of fantasy that are easily dismissed as wishful thinking. For Bloch, wishful thinking is itself a precursor of will-full action, so this utopian content is indispensable. The appropriate analogy here is mining – extracting the utopian essence from the ore of human culture.

Following Bloch, I opted for a much broader definition of Utopia: *the expression of desire for a better way of living*. This allows for variations in form, content, and location, and enables us to see that the function of Utopia may be compensation, critique, or change. Such a definition, however, does not help with the problem of boundaries. It is of no use to the bibliographer. It is, essentially, an analytic definition rather than a descriptive one. It provides a way of addressing the utopian *aspects* of a variety of cultural forms and expressions, rather than demanding fully-fledged utopias in the form of imagined societies. It allows Utopia to be fragmentary, partial, elusive, episodic (see Levitas, "Elusive Idea of Utopia").

The primary reason for adopting such a broad definition is that it enables us to see how "utopian energies" shift and change (see Sargent in this volume). Victorian, and especially *fin de siècle* utopians, such as Morris, but also Edward Bellamy and Charlotte Perkins Gilman, engaged in the imaginary reconstitution of society because they genuinely hoped and worked for its reconstruction in reality. Contemporary utopianism is very different. It has retreated into the private sphere. One might cite the exercise and diet regimes in pursuit of the perfect body that are so prevalent in contemporary western culture as utopian in Bloch's sense. Equally, the attempt to create a private utopian space is expressed in the emphasis on house and garden design: budget and luxury makeovers are the topic of countless magazines and television programmes, at least in Britain. Even the smallest rooms may be the setting for marketed constructions of desire, as instanced by the bathroom specialists called "utopia plc." Public and private gardens can be seen as little utopias squeezed into the interstices of space. Cornwall's Eden Project (part Eden, part Ark) reclaims an old china clay quarry to build bio-spheres to recreate a rain forest and preserve bio-diversity. Smaller gardens may be personal fragments of Eden. In January 2003, for example, the Oslo Museum of Modern Art displayed a photographic exhibition of small gardens, called *Temporary Utopias*, not just confined in space, but transient and limited in time (see Meyer). Holidays of course, always advertised as paradisical, are squeezed into the interstices of time. Zygmunt Bauman argues that in the era of "liquid modernity," happiness is sought not as a sustained state, but a fleeting moment.

And, of course, it is not only the content, form, and location of Utopia that shift and change, but also its function. These fleeting utopias function more as escape and compensation, rather than having transformative or even critical power. They are expressive rather than instrumental. Bloch himself makes a distinction between "abstract utopia," which is essentially expressive and wishful, and "concrete utopia," which is instrumental and transformative. Bloch's formulation echoes Morris's poem, *The Earthly Paradise*, whose first stanzas include the passage:

> Dreamer of dreams, born out of my due time,
> Why should I strive to set the crooked straight?
> Let it suffice me that my murmuring rhyme
> Beats with light wing against the ivory gate,
> Telling a tale not too importunate
> To those who in the sleepy region stay,
> Lulled by the singer of an empty day (1).

But it equally allows – and ultimately encourages – the closing words of *News from Nowhere*: "if others can see it as I have seen it, then it may be called a vision rather than a dream" (211). I say "encourages," since for Bloch the world is essentially unfinished and in process of becoming, so that such dreams can also be the reaching forward to a better future which humankind is instrumental in effecting. Bloch repeatedly quotes Marx: "the world has long possessed the dream of a matter, of which it must only possess the consciousness in order to possess it in reality" (155–6). But human agency is critical: thus Bloch also insists that "the hinge in human history is its producer" (249). Or, as Alan Titchmarsh (who has celebrity status in Britain as a television gardening presenter) put it, we have to put the "heave" in heaven.

The distinction between abstract and concrete utopia (what Bloch called *docta spes* or educated hope) has to be understood as process rather than classification (see Levitas, "Educated Hope"). This delivers a further understanding of the function of Utopia, or of the imaginary reconstitution of society as method: *the education of desire.* This term comes not from Bloch, but from debates about the interpretation of *News from Nowhere* which directly address issues of literalism and didacticism. Edward Thompson discusses the relationship between Utopia and Marxism through commentaries on *News from Nowhere* by Paul Meier and Miguel Abensour. Whereas Meier treats Morris's utopia as a more-or-less literal portrayal of the intended end-point of Marx's communism, Abensour makes a more complex methodological claim. While classical utopias such as those of More or the utopian socialists might have been intended as blueprints, from the mid-nineteenth century, utopias became heuristic rather than systematic. What Abensour means by this is that Utopia shifts from the construction of blueprints, which are meant to be taken literally as schema for the good society, to an exploratory project whose purpose is, as Thompson glosses Abensour, "to embody in the forms of fantasy alternative values sketched in an alternative way of life" (790). This is not IROS as goal or even as aspiration. IROS is a device firstly to defamiliarize the familiar, and secondly to create a space in which the reader is both brought to experience an alternative and called to judgment on it. We tend to think of experience and judgment as ontologically distinct processes, and indeed Thompson's own discussion reproduces this dualism between knowledge and desire. Martha Nussbaum, however, has argued, in *Upheavals of Thought*, that this is mistaken. Emotion involves judgment. Our feelings are necessarily dependent on judgment, our judgments on how things make us feel. We are, for example, angry because we judge something to be wrong. We judge it to be wrong because it involves pain for ourselves or for others. Abensour's view of the function of Utopia, of Utopia as method, does not insist on such a separation. When we enter into the imaginatively reconstituted society, two things happen:

> our habitual values (the "commonsense" of bourgeois society) are thrown into disarray. And we enter Utopia's new-found space: *the education of desire.* This is not the same as "a moral education" towards a given end: it is rather, to open a way to aspiration, to "teach desire to desire, to desire better, to desire more, and above all to desire in a different way" (Abensour, quoted in Thompson 790–1).

Abensour's view of what I have called the IROS method, then, is that it is not directly didactic. It is rather provisional, exploratory, up for negotiation – perhaps one might say an "invitation to treat." Moylan's *Demand the Impossible* offers a similar view of how the utopias of the late twentieth century work as "critical utopia," adding reflexivity and internal contestation to their characteristics, and thus to the possibilities of the IROS method.

My purpose in writing *The Concept of Utopia* was not to impose a new definition that would act as a constraint on the variety of work on and around Utopia. I hoped to provoke people to a greater clarity about their own usage of the term and its implications. To some extent this has happened, though not mainly because of the book. The general direction of utopian studies, of which that discussion was part, has been towards a greater openness concerning definition, substance, and method (see especially Sargisson; Moylan, *Scraps*). It has eschewed both holism and didacticism, and shifted the emphasis from content to process (see Levitas, "For Utopia"). The strongest exponent of this has been Fredric Jameson (see Fitting). As a Marxist, Jameson is explicit that imagining the future is, strictly speaking, impossible (a view that Morris shared). So what is important for Jameson – as for Abensour, and (up to a point) for Bloch – is not *what* we imagine, but *that* we imagine, at the same time exposing the limits of our imagination. So that the function of the utopian text becomes, as Jameson puts it, "to provoke [...] to jar the mind into some heightened but unconceptualizable consciousness of its own powers, functions, aims and structural limits" ("Islands and Trenches" 11).[2]

Well, all this openness is a bit much for me. We could do with a bit of closure. Abensour's commentary on Morris suggests that it does not matter whether you agree or disagree with the institutional arrangements. What matters is that the utopian experiment disrupts the taken-for-granted nature of the present and proffers an alternative set of values. Carried to the extremes of Jameson's argument, this position risks political evasion. First, for the estrangement effect to work, the posited alternative must have some degree of plausibility. Second, the *education* of desire rather than its simple indulgence requires judgment, not simply about the attractiveness of such abstract values as freedom, justice, inclusion, equality, but about how these might actually be played out in institutional form (see Levitas, "Utopia as Literature"). The strength of IROS or the utopian method is precisely that it deals with the concrete instantiation of values, enabling a level of real exploration and judgment. Without a certain element of closure, specificity, commitment, and literalism about what would actually be entailed in practice, serious criticism is impossible. If IROS were simply a method for literature or cultural studies, this might not matter. In so far as it is a method for addressing our possible future, it is crucial. If Utopia is *only* the expression of desire, without the drive to education, transcendence, and ultimately transformation, it

2   See also Jameson, *Postmodernism*, "Progress," and *Seeds*.

is in danger of becoming, as Raymond Williams said, merely a mode of living with alienation (203).

IROS Beyond Utopia

Utopian scholars are scattered across different disciplines. My academic career has been spent in sociology departments, chiefly at Bristol. My interest in Utopia has been accepted, but as a somewhat maverick interest, marginal to mainstream sociology. So marginal, in fact, that an abstract I submitted for the 2003 British Sociological Association conference about social futures was classified in the "open" stream reserved for contributions not related to the main theme of the conference. Yet H.G. Wells once argued in an essay on "The So-called Science of Sociology" that "the creation of Utopias – and their exhaustive criticism – is the proper and distinctive method of sociology" (*An Englishman* 204). Wells would have appreciated Auden's question:

> unless
> You become acquainted now
> With each refuge that tries to
> Counterfeit Atlantis, how
> Will you recognise the true? (87).

Wells's argument suggests that we should see Utopia as a form of speculative sociology. The reason why this did not catch on has to do with the emergence of sociology as a distinct discipline in the early twentieth century, and its self-justification as a social science. In pursuit of disciplinary respectability, sociology through most of the twentieth century insisted on a clear fact/value split, repressing the necessary predictive element in sociology as well as the evaluative content which drives every attempt to think about how society works.

Wells, of course, is concerned precisely with predicting what might be, in ways that invite judgment. And he was extraordinarily prescient. In 1909, he observed Louis Bleriot's first flight across the English Channel. Seventeen months later, he wrote "Off the Chain," which anticipates globalization, space-time compression, dis-embedding, and mass migration. The development of "swift, secure and cheapened locomotion" means, he says, that "the ties that bind men to place are being severed" (16). Humanity will return from a closely tethered to a migratory existence. Great multitudes of workers will move from place to place. Both in western Europe and, even more so, in the United States, there are, he says, increasing numbers of people who are uninterested in the affairs of their immediate locality because they are oriented to a wider arena. In prospect is a new kind of people, "uprooted, delocalised, and even, it may be, denationalised" (20). The forces of international finance and business will be with this trend, but existing structures of government will not:

> the history of the immediate future will [...] be very largely the history of the conflict of the needs of this new population with the institutions, the boundaries, the laws, prejudices and deep-rooted traditions established during the [...] localised era of mankind's career (Wells 21).

In the essay on sociology, Wells observes that there is:

> no such thing in sociology as dispassionately considering what is, without considering what is intended to be. [...] Sociologists cannot help making Utopias; though they avoid the word, though they deny the idea with passion, their very silences shape a Utopia (203–5).

Kumar has demonstrated, in *Prophecy and Progress*, how classical sociological theory embeds perceived tendencies in the social as fact – that is, the imagined future is collapsed back into the present. In this sense, one might, then, agree with Wells that all sociologists are necessarily utopians, even though their identity as sociologists requires them to deny this. One might add that sociology, like Utopia, works always through a method of estrangement. The very process of holding up our lives as in need of explanation requires that their patterns be denaturalized – that we first defamiliarize the familiar. Moreover, in the twenty-first century, it is impossible to avoid the fact that sociological representations of the social world are precisely that

– representations. A sociological model is itself an *imaginary reconstitution of society*. The IROS method *is* the method of sociology. At the same time, all utopians are necessarily sociologists. Sociological and utopian models share the characteristic of holism, of insisting on looking at how societies work as systems, and thus how their characteristics connect up. We might say that sociology and Utopia share a whole range of characteristics, being descriptive, explanatory, and present-oriented, as well as imaginary, critical, normative, prescriptive, and future-oriented. But sociology *foregrounds* the elements that Utopia *backgrounds*, and backgrounds – to the point of repression – the elements that Utopia foregrounds. Sociological models are also explicitly descriptive, explanatory, and present-oriented. These characteristics are present in utopian models as well. Since utopias work by implicit or explicit contrast with the society against which they are written, the extent to which they are explicit rather than implicit varies. Utopian models are also explicitly imaginary, critical, normative, prescriptive, and often future-oriented. In fact, as Wells said, these characteristics are present, although often implicit or actively repressed, in sociological models.

Such utopian elements in sociological thinking may be readily attributed to Marx, but the same is true of the far less radical mainstream sociologist, and key founder of the discipline, Émile Durkheim, especially in *The Division of Labour in Society* (published in 1893 as *De la division du travail social*). Durkheim's central thesis is that, as societies evolve from "primitive" to "advanced" forms, the mechanism of social cohesion – what holds the whole thing together – changes. Primitive societies cohere because their members are essentially similar in their social roles and in their beliefs and values, the latter forming what Durkheim calls the *conscience collective*. As societies become more complex, shared beliefs and values do not disappear, but become more abstract, and social cohesion depends on interdependence, on the variety rather than similarity of social roles. There are many problems with this thesis. Its utopianism, however, is apparent mainly in the final part, in which Durkheim posits a "normal" mode of development in which the division of labor should (and will) lead to social cohesion, as contrasted with the "pathological" forms evidenced in the class conflict of the late nineteenth century. Interestingly, Durkheim's implicit utopia has strong similarities with the explicit model set out in Bellamy's *Looking Backward* five years later.

But there is a problem. How do I square my definition of Utopia in analytic terms that reject the necessity of holism with the claim that what binds sociology and Utopia is, among other things, the characteristic of holism? One could go down the route of arguing that all holisms are necessarily partial – which is true, but not particularly helpful. More helpful is a clear distinction between Utopia as a concept, Utopia as an object of study, and Utopia or IROS as method. It is essential not to require holism in the definition of Utopia or in the object of study, for all the reasons outlined earlier. It is equally crucial to see that IROS as method does indeed depend on holism, on the connection that Morris originally offered. It also intrinsically demands evaluation and critique, as Wells maintained.

IROS as Archaeology

What the IROS method suggests is that we need to read back from utopian fragments a more total picture of the social origin of those shards. The work I have done across sociology, politics, and social policy (especially in *The Ideology of the New Right* and in *The Inclusive Society?*) uses a utopian method that is essentially *archaeological*. The excavations and reconstructions that archaeology undertakes, whether of artifacts or of cultures, are based on a mixture of evidence, deduction, and imagination, representing as whole something of which only fragments are actually available. Applied to ideas, IROS involves excavating and uncovering the implicit utopia or utopias buried in the political programs in question. This is *the imaginary reconstitution of the idea of the good society* that underpins them. It is my contention that all political programs (including feminism) are, in this sense, implicitly utopian. Where the New Right was concerned, the IROS method made it possible to explore the contradictions and continuities between its neo-liberal and neo-conservative strands and to show how, although these were philosophically contradictory, they were in practice complementary. Although neo-liberals emphasized freedom, efficiency, and accountability and claimed to be in favor of the minimal state, this disguised the extent to which they were, in fact, reliant on the strong state to police the negative effects of the market. Similarly, the neo-conservative position, though emphasizing authority, allegiance, and tradition, was fundamentally dependent on the market as a mechanism of social discipline (much as Tony Blair says the policy against crime is jobs). As in archaeology, this utopian method involves filling in some of the bits that are missing, or interpolating those elements about which there is significant silence. Again, the deconstructive methods of post-structuralism underline the importance of identifying and interrogating silences. Neo-liberalism repressed the fact that the so-called free market is a social construct embedded in laws and assumptions about property rights, as well as its need to enforce social order. It also, interestingly, repressed its dependence on unpaid labor, chiefly by women. Unlike neo-conservatism, which placed enormous stress on the merits of the nuclear family, neo-liberalism has always claimed to be gender-blind. Yet the kind of society implied in the aspirations and policy recommendations of, for example, the Adam Smith Institute, itself required an army of shadow workers.

In the 1990s, I undertook a similar deconstruction of New Labour's rhetoric and policy, focusing on the slippery usage of the term "social exclusion" (see Levitas, *Inclusive Society*). The contradiction in New Labour's policy also hinges on the limitations of the market and dependence on unpaid labor. In their case, "community" fills the role occupied by the repressive state in Thatcherism, and the welfare state in Fabianism. Rather than the free market and the strong state, or the regulated market and the welfare state, we have the global market and the active community. But active communities rely on unpaid work – much of which is undertaken by women and which only becomes visible when it does not get done. Charity shops are finding it much more difficult to recruit volunteers now that so many more women in their fifties are in paid work and not available for unpaid work, or indeed informal child care. A policy which is dedicated to increasing the labor force participation rate, and which aims its Welfare to Work strategy at lone parents, is profoundly problematic. The work of raising children is rendered invisible by being wrapped up either in "parental responsibility" or the "life" side of the "work-life balance." As Michael Moore shows in *Bowling for Columbine*, this blindness can have fatal consequences. A six-year-old boy took a gun to school and fired it, resulting in the death of a class-mate. The gun belonged to his uncle, with whom the boy and his mother were staying because they were homeless. No one knew he had taken the gun, because his mother was not there when he left the house. She was being bussed to work miles away, as part of a workfare scheme to prevent welfare dependency.

The kind of society Blair envisages for Britain is, of course, a meritocracy. The IROS method was used to brilliant effect by Michael Young in his 1950s dystopian text, *The Rise of the Meritocracy*. Young's book demonstrated the instability of an unequal society in which position was based on merit, where "IQ plus effort equals merit," or, in more Blairite language, "talent plus work equals merit." Those in higher positions would go to any lengths to prevent the downward mobility of their less-bright offspring. And those in lower positions would not be reconciled to their unequal share by being told it was all they deserved. Such an ideology would fuel resentment and conflict, rather than build social cohesion. More recently, the idea of meritocracy has been satirized in the account of Aramanth in William Nicholson's *The Wind Singer*. This book describes the operation – and eventual downfall – of a society based on tests applied to individual members from the age of two. In both these fictional accounts, an image of a society rooted in a particular value is created in order to demonstrate the implications of its concrete instantiation, and to call it into question. At the moment, the value the European Union (EU) is asked to pursue is social inclusion (except for asylum seekers). Since 2001, every member-state has been required to produce a National Plan for Inclusion, a title contracted, with Orwellian echoes, to NAPinc. You can read these plans on the European Commission website. Inclusion, as far as the EU is concerned, is very largely about labor market participation and opportunities to compete in an increasingly unequal system. The reconstituted image that can be excavated from these plans is not unlike Blair's meritocracy. And in both fictional and factional versions of this process, IROS has both an archaeological and a critical element. The purpose of the imaginary reconstitution of society is to expose it to judgment.

IROS as Architecture

When the theologian Peter Askonas argues without derogation that social inclusion is at least potentially a utopian idea, he means something else (see Askonas and Stewart). What would an inclusive society look like, and how could it be attained? Such a question implies IROS not as archaeology or as critique, but as aspiration, as architecture. In a recent piece on the application of utopian method to social policy, I contrasted this approach with the more common piecemeal extrapolative approach (see Levitas, "Against Work"). Most social policy addresses present problems, or at best engages in short-term projection of present trends, and suggests modes of damage limitation. Such an approach naturalizes the major contours of present society, the structures of global capitalism, the dominance of paid work, and the inequalities of the market. The alternative is to think about where we might want to get to, and what routes are open to us. This is the more usual understanding of utopianism. The imaginary reconstitution of society is presented as aspiration, as goal – but one that must necessarily be a proposition for discussion and negotiation, the beginning of a process, not a statement of closure. In this sense, IROS can be understood as a quasi-Brechtian method. As Jameson construes Brecht, techniques of estrangement are used to didactic effect (see Jameson, *Brecht and Method*). But Brecht's didacticism is neither a closed system, nor a moral education towards a given end. It involves a call to judgment, or to judgment on a judgment, rather than simply the presentation of a judgment in itself. Both Brecht and IROS as method demand responsibility from the audience as much as the writer.

A potential project might be to take forward the question of the nature of an inclusive society. This could employ IROS in both archaeological and architectural modes. Archeologically, such a project could explore or expose the versions of the good society currently being promoted under the banner of "social inclusion," a term that has been taken up in Canadian social policy as well as across the EU. Architecturally, it could construct at least one alternative vision of what an inclusive society could look like: freed from the constraints and assumptions of contemporary political and social policy agendas, and broadened in its definition of inclusion. In so doing, it could demonstrate the potential of Utopia as method, to change the way we think about our possible future. Such a project involves politics, philosophy, sociology, and social policy as well as the accumulated resources of utopian speculation and desire. It thus transgresses disciplinary boundaries. It is a defining characteristic and strength of IROS and the utopian method that it explodes artificial disciplinary boundaries and constraints. If it cannot return us to the pre-disciplinary era of Marx, Morris, Bellamy, Gilman, it might well give us a much-needed push towards what some writers are now terming post-disciplinarity.

My current project, in fact, might also be described as post-disciplinary – and my focus is once again on Morris. In *Spaces of Hope*, David Harvey insists that utopian thinking is essential to any possibility of social transformation, but that it is problematic because in practice it tends either to emphasize process, resulting in evasion, or to emphasize form and content, resulting in closure. He suggests we need a more dialectical approach. However, Harvey's thesis also insists on a degree of necessary closure, effected by the physical embeddedness of social life. As a Marxist geographer, his discussion focuses on the way capitalism constantly tears down and rebuilds the physical infrastructure in the interests of profit. His discussion suggests more of a three-way interaction between the social, the spatial, and the historical (see Levitas, "On Dialectical Utopianism"). Morris's utopia embodies all these. I am trying to read Morris's imaginary reconstitution of society against its historical and *spatial* context, by imaginatively reconstructing the *place* in which *News from Nowhere* was composed through maps, documents, and contemporary accounts.

Doing this suggests Morris was writing against recent and continuing changes in Hammersmith, rather than simply evoking or invoking a medieval past. It is not that a different reading of Morris's text is suggested, but it is apparent that Morris's concerns have continued to be points of conflict through the twentieth century, into debates in our own time about the sustainable city. Yet if we look at these debates through the lens of IROS as archaeology, we can see that there are significant silences in place of Morris's holism. They consistently evade the deeper question of the social and economic arrangements that would make sustainability a real option – that is, they do not confront the endemic and overriding problem of the age, rampant global capitalism. The imaginary reconstitution of society of Morris's utopian vision provides a "base outside" from which the actual Hammersmith, the emergent Hammersmith, and hopes for Hammersmith (and other places) can be called into question. But this base outside does not have to be adopted as a viable solution. It can function to produce estrangement, to insist that it does not have to be like this. It can stand as a possibility for consideration, if not necessarily a possibility. And both Morris's vision and any commentary I might make on it stand less as a platform than a provocation: an invitation to consider "how should we live" and "how can that be"?

Works Cited

Amis, Martin. *Koba the Dread: Laughter and the Twenty Million.* London: Jonathan Cape, 2002.
—— "The Books Interview." *The Observer* 8 September 2002, 18.
Askonas, Peter, and Angus Stewart. *Social Inclusion: Possibilities and Tensions.* London: Palgrave, 2000.
Auden, W.H. "Atlantis." *W.H. Auden.* Harmondsworth: Penguin, 1958. 86–8.
Bauman, Zygmunt. "Utopia with No Topos." *History of the Human Sciences* 16.1 (2003): 11–26.
Bloch, Ernst. *The Principle of Hope.* Trans. Neville Plaice, Stephen Plaice, and Paul Knight. 3 Vols. Oxford: Blackwell, 1986.

Davis, J.C. *Utopia and the Ideal Society: A Study of English Utopian Writing, 1516– 1700*. Cambridge: Cambridge University Press, 1981.

Durkheim, Emile. *The Division of Labour in Society*. New York: Free Press, 1964.

Eliot, T.S. "Little Gidding." *The Complete Poems and Plays of T.S. Eliot*. London: Faber, 1969. 191–8.

Fitting, Peter. "The Concept of Utopia in the Work of Fredric Jameson." *Utopian Studies* 9.2 (1998): 8–17.

Foden, Giles. "War of the Worlds." *The Guardian* 24 August 2002.

Harvey, David. *Spaces of Hope*. Edinburgh: Edinburgh University Press, 2000.

Hepworth, Barbara. *A Retrospective Exhibition of Carvings and Drawings from 1927 to 1954, Whitechapel Art Gallery, 8th April–6th June, 1954*. London: Whitechapel Art Gallery, 1954.

Jameson, Fredric. *Brecht and Method*. London: Verso, 1998.

—— "Of Islands and Trenches: Naturalization and the Production of Utopian Discourse." *Diacritics* 7.2 (1977): 2–21.

—— *Postmodernism: Or, The Cultural Logic of Late Capitalism*. London: Verso, 1991.

—— "Progress Versus Utopia: Or, Can We Imagine the Future?" *Science-Fiction Studies* 27.9 (1982): 13–92.

—— *The Seeds of Time*. New York: Columbia University Press, 1994.

Kumar, Krishan. *Prophecy and Progress*. Harmondsworth: Penguin, 1979.

—— *Utopianism*. Milton Keynes: Open U, 1991.

Levitas, Ruth. "Against Work: A Utopian Incursion into Social Policy." *Critical Social Policy* 21.4 (2001): 449–65.

—— *The Concept of Utopia*. Hemel Hempstead: Philip Allan, 1990.

—— "Educated Hope: Ernst Bloch on Abstract and Concrete Utopia." *Not Yet: Reconsidering Ernst Bloch*. Ed. Jamie Daniel and Tom Moylan. London: Verso, 1997. 65–79.

—— "The Elusive Idea of Utopia." *History of the Human Sciences* 16.1 (2003): 1–10.

—— "For Utopia: The (Limits of the) Utopian Function in Late Capitalist Society." *The Philosophy of Utopia*. Ed. Barbara Goodwin. Ilford: Cass, 2001. 25–43.

—— *The Inclusive Society? Social Exclusion and New Labour*. Basingstoke: Palgrave Macmillan, 2005.

—— "On Dialectical Utopianism." *History of the Human Sciences* 16.1 (2003): 137– 50.

—— "Utopia as Literature, Utopia as Politics." *Zeitgenössische Utopieentwürfe in Literatur und Gesellschaft: Zur Kontroverse seit den achtziger Jahren*. Ed. Rolf Jucker. Amsterdam: Rodopi, 1997. 121–38.

Levitas, Ruth (ed.). *The Ideology of the New Right*. Cambridge: Polity, 1986.

Meyer, Siri (ed.). *Midlertiidige Utopier*. Oslo: Museum of Contemporary Art, 2003.

More, Thomas. *Utopia: A New Translation, Backgrounds, Criticism*. Ed. and trans. Robert M. Adams. New York: Norton, 1975.

Morris, William. *News from Nowhere. Collected Works of William Morris.* 1891. London: Routledge, 1992.

—— *The Earthly Paradise. Collected Works of William Morris.* 1868. London, Routledge, 1992.

Moylan, Tom. *Demand the Impossible: Science Fiction and the Utopian Imagination.* London: Methuen, 1986.

—— *Scraps of the Untainted Sky: Science Fiction, Utopia, Dystopia.* Boulder: Westview, 2000.

Nicholson, William. *The Wind Singer.* London: Egmont, 2000.

Nussbaum, Martha. *Upheavals of Thought: the Intelligence of Emotions.* Cambridge: Cambridge University Press, 2002.

Popper, Karl. *The Open Society and its Enemies.* London: Routledge, 1945.

Sargent, Lyman Tower. *British and Utopian Literature, 1516–1985.* New York: Garland, 1988.

—— "Is There Only One Utopian Tradition?" *Journal of the History of Ideas* (1982): 681–89.

—— "The Three Faces of Utopianism Revisited." *Utopian Studies* 5.1 (1994): 1–37.

Sargisson, Lucy. *Contemporary Feminist Utopianism.* London: Routledge, 1996.

Thompson, E.P. *William Morris: Romantic to Revolutionary.* London: Merlin, 1976.

Titchmarsh, Alan. Trailer for Spring Series of *How to Be a Gardener.* BBC2. February 2003.

Wells, H.G. *An Englishman Looks at the World.* London: Cassell, 1914.

Williams, Raymond. "Utopia and Science Fiction." *Problems in Materialism and Culture.* London: Verso, 1980. 190–212.

Yeats, William Butler. "He Wishes for the Cloths of Heaven." *The Poems.* Ed. Daniel Albright. London: Dent, 1990. 90.

Young, Michael. *The Rise of the Meritocracy.* London: Thames and Hudson, 1958.

VINCENT GEOGHEGAN

Political Theory, Utopia, Post-Secularism

> We do not wish to be sans-culottists, nor frugal citizens, nor unassuming presidents; we are for founding a democracy of terrestrial gods, equal in glory, in blessedness, and in sanctity. You demand simple modes of dress, austere morals, and unspiced pleasures; we, on the contrary, desire nectar and ambrosia, purple mantles, costly perfumes, luxury and splendour, dances of laughing nymphs, music and comedies. Be not therefore angry with us, virtuous republicans!
> Heinrich Heine, *Religion and Philosophy in Germany*

> They that start by burning books will end by burning men.
> Heinrich Heine, *Almansor*[1]

Political Theory

When I was an undergraduate at the beginning of the 1970s, the political theorists I studied had one noticeable thing in common: *they were all dead.*[2] And I mean *dead*! Political theory, in this context, was an activity carried out only by historical figures such as Thomas

1   Inscription on memorial, Dachau concentration camp. When the Nazis invaded France, Hitler ordered that the grave of Heine (who was born of Jewish parents) should be destroyed.
2   I would like to thank my (very much alive!) political theorist colleagues at Queen's University, Belfast – Chris Armstrong, Keith Breen, Susan McManus, and Shane O'Neill – for their comments on earlier drafts; also Tom Moylan for organizing the seminars in Limerick and Galway, where the chapter was given its first outings; Mike Kenny of Sheffield University also made useful comments, as did the participants in a seminar held in the School of Politics, University of Nottingham.

Hobbes, John Locke, and John Stuart Mill. The most recent theorist I studied, Karl Marx, had died in 1883. This was not the result of an unambitious syllabus, or negligent teaching staff, but of something deeper. The apparent reduction of political theory to the history of political thought was indicative of a profound shift that had begun earlier in the century, one that had opened up an abyss between the political theorists of the past and contemporary understandings of "Politics" (see Horton; Miller; and Parekh). A number of writers in the 1950s and 1960s registered this fact. In 1956, the historian Peter Laslett wrote that "for the moment, anyway, political philosophy is dead" (vii); whilst Isaiah Berlin, whose Oxford Chair was actually in Political and Social Theory, and no advocate of the "death of political theory" thesis, still felt impelled in 1961 to pen an article with the defensive title: "Does Political Theory Still Exist?" Writing in 1970, Brian Barry wittily summed up the mood of this period:

> until fairly recently, political theory had for many years been regarded as something that had occurred in the past, but could hardly be expected to happen nowadays – rather like the Church of England's view of miracles (1).

What therefore had happened? From the end of the nineteenth century, political theory was effectively torn apart by far-reaching shifts in intellectual life, these shifts in turn resting on more basic socio-economic change. One source of disintegration was the rise of the social sciences. A positivist and scientistic climate sought to model social enquiry on the natural sciences. Theorizing about politics was to take the form of an empirical theory, a political science. This was part of a broader separation of fact from value. Just as political science annexed the factual aspects of political theory, so the value dimensions of political theory were deemed to be in the realm of ethics and moral philosophy. This left the vigorous past of political theory to be hived off into the history of political thought. Furthermore, in Britain, where courses involving the study of politics had emerged partly in response to the need to train imperial officials, the retreat from empire destroyed the internal coherence of syllabi predicated on the assumption of British "greatness." As Stefan Collini and his co-authors argue, the familiar mixture of the history of political thought, the British Constitution, and comparative political institutions to be found in twentieth-century syllabi became detached from the ideological project that generated them (353–7).

By the 1950s, this process was further assisted by the dominant trends in Anglo-American philosophy. Logical positivism and linguistic philosophy played skittles with the venerable concepts of political theory, claiming to see in them a mass of tautological, logically contradictory, or simply meaningless statements. T.D. Weldon's *The Vocabulary of Politics* of 1953 was an important representative of this approach. Its subtitle, *An Enquiry into the Use and Abuse of Language in the Making of Political Theories*, left little room for doubt about its intentions – namely, to demonstrate the intellectual nullity of whole swathes of political theory. Weldon had a noble concern – the misuse of words – but it was a discouraging moment. There may have been the promise of a constructive turn, but Weldon never really got beyond the moment of destruction.

This, then, was the context in which I began my study of politics. The fact that I was studying dead political theorists was not a cause for concern – quite the opposite – for the last dead thinker we studied (Marx, whose work had a powerful fascination for my generation of students) had provided an analytical framework that could explain why this had happened, and why it was part of a "progressive" development. Political theory was part of a division of academic labor, which itself reflected the broader division of labor. The speculations of the dead thinkers were to be superseded by a new unity of theory and practice. Marx was the last "great thinker," who pointed to the diffusion and democratization of genius. The canon of great sages was itself a testimony to the elitist individualism of the capitalist mode of production. Political theory, in this sense, was therefore rightly to be understood as an historical issue.

Needless to say, political theory had not gone away. Throughout this period there had been intense reflection and speculation on matters political – hardly surprising, given the cataclysmic events of the century – but this activity was dispersed in activities and disciplines other than political theory: in history, philosophy, economics, and in the creative work of writers and artists. Furthermore, much of the best theoretical work came, not from the Anglo-American tradition but

from the so-called Continental schools of thought. However, within
the Anglo-American tradition things were about to change. Indeed
claims about the "death" of doctrines and movements are frequently
part of the process of recovery for the supposed deceased. Genuinely
dead dogs tend to lie in silence. And so it was with political theory.
When I went to university in 1971, I was oblivious to the fact that this
very year would, in retrospect, be seen as the year political theory was
reborn, for in that year the American philosopher John Rawls published *A Theory of Justice*. This book was hailed as a return to the
grand tradition of political theory. In fact, the book was based upon
material that Rawls had been developing in the 1950s and 1960s
(again casting doubt on a simplistic "death of political theory" thesis).
Certainly by the time I ceased to be a student in 1977, Rawls had been
tacked on the list of the great tradition of political thought – seemingly
the one example of a political theorist still breathing.

However, all was not as it seemed. First we must ask, why did
this revival occur at this point in time? Important changes were occurring in the intellectual and social spheres. At the intellectual level,
the old positivist and scientistic orthodoxies were breaking down. The
attempt to import the methods of the natural sciences into the social
had come under sustained attack, assisted by developments in natural
science itself, which had been moving away from its traditional
models. Facts and values were coming together once more. Furthermore, the philosophical climate was also changing as the dead hand of
logical positivism was removed, and linguistic philosophy began to
develop a more constructive project. Political theory's theoretical
space, annexed earlier in the century, seemed to be up for grabs once
more. At the social and political level, post-war development had
created an increasingly educated population, with new agendas and
demands. The radicalization surrounding the Vietnam War was an
important reflection of this process.

But was the new theory adequate to cope with the context that
had given birth to it? Rawls was a philosopher – a liberal philosopher.
Much of the resurgence of political theorizing that appeared after *A
Theory of Justice* was very much in the mould of *liberal political
philosophy*. This new hegemony in political theory claimed continuity
with the past through the selective annexing of the various theolo-

gians, courtiers, politicians, tutors, civil servants, revolutionaries, and so forth who made up the historical canon of political thought; but this was a new phenomenon. This Rawlsian moment represented the triumph of one particular mode of political theory within Anglo-American political theory.

But the world outside was one of seething particularism. To put it at its most basic: the new political theory had to come to terms with the fact that society was composed of individuals and groups with differing, though legitimate, interests and wishes, and that these differences were likely to be salient for some considerable time to come, if not permanently. Liberalism was attractive because it seemed to provide theoretical and institutional means of coping with these claims of diversity. This new liberal orthodoxy seemed to offer the prospect of various forms of difference co-existing in a tolerant society, protected by a state committed to the protection of freedom of thought and action. The difficulties with this hope soon became apparent. For some groups and thinkers liberalism was not the solution but the *problem*. Whilst some self-consciously religious fundamentalist groups argued that liberalism was a value-laden project, committed to ungodly moral anarchism, some ethnic minorities within western society rejected what they saw as the spurious universalism of liberalism. Furthermore, although a commodious ideology, liberalism was not infinitely elastic; it could not necessarily be adapted and re-configured to embody emerging values and visions. Thus, although the Rawlsian conversation included thinkers as ideologically distinct as G.A. Cohen and Robert Nozick, the possibility of new dialogues needed to be seriously entertained. Francis Fukuyama's tendentious *The End of History* stands as a warning of the dangers of a hegemonic liberalism.

Rawls's own theoretical development after 1971 can be seen as an attempt to deepen and thicken his perspective, to make it more adequate to the complexities of the world. Two areas, in particular, I want to mention, because they deal with areas I want to cover in the rest of this essay: the need for utopianism, and the need for a more nuanced approach to religion. In *Justice as Fairness: A Restatement* (largely completed by 1989), Rawls outlines the four roles of political philosophy, and of the fourth role he says: "We view political philosophy as realistically utopian: that is, as probing the limits of practical possibility" (4). This is a fairly modest form of utopianism, but it does recognize the necessary utopian dimension in any adequate political theory. In *Political Liberalism*, Rawls, at first sight, appears to be retreating from the utopian in his reference to "the unrealistic idea of a well-ordered society as it appears in [*A Theory of Justice*]"; but this in fact hinges on a rejection of an underlying assumption in *A Theory of Justice* that a comprehensive philosophical doctrine could serve as the basis of such social arrangements (xvi). Since writing that earlier text he had become convinced that the existence of opposed but reasonable comprehensive doctrines (including some based on religious conceptions) meant that the principles of a just society had to be grounded in a "reasonable pluralism." This shift, therefore, was not a retreat from the utopian, but an acknowledgement of the complexities involved in creating a good society in a world of immense differences. In *The Law of Peoples*, the "realistic utopia" takes center stage, where he offers a self-consciously utopian vision of international justice (and explicitly takes issue with E.H. Carr's critique of utopianism). His conclusion is unambiguous:

> by showing how the social world may realize the features of a realistic utopia, political philosophy provides a long-term goal of political endeavour, and in working toward it gives meaning to what we can do today (128).

In the case of the issue of religion, whilst *A Theory of Justice* had relatively little to say on the matter, and sounded a distinctly secular tone, *Political Liberalism* is greatly concerned with the consequences for liberal democracy of the relationship between the religious and the secular. As Rawls put it in an interview in 1998:

> *A Theory of Justice* was a comprehensive doctrine of liberalism designed to set out a certain classical theory of justice [...] so as to make it immune to various traditional objections. The difference is that, in *Political Liberalism*, the problem is how do you see religion and comprehensive secular doctrines as compatible with and supportive of the basic institutions of a constitutional regime (617).

This latter stance is beginning to take us into the terrain that I term post-secular.

Utopia

Utopia is unique amongst political concepts in having an intentional ambiguity built into it from its very inception. Thomas More punned on the sound of two Greek words, *eu* and *ou*, to make "utopia" mean simultaneously good place and no place. This introduced a dynamism into the concept that has made it potentially very powerful. First, there was the dynamism of the "good" and the "no." In a positive sense it could mean the good place that, *as of yet*, has found no place. Or, negatively, it was a desire for goodness that could never realistically find a place. Hence, two completely opposed positions could use the same word in their argument. Second, there was also the dynamism of the next element of the word – derived from *topos*, the Greek for "place." Although More used it in a spatial sense (Utopia was a geographically distant island), the fact that it was no place meant that it could fairly easily be construed as a temporal or historical category: utopia as a place lying in the future. Historically the dynamic ambiguity contained in More's text bifurcated into distinct and opposing activities. On the one hand, the search for the good place continued in the so-called utopian literary genre – the result being, with a few notable exceptions, virtually unreadable accounts of quite tedious goodness. In this respect More's *Utopia* was, to this day, the first and *last* example of its kind. The utopian impulse also entered various forms of progressive social theory – notably liberalism and socialism. On the other hand, the anti-utopian deployment of the category of Utopia entered both conservative social theory and the distinct genres of the anti-utopia and the dystopia (both of which dwelt on the horrific consequences of arrogant attempts at social engineering). If the utopias were dull but worthy, the anti-utopias and dystopias were depressing but much greater fun to read. It is only in recent years that the original intentions of More have been reproduced. Tom Moylan has developed the concept of the "critical utopia" in his *Demand the Impossible* to show how a single text can explore the good through a dialectic of good and bad.

The hybrid nature of the utopian form – part literary, part philosophical – has had an important positive consequence. If, as Wendy
Brown has argued, the modern academy has seen the emergence of a
restrictive professionalization, even Balkanization, of disciplines
(111–21), then work on the utopian tends to encourage the counter-
tendency of inter-disciplinarity. Without wishing to be too fanciful,
there is an echo here of the young Marx's utopian evocation of
communism, where one would engage in many functions and not be
defined by any of them. Anyone who has ever attended a conference
discussing the utopian could not but notice both the large range of
disciplines represented and the relative ease of communication between them – the shared study of the utopian to some extent detaching
the participants from their conventional disciplinary homes. There is
something of the *flâneur* in those who peruse utopias (the purposeful
purposelessness of the dreamy stroll around the streets of the city),
for, as Walter Benjamin noted, "the idleness of the flâneur is a
demonstration against the division of labour" (427). It is surely no
coincidence that the single most important modern text on the utopian
– Ernst Bloch's *Principle of Hope* – is so frequently described as
encyclopedic; but it is a *flâneur*'s encyclopedia, a great sprawling
assemblage of the sublime and the gimcrack drawn from myriad times
and places, and a dizzying array of disciplines.

Implicit in all of this is a greatly expanded concept of the utopian. Establishing the boundaries of the utopian continues to tax
scholars in the field of utopian studies. Whilst not wishing to reduce
the concept to a literary device supposedly invented by More in 1516,
it is necessary to resist the urge to expand the concept so that it can
encompass any form of hope, imaginative construction, or counter-
factual, to the point that in referring to everything it ends up referring
to nothing at all. A lot of good work attempting to draw boundaries
has been done by, amongst others, Lyman Tower Sargent, Ruth Levitas, and Moylan. My concern here is to explore the role of the utopian
in political theory.

Historically, the adoption of a positive or a negative definition of
Utopia determined the conceptual framework within which Utopia
was to be inserted. In a negative appraisal, utopian became contrasted
with realistic, where this dualism was used to contrast an impractical

approach with a hard-headed practicality. From a positive perspective this distinction was unhelpful. First, "realistic" is itself a highly contested concept; second, it has often been deployed historically by those opposed to change of any sort. Finally, the distinction leaves the approach to the future extremely undertheorized: how does the new come about? Indeed, given the immense problems we face today, utopianism might be the most realistic of all responses; this is the substance of Roberto Unger's demand that "we must be visionaries to become realists" (74). In short, if one does not succumb to a simplistic utopianism/realism distinction, one is left with a cluster of ways of thinking about the future, each possessing different objectives, forms, contents, methods of assessment, and, let it be said, differing strengths and weaknesses.

Let me take as an example the classic target of the realist anti-utopian: Utopia as a vision of perfection. I am more than happy to resist this attack. However, even within utopian studies there has been a degree of reticence about this category. Stung by conservative and Cold War liberal attacks on the dangerous ambitions of utopian think-ing, a retreat from visions of perfection began. Utopias, it was now claimed, merely looked forward to a *better* society, not a perfect society. Likewise, as in the conception of the critical utopia, it was felt that utopian forms should incorporate blemishes and dissonance. The danger with this approach (a danger Moylan avoids) is that utopias may become attenuated and lose that element of uncompromising marvelous otherness that is at the heart of genuine transcendence. "Where wast thou," thunders Jehova in the *Book of Job*, "where wast thou when I laid the foundations of the earth [...] When the morning stars sang together and all the sons of God shouted for joy?" The utopian tradition can cease to be a source of powerful images and instead become a source of embarrassment. Indeed one of Bloch's great contributions was that he wished to celebrate the commanding achievements of the human imagination, artistic and religious con-ceptions of the sublime, which lay far beyond any possibility of accomplishment in the conceivable future.

But forward thinking *need not* be concerned with the perfect; the search for the *better* is an entirely legitimate enterprise. The strong normative element in recent political philosophy can lend itself to this

project. Rawls's realistic utopia, in effect, taps into this latent utopianism. The problem is that for many of the writers belonging to the
Anglo-American tradition of political theory, this latent utopianism
remains undertheorized, abstract, and a trifle shame-faced. It was
Marx, in his early work, who suggested that the *apparent* evacuation
of history from the abstract normative structure of modern civil
society was *actually* a testimony to the intense historical coloration of
those norms. The abstractions of liberalism are aspects of a withdrawal of the state from society, or, more accurately, the recon-
figuration of the political use of the state, and reflect the project of a
new hegemonic social class that needed a politically depoliticized
society. We might also note Alasdair MacIntyre's characterization of
the abstract rationalist:

> an individual whose distinctive identity consists in key part in the ability to
> escape social identification, by always being able to abstract him or herself
> from any role whatsoever; it is the individual who is potentially many things,
> but actually in and for him or herself nothing (30).

There is also Avishai Margalit's useful distinction, in *The Ethics
of Memory*, between the "moral" with its "thin" description of "thin
relations" between humans, expressible in general principles, and the
"ethical" with its "thick" descriptions of "thick human relations,"
which more appropriately depends on "comparisons to paradigmatic
cases." In Margalit's own exploration of the question, "who is my
neighbour?," the moral involves a discussion of Kantian principles,
whilst the ethical takes the form of an engagement with the New
Testament parable of the Good Samaritan; although I do not subscribe
to Margalit's defense of ethical partiality – that a husband has an
ethical obligation to save his wife rather than a stranger, when one of
them has to drown (7–8, 38–9, 41–4). In short, the recognition of the
historicity of norms can act as a springboard for a fuller universality
that includes, as an integral part, the anticipations, of concrete individuals, groups, and communities.

Post-Secularism

Anyone familiar with recent political theory, whether Anglo-American or Continental, could not fail to be struck by a new concern with religion. I have already referred to this development in the work of Rawls, but it can be found in thinkers as diverse as William Connolly and Cohen, Jacques Derrida and Jürgen Habermas. Even a thinker like Charles Taylor, whose Catholicism is of long vintage, has only recently explicitly brought his religious concerns into the heart of his work. In terms of the Anglo-American tradition, it would appear that the revival of political theory in the 1970s, after its mooted death in the 1950s, produced a body of work (rooted in transatlantic analytic philosophy, and liberal in cast) too thin to meet the tumultuous social changes that had called it from its purported grave. To gain a purchase on this new terrain, theorists have had to look to alternative resources to thicken their responses, and religion has provided one such resource. More modestly, the peripheral status of religion as a serious issue became untenable. Within Continental traditions of philosophy, complex modern processes of globalization, the information revolution, the rise of fundamentalism, and so forth, have thrust religion to the center stage and generated an imperative to involve the religious in the response. As Derrida noted:

> the said "return of the religious," which is to say the spread of a complex and overdetermined phenomenon, is not a simple *return*, for its globality and its figures (tele-techno-media-scientific, capitalistic and politico-economic) remain original and unprecedented (42).[3]

3   A distinctly acerbic note on the "turn to religion" in general, and on its presence in Derrida in particular, is struck by Christopher Norris: "this whole revival of religious or theological interests among literary theorists is something that I find pretty hard to take [...] I expect it was reading Bertrand Russell's *Why I Am Not a Christian* – at an impressionable age, no doubt – that cured me of religion once and for all [...] I want to say that this is a highly undesirable, as well as philosophically confused, way of thinking, especially at a time when so many barbarous acts are condoned in the name of this or that revived fundamentalist creed [...] the recent 'religious' turn in Derrida's writing [...] is in striking contrast with his early work" (128–30).

I term this development *post-secular* in that it represents an attempt to reconfigure the Enlightenment dualism of the religious and the secular, whereby the secular moment is defended and cherished, but not at the expense of the rich resources of religious traditions.

This can take a number of forms. There is sensitivity to some of the religious roots of modern concepts, and a desire to enrich these concepts through an exploration of this genealogy. There has also been a kind of "return of the repressed" as thinkers have come to realize that whilst religious ideas have haunted their work, they have either denied this to themselves in the past, been previously genuinely unaware of the fact, or have, till now, for fear of professional ridicule, been unwilling to introduce religious themes into serious works of philosophy. There has been a recognition that religious traditions offer concepts, insights, imagery, vistas that are often absent in the attenuated abstractions of modern secular thought. There is also an attempt to distinguish this approach from another use of the term post-secular by those with a deeply antagonistic stance towards secularism, those who call for a resurgent religiosity that dismantles the secular world and returns to a mythic religious age. Here *post*-secular betokens *pre*-secular.

The threat from the latter quarter, in the form of religious fundamentalism, is part of the reason why an adequate post-secularism is so necessary. Partly as a reaction to the experience of secularism, fundamentalism in both affluent and impoverished societies has sought to forge a political/religious project out of the religious resources of specific faiths. Having consigned the religious to a realm beyond rational discourse, advocates of secular traditions of thought have found it very difficult to engage with this phenomenon. Confronted with a passage of scripture, they are rendered speechless. I got some sense of this context when I decided to use a twice-weekly lengthy train journey in England to read, for the first time, the Bible from start to finish. The levels of studied indifference, embarrassment, and hostility, but also of zealous encouragement and righteous affirmation in those who noticed my reading matter were palpable! Furthermore, there is a sense in which the two elements of the belief/unbelief dualism have been mutually reinforcing. One might recall Marx's rejection of the term "atheism" on the grounds that the continued presence of the word "theism" in atheism indicated that belief had not been overcome; likewise, contrary to the project of proselytization, it could be argued that faith has drawn sustenance from lack of faith, gaining a sort of validation for its choice (395). In short, the post-secular reintegration of the religious into the secular may thus be a means of generating empathy, dialogue, and, where necessary, contestation, in a century that might readily generate appalling levels of religious conflict (with September 11th as a terrible warning).

One can explore the possibility of a utopian post-secularism in the two forms of utopianism previously discussed – the search for the good (or, if one prefers, the "better"), and the search for the perfect. In terms of the former, one might consider the recent work of Habermas. Given the themes of this essay, Habermas is particularly interesting in that, although a product of the Frankfurt School, he has had a long and fruitful conversation with Anglo-American political theory. He also has registered the broader significance of September 11th, when "the tension between secular society and religion exploded in an entirely different way" ("Faith and Knowledge" 101). Some may be non-plussed by the description of Habermas as utopian. A distinction has grown up in the literature between the "theory of the good" and the "theory of the right," where the former is deemed to be concerned with the question of what constitutes the good society and the latter with the criteria to be used when there is a choice of competing goals (Pettit 22). Within this distinction, Habermas has been conventionally defined as concerned with the theory of the right, and therefore in no way utopian. However, even within the terms of reference of Anglo-American political philosophy this distinction appears distinctly unstable, for clearly the search for criteria to decide when goals come into conflict must itself be grounded on broad assessments of the nature of human behavior, capacities, and entitlements – in short, on some conception of the good. From this perspective, therefore, Habermas can be discussed under the rubric of the utopian.

In a recent intervention, "Religious Tolerance – The Pacemaker for Cultural Rights," Habermas builds upon the later Rawls's deeper grounding of his theory of justice and his greater attention to the issue of religion. Rawls, he argues, in his attempt to validate the norms of liberal democracy in the context of powerful "comprehensive doctrines" of religion, wishes to see the "embedding" of liberal political morality in the various religious traditions (11–12). Habermas, in turn, noting "the highly developed conceptual resources of [...] the great world religions," likewise argues for the grounding of the valuable normative elements of the secular moment in the various religions by the adherents of those religions: the development of "the normative principles of the secular order from within the view of a respective religious tradition and community" (17, 12). He is aware of the great problems involved in this enterprise, notably the presence in religious traditions of pre-secular anathemas and condemnations directed against certain forms of human behavior. The secular gains must, however, be defended. It is the religious traditions that must reconsider their positions on these issues: it is "necessary to revise attitudes and prescriptions that (as with the dogmatic prejudice against homosexuality for example) claim support from [...] long-standing traditions of interpretations of the holy scriptures" (13).

In the case of religious visions of perfection, I have yet to find a starting point that surpasses the work of Bloch. The fact that he was an atheist and a Marxist does not seem a promising beginning for an analysis of the virtues of religion. However, his rejection of theism enhanced his sense of the wonder of the universe; there was something infinitely more miraculous in nature creating such diversity than in the genuinely mundane hypothesis of divine creation. This further meant that religion was a distinctive form of human discourse, a special form for talking about the deepest and most profound aspects of human experience. Unlike many secular analyses of religion, Bloch's did not seek to reduce religion to its supposed rational substratum: religion brought its own gifts to the table. His Marxist divergence from Marx's excoriation of religion can, perhaps, be grasped in terms of different readings of Ludwig Feuerbach. Whilst Marx's analysis is saturated with the second part of *The Essence of Christianity*, and Feuerbach deals with "the false or theological essence of religion" (185), Bloch's approach is much more consonant with the first part: "the true or anthropological essence of religion" (33; see Geoghegan, "Religion and Communism"). Religion for Bloch is suffused with the most sublime utopian imagery; and it pays the ultimate compliment to humanity, in that "it cannot think highly and mysteriously enough of man" (1197). The religious traditions of humanity contain the gold-bearing seams of utopian hope – in many ways the most distant from existing reality, but also grounded in the most intimate of human concerns. In his explorations of these *traditions* therefore Bloch brings out the Janus-faced quality of utopia – the forward look and the backward look – where the latter feeds into what one might term "remembering the future."[4] But he is clear that past visions have to be used with care since they can act as a brake on the necessary production of novelty. The religious sphere is not simply a storehouse of historic utopian imagery; it is a space where the new can be incubated. Hence his advocacy of "recognition" rather than "recollection." He also brings out the political salience of this project. Reflecting on the collapse of Weimar Germany and the triumph of fascism, he points to the dangers of abandoning religion as mere archaic superstition, as did the hyper-rational Marxists of that time. By vacating the territory of deep religious longings they left it to be oppressively colonized by the forces of National Socialism. For Bloch religion is too important to be left to the religious.

Conclusion

Let me conclude by returning to the opening theme of this essay – dead political theorists. Rawls himself is now dead. It is too early to say whether with his death what I earlier called the Rawlsian moment will also begin to dissipate. But as we saw, Rawls, in his later work on the utopian and the religious, was moving in a direction that allowed someone like myself, raised in the theoretical traditions of Marxism, to find some common ground with him. Perhaps, instead of using the imagery of death, we might use, as Derrida has, the imagery of the ghostly. Ghosts, as Derrida reminds us, although in one sense dead, are nonetheless very much alive. This spectral language does seem to lend itself to our themes. Coming out of religious traditions, the ghost-

4   See Geoghegan, "Remembering"; and Baccolini.

ly has precisely those extra dimensions of meaning for which post-secularism is looking for. There is also something of the ghostly in the utopian – the inherent ambiguity, the playing fast and loose with time and space, the prophetic and unmasking voices, and the deeply disreputable connotations. Derrida suggests that there is much to be gained in having conversations with ghosts (in his case the specter of Marx), and this seems eminently good advice. In these challenging times we need to be genuinely catholic in our exploration of the sources of hope.

Works Cited

Baccolini, Raffaella. "'A useful knowledge of the present is rooted in the past': Memory and Historical Reconciliation in Ursula K. Le Guin's *The Telling*." *Dark Horizons: Science Fiction and the Dystopian Imagination*. Ed. Raffaella Baccolini and Tom Moylan. New York and London: Routledge, 2003. 113–35.

Barry, Brian. *Sociologists, Economists and Democracy*. London: Collier-Macmillan, 1970.

Benjamin, Walter. *The Arcades Project*. Trans. Howard Eiland and Kevin McLaughlin. Cambridge, Massachusetts: Harvard University Press, 1999.

Berlin, Isaiah. "Does Political Theory Still Exist?" *Philosophy, Politics and Society: Second Series*. Ed. Peter Laslett and W.G. Runciman. Oxford: Blackwell, 1962. 1–33.

Bloch, Ernst. *The Principle of Hope*. Trans. Neville Plaice, Stephen Plaice, and Paul Knight. 3 Vols. Oxford: Blackwell, 1986.

Brown, Wendy. "At the Edge." *What Is Political Theory?* Ed. Stephen K. White and J. Donald Moon. London: Sage, 2004. 103–23.

Cohen, G.A. *If You're an Egalitarian, How Come You're So Rich?* Cambridge: Harvard University Press, 2001.

Collini, Stefan, Donald Winch, and John Burrow. *That Noble Science of Politics: A Study in Nineteenth-Century Intellectual History*. Cambridge: Cambridge University Press, 1983.

Connolly, William. *Why I Am Not a Secularist*. Minneapolis: University of Minnesota Press, 1999.

Derrida, Jacques. "Faith and Knowledge: The Two Sources of 'Religion' at the Limits of Reason Alone." Trans. Samuel Weber. *Religion*. Ed. Jacques Derrida and Gianni Vattimo. Oxford: Polity, 1998. 1–78.

—— *Spectres of Marx*. Trans. Peggy Kamuf. New York and London: Routledge, 1994.

Feuerbach, Ludwig. *The Essence of Christianity*. Trans. George Eliot. New York, Evanston and London: Harper & Row, 1957.

Fukuyama, Francis. *The End of History and the Last Man*. New York: Free Press, 1992.

Geoghegan, Vincent. "Religion and Communism: Feuerbach, Marx and Bloch." *European Legacy* 9.5 (2004): 585–95.

—— "Remembering the Future." *Not Yet: Reconsidering Ernst Bloch*. Ed. Tom Moylan and Jamie Owen Daniel. London: Verso, 1997. 15–32.

Habermas, Jürgen. "Faith and Knowledge." Trans. Hella Beister and Max Pensky. *The Future of Human Nature*. Oxford: Polity, 2003. 101–15.

—— "Religious Tolerance – The Pacemaker for Cultural Rights." *Philosophy* 79 (2004): 5–18.

Heine, Heinrich. *Almansor*. Quoted in Cunningham, Hugo. S. 'Yes, he really said it!' 12 November 2003 <http://www.cyberussr.com/hcunn/quo-heine.html>.

—— *Religion and Philosophy in Germany. Marx, The Young Hegelians, and the Origins of Radical Social Theory: Dethroning the Self*. Ed. Warren Breckman. Cambridge: Cambridge University Press, 1999. 191.

Horton, John. "Weight or Lightness? Political Philosophy and its Prospects." *New Developments in Political Science*. Ed. Adrian Leftwich. Aldershot: Elgar, 1990. 126–42.

Laslett, Peter. "Introduction." *Philosophy, Politics and Society: First Series*. Ed. Peter Laslett. Oxford: Blackwell, 1956. vii–xv.

Levitas, Ruth. *The Concept of Utopia*. Syracuse: Syracuse University Press, 1990.

MacIntyre, Alasdair. "Practical Rationalities as Forms of Social Structure." *Irish Philosophical Journal* 4.1–2 (1987): 3–19.

Margalit, Avishai. *The Ethics of Memory*. Cambridge, Massachusetts: Harvard University Press, 2002.

Marx, Karl. "Letter to Arnold Ruge." Trans. Clemens Dutt. *The Collected Works of Marx and Engels*. Vol.1. London: Lawrence & Wishart, 1975. 393–5.

Miller, David. "The Resurgence of Political Theory." *Political Studies* 38.3 (1990): 421–37.

Moylan, Tom. *Demand the Impossible: Science Fiction and the Utopian Imagination*. New York and London: Methuen, 1986.

Norris, Christopher. "Music, Religion and Art After Theory: Frank Kermode and Christopher Norris." *life .after. theory*. Ed. Michael Payne and John Schad. London and New York: Continuum, 2003. 115–32.

Nozick, Robert. *Anarchy, State, and Utopia*. Oxford: Blackwell, 1974.

Parekh, Bhikhu. "Political Theory: Traditions in Political Philosophy." *A New Handbook of Political Science*. Ed. Robert E. Goodin and Hans-Dieter Klingemann. Oxford: Oxford University Press, 1996. 503–18.

Pettit, Philip. "Analytical Philosophy." *A Companion to Contemporary Political Philosophy*. Ed. Robert E. Goodin and Philip Pettit. Oxford: Blackwell, 1993. 7–38.

Rawls, John. "*Commonweal* Interview with John Rawls." *Collected Papers*. Cambridge, Massachusetts: Harvard University Press, 1999. 616–22.

—— *Justice as Fairness: A Restatement*. Cambridge, Massachusetts: Harvard University Press, 2001.

—— *The Law of Peoples*. Cambridge, Massachusetts: Harvard University Press, 1999.

—— *Political Liberalism*. New York: Columbia University Press, 1993.

Sargent, Lyman Tower. "The Three Faces of Utopianism Revisited." *Utopian Studies* 5.1 (1994): 1–37.

Taylor, Charles. "A Catholic Modernity." *A Catholic Modernity?* Ed. J.L. Heft. New York: Oxford University Press, 1999. 13–37.

Unger, Roberto. *Democracy Realized: The Progressive Alternative*. London: Verso, 1998.

Weldon, T.D. *The Vocabulary of Politics*. Harmondsworth: Penguin, 1953.

GREGORY CLAEYS

Rethinking Modern British Utopianism: Community and the Mastery of Desire

The Pursuit of Utopia

Speaking to the theme of how I came to Utopia and utopian studies –
and how this pursuit has altered both my own view of the world and of
my particular academic subject, modern British political thought – I
consider that I gravitated naturally to the field as a consequence of
growing up in a period of enormous social and political idealism – the
generation of *soixante-huit* – and of being possessed of a juvenile bent
for philosophic and religious speculation. Like many of us, perhaps,
the final departure of religious faith even metaphysical faith (Budd-
hist, in this case), which in my case occurred in my early twenties, left
a space into which Utopia would naturally gravitate.

As for many of my generation, the appeal of Karl Marx in such a
vacuum was immediate and compelling. When I began studying for
my doctorate, the first of my (I believe it was) thirteen Ph.D. topics
was Marx's political thought: the problem I sought to solve was why
there was so little of it; why Marx, in other words, presumed that so
much pre-existing conflict would be eliminated in the glorious communist society of the future. I found that political science, my disciplinary starting-point, was largely unhelpful in its approach to such
problems. At Cambridge, such questions were posed more historically, and as I moved to the Faculty of History I converted to the
historical method of approaching ideas, no doubt with some degree of
zealotry carried over from my recent religious past.

Regressing, as historians inevitably must, to seek the sources of
this somewhat implausible assumption, I reached William Godwin,
whose *Enquiry Concerning Political Justice* seemed less well mined
than the overworked seams of the Marxian field. And then, by what

now seems an amazing stroke of luck, I stumbled across the largest archive of hitherto unmined literature in the general field, the Goldsmiths' Library collection of Owenite literature at the University of London. There existed one highly respected secondary study of the Owenite movement, J.F.C. Harrison's *Robert Owen and the Owenites in Britain and America.* But I soon realized that the hundred-page bibliography appended to this work, compiled by Harrison and his research assistants, while reasonably complete, had not by any means been read completely, much less subject to a reasonably rigorous contextualization. The result was my first two books, *Machinery, Money and the Millennium: From Moral Economy to Socialism* and *Citizens and Saints: Politics and Anti-Politics in Early British Socialism,* the first resulting from working under Istvan Hont and Michael Ignatieff on a King's College Research Centre project on the history of political economy, the second answering my original question about Marx's political thought.

I did not at this point consider myself a "utopian" scholar as such; indeed I did not define the field in this way, but rather saw myself as an historian of socialism fortunate enough to have lighted upon such a rich trove of materials. Teaching in Germany in the early 1980s, however, I began to expand into other aspects of the utopian and communitarian traditions. My Marxism, never too dogmatic, was now increasingly tempered by the perception that "utopia" could have a non-pejorative echo, and need not be contrasted unfavorably with a "scientific" view of the world. By the time the Soviet Union and its affiliated regimes collapsed, I considered Marxism as merely the greatest of the modern utopian movements, flawed inevitably by its reluctance to embrace democratic theory adequately enough to avoid the emergence of one-party dictatorship of the totalitarian type, and uncomfortably theological in its assumption of its own superiority. I also became increasingly convinced that Marxism's disdain for intellectual history as "idealist" was misplaced, and that psychologically the power of ideas over the human mind has always been enormous.

As I began then to consider myself as a "utopian" scholar, first with producing editions of Owen's writings, then with bringing out the first sets of what would eventually be twenty-seven volumes of reprinted utopian primary sources, my sense of how a better future might be imagined did not diminish. Indeed, in some respects it was intensified by a growing interest in ecology, which demanded a better future on the grounds of necessity rather than on moral or economic justice. But I came increasingly to believe that if Utopia represented that intellectual space in which we can conceive of a world perhaps dramatically different from our own, that space could not be filled by some quasi-theological image of human perfectibility. Here the curious juxtaposition of my loss of religious faith and my embrace of the concept of Utopia took a firm hold. I became convinced that what had gone wrong with one variant of Utopia – Marxism – was that it remained overtly theological. The perfect society could only be heaven – but creating it was a religious exercise, and thus doomed to fail. By contrast, I came to believe, Utopia was by definition flawed. My understanding of how we should adjust our understanding of the various sub-genres of utopian literature has been much influenced by J.C. Davis's *Utopia and the Ideal Society* in particular. Utopia as a concept is, to my mind, only usable provided this premise is accepted; otherwise we follow the common-language definition of Utopia as the impossible or unrealistic, rather than Utopia as an image of a better-ordered society, warts and all. As I began to concentrate on the study of modern British utopianism, it soon became evident to me that much utopian writing focuses on the theme of degeneration and corruption, and the prospect of social regeneration and renewal, which are the central themes of what follows. These are, of course, also themes in mainstream social and political thought in the modern period. But if our mapping of that intellectual history excludes the utopian dimension, or includes only an accounting of the rise and development of the socialist tradition, we lose a vital sense of the richness and variety of the modern reform movement. We should still study Marx, yes; but William Morris may offer us a better account of how democracy might work in a future society.

History and Utopia

In what follows, I demonstrate my method of utopian analysis as I extend thematically and chronologically certain interpretations of the utopian genre that I offered previously in several editions of British utopian texts.[1] I begin with the presupposition that the utopian genre focuses principally on imaginatively portraying more orderly, just, and equal societies than those in which its authors live, and that confronting the problem of the maintenance of order involves theorizing different approaches to desire and want in particular. In the period under discussion, contemporaries frequently noted that Britain's immense wealth had unleashed hitherto restrained or invisible passions for wealth and power, notably blurring existing boundaries of class and status and unsettling definitions of ideal personality. Utopian texts face a similar fear of degeneration through corruption, especially by the consumption of and desire for luxuries and the obsession with money-getting attendant on it, but including the lust for political and imperial power, and the desire for social advancement. The answers to such problems provided by utopian texts are indicative not only of characteristic fears of the epoch, but of the increasing popularity, with the rise of socialism in the early decades of the nineteenth century, of what were traditionally regarded as "impossibly" utopian solutions to social problems and the threat of decline and/or decadence.

The chief characteristic of the utopian form is its fantastic portrayal of successfully institutionalized societies or communities in which greater virtue and (usually) equality is maintained over a lengthy period. Such societies, as Davis has stressed, are not perfect, but they recognize deficiencies in human nature, such as the conflict of passion with reason, the possibility of crime, the collision of desires, and so on. In the eighteenth and nineteenth centuries, the genre functions as a means of assessing how far greater virtue might be possible, and how widely actual moral and social corruption had

---

1   See Claeys, *Utopias of the British Enlightenment* and *Modern British Utopias*. I
    am particularly here extending arguments first offered in the latter, vol.1
    (xxxii–xxvii).

become pervasive. The utopian genre is thus characteristically a discourse on corruption, which centrally confronts both at the individual and national level the problem of maintaining virtue in time. As the genre evolves in this period, it provides an alternative ideal of sociability, community, and moral harmony which collides increasingly with the widening social divisions and perceived selfishness which characterized the development of commercial society. Virtually all British utopias in this period conceded that British national character had become debauched and dissipated by the growth of wealth; their own characteristic question was whether an alternative development could be imagined. This essay traces five stages of the unfolding of this imaginative process: the use of *simplicity* to define the process of restraining desire; the analysis of the passion for luxury goods; the solutions provided to this problem; the redefinition of manners thereby entailed; and the ways in which the passions were to be mastered in order to maintain order.

The Centrality of Simplicity in British Utopianism

With the exception of the Baconian tradition of scientific improvement, most utopian thought prior to 1700 relied on some ideal of restraint to guarantee social order. As I have indicated in *Modern British Utopias*, four models of virtuous restraint dominate eighteenth- and nineteenth-century debates: the idea of an Arcadian state of nature, often without private property, where luxury has not yet been invented; the primitive Christian community, often with a uniformity of dress and consumption, and a virtual prohibition of frivolity and luxury; the classical republican ideal, where property and often trade are limited; and a Tory or Country Party ideal, in which corruption is associated with the growing predominance of a Whiggish commercial interest, by contrast with a virtuous landed interest and patriot-king (see vol.1, xxviii–xxxii, where examples are given of each type). Most utopian texts of the period advert to a period of previously greater virtue; in John Elliott's *The Travels of Hildebrand Bowman* (1778), for instance, it is under the rule of "Queen Tudorina" that the people were brave and virtuous, wine was drunk only in moderation, and lawyers and physicians returned their fees when they failed to protect their clients. In some texts, notably *Private Letters from an American in England to His Friends in America* (1769), Britain is described as having already suffered a "decay of virtue for near a century past" as to be beyond redemption (*Modern British Utopias* vol.3, 367). Such texts thus echoed the wider debate of the period between opponents of unrestrained commercial development, notably Jean-Jacques Rousseau, and its votaries, such as David Hume and Adam Smith.

At the other end of the utopian spectrum, of course, proposals to revert to a simpler life, and the association of virtue with primitivism in general, were satirized mercilessly, notably in Samuel Johnson's *Rasselas* (1759) and Edmund Burke's *Vindication of Natural Society* (1756), in which the many inconveniences of the state of nature are linked to an inability to renounce artificial wants once they have been instilled.

Utopian Accounts of the Diffusion of Luxury: The Role of the Passions

Utopian writers mirrored contemporary assessments that the immense diffusion of luxury goods following Charles II's restoration in 1660, and escalating sharply in the eighteenth century, had engendered the most powerful instance of the wider social emulation of the manners of the upper ranks ever witnessed. The cause of this was perceived to be Britain's relatively greater social equality and fluidity of class boundaries. Its result was not only a vastly enhanced desire to ape the upper classes in fashionable dress and much else, but an astonishing blurring of social boundaries as they were perceived physically, without the adequate demarcation of a uniform for rich and poor, in public spaces. Bernard de Mandeville had noted as early as 1714 that "fine

Feathers make fine Birds, and People, where they are not known, are generally honour'd according to their Clothes, and other Accoutrements they have about them" (*Fable of the Bees* online). Utopian writers agreed that national degeneration was chiefly occasioned by the emulation of the upper by the lower orders: in *Private Letters* servants are satirized for learning Italian and fencing; while in *Memoirs [...] concerning Captain Mackheath* (1728) the middle ranks are described as enfeebled by luxury through following their betters, and the lower in turn imitating them. By the time of Henry Forrest's *A Dream of Reform* (1848), we thus find the statement that "human nature is imitative, and in no other case is that fact so striking as between the patrician and royalty" (*Modern British Utopias* vol.8, 410). A court-centered model is thus widely assumed to dictate trends in fashion, with the nobility frequently satirized in utopian works for its avarice, folly and debauchery. In John Francis Bray's *A Voyage to Utopia* (1842), thus, the "aristocs" are described as passing "their lives either in debasing inaction or in the most silly and frivolous pursuits," such as breaking the windows of the "commos" when drunk (*Modern British Utopias* vol.7, 368). But again emulation is singled out as a marked attribute of contemporary Britain:

> I was at first much surprised to view the commos thus anxious to imitate and as much as possible identify themselves with the aristocs, my astonishment vanished when I came to regard all the engines made use of to elevate the latter in public estimation, by exhibiting them almost as beings not of this earth. Man is naturally imitative; and, when grossly ignorant, will imitate anything, merely to exercise his powers. As he becomes more enlightened, however, he seeks to imitate something that is or appears to be greater and better than himself; and he is in a great degree guided in his opinions as to what constitutes greatness and goodness by those who surround him (*Modern British Utopias* vol.7, 435–6).

For constructors of utopias, therefore, a crucial problem was how to break this cycle of emulation, and to redirect the passions which evidently underpinned it: imagining a simpler society provided a widely-accepted solution to many of these issues.

Utopian Approaches to Simplicity

The restraint of the passions associated with consumption tends to assume three forms in this period. The first chiefly enjoins a reinforcement of personal virtue within a society which remains corrupted. In the alchemical treatise, *The Sophick Constitution* (1700), for instance, "adepts" are described as being most approving of "simplicity of Life":

> an Adept will not have rich Cloths, Furniture and Equipage, nor will accept of Titles, or Honour; those Things, and Philosophy are inconsistent: He looks upon all Men as being equal and Brethren, and upon himself as no better than others; he would not have others respect him, more than he would respect them: As for Titles and Dignities, he looks upon them, as Things very dangerous, and not easily reconcileable with Christian Humility; he would have all Men go plain, even plainer than the Quakers (*Modern British Utopias* vol.1, 12).

A collective dimension presents another variation on this theme, where withdrawal from mainstream society is possible in some institutional form, such as the "College" described in John Bellers's *Proposals for Raising a College of Industry* (1696). The existence of a monastic tradition provided a realistic dimension for such schemes.

The second strategy adopted by utopian writers imagines institutionalized restraint practiced on a national scale, following the models of Sparta and Thomas More's *Utopia* in particular. This was of course widely recognized to be an infinitely more daring and less realistic alternative than the reinforcement of virtue in a small-scale community. Yet there are many instances of such proposals. In James Burgh's *Account ... of the Cessares* (1764), for instance, the mining of gold and silver is prohibited, the prices of food and labor are regulated, and sumptuary laws inhibit luxury. William Hodgson's *The Commonwealth of Reason* (1795) describes the regulation of agriculture, trade, and provisions in order to ensure adequate food supplies, with a fixed minimum wage and the creation of national manufactories to ensure employment. I note, here, however, an emphasis upon regulation rather than restraint as such; not only is the influence of a pro-commercial, Paineite ideal evident, but also an unwillingness to push the issue of simplicity unduly, unlike John Lithgow's *Equality – A Political Romance* (1802), in which, we are told "Variety of dress and equipage" are simply "unknown," beyond some difference in neatness and decoration, each citizen being issued with standard clothing. Other texts, however, remain more traditional in this regard. In John Kirkby's well-known *The Capacity and Extent of the Human Understanding* (1745), a central contrast is of the "life of luxury" with that of "following nature," and a shipwrecked couple discover:

> more true and solid Felicity than what their former Condition had ever afforded them [...] They now looked upon themselves to be as sufficiently supplied with all the real Necessities of Life; as ever, though not in so splendid a Manner. Their homely Fare went down with as good a Relish, as when they were entertained with more costly Dishes; and their Sleep was as sweet upon their Beds of Moss, as what they formerly enjoyed upon those of Down: The Reason was, because they now eat and slept only to satisfy Nature, and not Luxury (*Modern British Utopias* vol.2, 68–9).

Similarly, in G.A. Ellis's *New Britain* (1820), which describes a colony of British settlers in the wilds of the American frontier, the inhabitants drink chiefly water, are "free from the cares of riches and the fear of poverty," have no more land than is "requisite for comfortable subsistence," and generally practice "moderation and equity":

> we do not consider it just for a man to acquire all he can: such conduct would tend to deprive his neighbours of their rights, and to enslave his equals. Prevailing luxury and general happiness are the opposing scales of human life [...] commerce is, too generally, a system of injustice, thriving upon, or using particular information to take advantage of the want of it in others; and that all manufactures for commerce, contribute to the vices of avarice and unjust accumulation. That its obvious tendency is, to all improper state of labour and danger to many, for the advantage of a few, dividing society into slaves and tyrants, though the odious fact be attempted to be softened down by other appellations. It sacrifices, to furnish a few with contemptible luxuries, which add nothing to real comfort, but most of which generate disease, and shorten life, the liberty, the certainty of competence, and consequently, the happiness of all. Commerce, and the manufactures, which support it, when successful, increase population, by causing early marriages (where there is no restraint) and by other means, so that the consumption of the necessaries of life cannot be supplied by the country. It still increases while this deceitful appearance of

good continues, and supplies itself with the necessaries of life from other countries. When those countries manufacture for themselves, the demand fails; the means of importing the necessaries of life fail with it; the produce of the country is insufficient for its inhabitants; and the dreadful consequences are famine and misery, and not unfrequently anarchy and bloodshed. It is therefore enacted, that no commerce, or manufactures for commerce, be allowed on any pretence (*Modern British Utopias* vol.6, 177).

The third model for institutionalizing the restraint of wants through some form of greater simplicity envisions a compromise between a thoroughgoing antipathy to luxury and the abandonment of such attempts. Here luxury is limited and reduced rather than abolished, or rendered a function of public reward more than private accumulation. In Simon Berrington's *The Adventures of Sig. Gaudentio di Lucca* (1737), for instance, a land is discovered hidden in the African deserts in which grain, gold, fruits, and inventions permit even "the Magnificence of Life." But its laws aim "to keep up the equality of Brotherhood and Dignity, as exact as they can," and to this end its patriarchal rulers distribute property for the benefit of the public (*Modern British Utopias* vol.1, 363).

The general trend of nineteenth-century utopianism was for the increasing adoption of the latter model; in other words, acknowledging the advantages of a higher standard of living for the working classes in particular, as well as their practical desire to benefit by both greater wealth and science and technology. The two most prominent utopian ideals of the century, the communism of Marx and Friedrich Engels and the technologically-based, consumerist ideal described in Edward Bellamy's *Looking Backward* (1888), both evidence this renunciation of the primitivist trend within utopian thought. Luxury is plentifully in evidence, indeed, even in Morris's critique of Bellamy's "cockney utopia," *News from Nowhere* (1890), though any evil effects associated with its consumption are mitigated by a widespread acceptance of aesthetic ideals and the value of free time.

The Restraint of Passion Anatomized

I have argued so far that eighteenth- and nineteenth-century British utopian writers described their existing national obsession with money-getting and ostentatious display as tending to the degeneration of both individual and national character, and they envisioned in their alternative societies a range of ways of restraining such passions. It was widely recognized that utopian order could be subverted from a number of directions. Here, I introduce three examples: the desire for power; sexual desire; and the quest for property and ostentation.

The Desire for Power and Dominion

Greater social equality characterizes virtually all utopias, though such equality is often combined with some variation on patriarchalism, for instance in Ambrose Evans's *The Adventures and Surprizing Deliverances of James Dubourdieu* (1719):

> the oldest men among them were the heads of their families, or little tribes, and to them there was a respect and deference paid, and all publick actions were directed by them; as general meetings, approbation of marriages, the order of all solemnities, and who should speak or dance in them (*Modern British Utopias* vol.1, 84).

Rotation of task is sometimes enjoined as the best means of achieving this, as had been commended in the leading republican texts of the seventeenth and eighteenth centuries: see, for instance, Catherine Macaulay's *A Short Sketch of a Democratical Form of Government in a Letter to Signior Paoli* (1767), where a third of the senate is changed annually; Burgh's *Account ... of the Cessares*; or William Hodgson's *The Commonwealth of Reason*. In *The Adventures of Sig. Gaudentio di Lucca*, for instance, it is said that "they are all Masters, and all Servants, every one has his employment [...] the younger sort wait on the elders, changing their Offices as it is thought proper by their superiors, as in a well regulated Community" (*Modern British*

Utopias vol.1, 366). Similarly in Robert Owen's socialist communities
– represented in literary form in a number of texts, including John
Minter Morgan's *The Revolt of the Bees* (1826) and Bray's *A Voyage
to Utopia* – contest for power and governance was to be eliminated by
defining the governing classes as one adult age-group, such that all
succeeded to the task eventually, but no contest for power was ever
possible. This scheme seems to have been first mooted in Lithgow's
Equality, where a scheme of universal labor lasts from ages fifteen to
fifty, thereafter the general direction of the nation being under the
supervision of its elder members. The more republican utopias define
public service as an honor and duty but often leave it unpaid, as in
New Britain; in *The Travels of Hildebrand Bowman* public salaries are
declined in the virtuous state of Bonhommica. The influence of money
in corrupting politics is a constant theme in satires of this period; see
for instance Aratus's *A Voyage to the Moon* (1793), which assails the
Pittite regime. In Lithgow's socialistic *Equality*, "love of country" is
used to occasionally extract feats of extraordinary labor from the
inhabitants.[2] In utopias, the priority given to public over private good
is, of course, especially marked. In *Gaudentio di Lucca*, again, public
employments are described as being "rather an honorary Trouble than
an Advantage, but for the real Good of the whole." As a result:

> they place their great Ambition in the Grandeur of their Country, looking on
> those as narrow and mercenary Spirits, who can prefer a part to the whole; they
> pride themselves over other Nations on that Account, each Man having a pro-
> portionable share in the publick Grandeur, the Love of Glory and Praise seems
> to be their greatest Passion. Besides, their wise Governours have such ways of
> stirring up their emulation by publick Honours, Harangues, and Panegyricks in
> their Assemblies, with a thousand other Arts of Shew and Pageantry, and this
> for the most minute Arts, that were it not for that fraternal Love ingrafted in
> them from their Infancy, they would be in danger of raising their emulation to
> too great a height. Those who give Indications of greater Wisdom and Prudence
> in their Conduct than others, are marked out for Governours, and gradually
> raised according to their Merit (*Modern British Utopias* vol.1, 367).

---

2   Although this text is first published in the United States by an émigré, it is
     clearly written against a background of British political and intellectual history
     during the 1790s.

Here, however, it is worth noting a tension between patriotism and cosmopolitanism which emerges in British utopianism from the later eighteenth century onwards. Many utopias, at least in passing, acknowledge the dangers of submerging private desire in the pursuit of public good. *New Britain*, for instance, derides patriotism as not "the first of virtues, whereas, it is at best but a partial one, and very often a most mischievous vice, leading to innumerable and dreadful evils and excesses" and dismisses "the seductive splendour cast around military achievements, by the Grecian, Roman, and other historians and poets" as "a lasting injury to mankind" (*Modern British Utopias* vol.6). Patriotism is here thus replaced by philanthropy, and a republican idea of national glory by a Christian and socialist ideal of universal benevolence, which was first popularized in Godwin's *Enquiry Concerning Political Justice* (1793). Correspondingly, where the utopian genre is deployed satirically to discuss dominion over other nations, as in Horace Walpole's *An Account of the Giants Lately Discovered* (1766), encounters with native peoples are often described in terms of fruitful ground for national and imperial expansion, particularly where any wealth is to be had. A similar intent is evident in Benjamin Disraeli's *The Voyage of Captain Popanilla* (1827), where an innocent unspoilt people is contrasted to one obsessed by Whiggish utility and liberal political economic maxims: much like *Private Letters from an American in England to his Friends in America* a half-century earlier, the text is veritably a study in the consequences of a commercialized market economy on a society previously defined by more limited wants. In a similar vein, the satirical maxim in *The Voyages of Captain Holmesby* (1757) is evident in the following:

> I want to enslave such a Province. Make some rotten Title; then invade it with Fire and Sword. If the People submit, you have a Right of Conquest: If they resist, they are Rebels and Traitors. In both cases, if you win, it is Glory (*Modern British Utopias* vol.3, 68).

Not satirically, too, I note the attack on Julius Caesar, Alexander, and other conquerors in Burgh's *Account of ... the Cessares* as "who by fawning flatterers have been styled heroes – heroes! rather the butchers of the human race, and the enslavers of the world!" (*Utopias of the*

British Enlightenment 89). At the time of the French Revolution, Thomas Northmore's *Memoirs of Planetes* (1795) also assailed the "system of warfare" by which European policy had hitherto been dictated, citing Godwin's *Enquiry concerning Political Justice* on the essential incompatibility of true republicanism and warfare. So did Hodgson's *Commonwealth of Reason*, whose universal armed militia force was intended to deter any external invader, but is prohibited from entering upon any offensive war. Indeed, it is tempting to see a Quakerish tinge in much utopian writing on politics in the revolutionary period and afterwards, in the emphasis given to both peace and universal benevolence.

In terms of later nineteenth-century developments, where real, often devastating, encounters with native peoples are increasingly the norm, it is worth recalling the innovative regime of racial toleration described in Richard Whately's *Account of an Expedition to the Interior of New Holland* (1837), where a land is discovered in which "the European and aboriginal races became in time completely blended together" (*Modern British Utopias* vol.7, 264).

In the period after the French Revolution the problem of the pursuit of power was commonly settled by the introduction of some form of representative government. In Thomas Erskine's *Armata* (1817), for instance, there is a loosely-disguised account of how the parliamentary reform movement might evolve in Britain – as the sole means of remedying governmental abuses, and particularly that flowing from arbitrary monarchy. Here I note that, as Erskine puts it, "the principles of civil freedom" are a key element in utopian thinking: liberty is associated not with disorder, but the maintenance of order on behalf of the interest of the whole people (*Modern British Utopias* vol.6, 18).

Sexual Desire

Sexual desire was not a problem to be entertained lightly in Utopia either. In some separatist communities, the issue was eliminated, at least formally; such is the case in Sarah Scott's *Millennium Hall* (1762), where women consort only with women. And it could be avoided by the proto-Fourierist device of liberating libidinal desire as such: in James Lawrence's *Empire of the Nairs* (1811), women choose their lovers freely, the idea of "father" is unknown, motherhood in any form is socially rewarded, and "matriotism" is the prevailing national ideal. Nonetheless, these are uncommon solutions. Most utopias presume that competition for marriage will persist; indeed, in *Gaudentio di Lucca* we are told of the ideal society that "as for their women [...] it was what gave them the most trouble of any Thing in their whole Government" (*Modern British Utopias* vol.1, 369). The solution provided is that:

> at all publick exercises the Women are placed in view to see and be seen, to enflame the young Men with emulation in their Performances. They are permitted to be decently familiar on those publick Occasions, and can chuse their Lovers respectively, according to their liking, there being no such thing as Dowries, or Interest, but mere personal Merit in the Case (*Modern British Utopias* vol.1, 368).

Here, a romantic ideal appears to inhibit the possibly socially destructive results of sexual desire: "we don't allow Temporal Interest to interfere in the choice, but rather wish our young People should fall in love. Our whole Business is to prove their constancy." A similar concern with upholding the institution of marriage and condemning affairs outside of it is evident in, for instance, Robert Paltock's extremely popular *Life and Adventures of Peter Wilkins* (1751) and in Evans's *The Adventures ... of James Dubourdieu* (1719), where the marital relationship is described as "so sacred, that no one ever invaded it, so that adultery was a crime unknown among them" (*Modern British Utopias* vol.1). By contrast, however, marriage, in Lithgow, is described as:

sacred here as in other countries; but when property became in common, it fell gradually into disuse – for the children being the property of the state, educated and brought up at the public expence, and as women could live as well single as united young people were seldom at the trouble to make such a contract. Children were born and no one thought it his business or interest to enquire who was the father (*Equality – A Political Romance*).

Elsewhere, a greater degree of equality is extended to women, as in *The Island of Content* (1709), where women are given:

the Precedency in all Cases, excepting Family-Government: They chuse first, eat first, drink first, go to Bed first, and have a peculiar Liberty in discovering their Affections, without incurring thereby the least Scandal or Reflexion (*Utopias of the British Enlightenment* 12–13).

As we move into the revolutionary period, divorce is increasingly accepted; in Northmore's *Memoirs of Planetes*, for instance, we are told that:

their women are chaste, handsome, and well educated. It is rare to see a woman of twenty years of age married, or one of thirty unmarried. They think that the fruit of too early marriages is debilitated. The mother, unless incapacitated by disease, never fails to suckle her child; to do otherways would be deemed criminal, and she would be severely reprimanded for it by those around her. Adultery is unknown. If a man and wife are unhappy in each other's company, and are resolved to separate, they have no more to do than to signify in writing such resolution to the witnesses of their marriage, which, if such resolution remain in the mean time unaltered, is dissolved accordingly after a lapse of half a year (*Utopias of the British Enlightenment* 193–4).

Property and Ostentation

More important still for the security of Utopia than the desire for power over others, or for sexual conquest, is the desire for property. An obsession with money-getting and spending was a notoriously dominant passion in eighteenth-century Britain, and while the growing taste for luxury, and its diffusion amongst the middle and even lower ranks, were often satirized in utopian form, serious architects of greatly improved societies found themselves in an increasingly difficult position as the century advanced. For while Plato might advert to an actually existing Spartan regime, and while the backdrop against which More's *Utopia* is set is an essentially agricultural society in which sumptuary regulations were, across early-modern Europe, still in use or within common memory, eighteenth-century Britain had witnessed an aggressive universalizing of the desire for consumption on a scale hitherto unimaginable. Utopia seemed, in such circumstances, inevitably in retreat, destined to represent a recurrent minor theme within modern European intellectual history, a primitivist impulse adverted to across the generations from Rousseau to Paul Gauguin and beyond, but nothing more than an essentially nostalgic, invariably reactionary, response to the extension of the market, consumption, and modern technology. Very few utopias, notoriously, are set in urban contexts; Lithgow's *Equality* is an important exception, describing "Lithconia" as "only one large city upon a grand scale"; Morris's *News from Nowhere* is another. Thomas Spence's works, despite their foundation in agrarian doctrine, also describe town life as central to the ideal society in, for instance, *A Supplement to the History of Robinson Crusoe* (1782).

Nonetheless, from the mid-nineteenth century onwards, the mainstream of modern utopianism remains resolutely modernist, whether it is rendered by Marx or Bellamy, the two most influential utopian writers of the epoch. A century earlier, the story is rather different, and two centuries earlier, in works like *The Isle of Pines* (1668), even more so.[3] The common utopian device of discovering an unknown land – often in the South Seas or Australasia, with irritated natives usually conveniently removed, and where the pursuit of gain and riches is unknown – is adopted in, for instance, *The Island of Content*, where "Nature is here so lavish of her Plenty, that we abound in Variety of Dainties, without human Labour" (*Utopias of the British Enlightenment* 5). Similarly, in *The Adventures ... of James Dubourdieu*, where the people, a group called the "children of love" chosen by God for their innocence of sin, live without magistrates, for:

> indeed there was no occasion for magistrates, when there was no ground for contention; there being no property among them, but a perpetual and uninter-

---

3   See Claeys, *Restoration and Augustan British Utopias* 115–31.

rupted course of a perfect love of one another. What the earth produced was a
sufficient stock, plentifully to provide for their subsistence; and their cultivation
of these products was so far from being laborious to them, that it was only their
exercise and diversion (*Modern British Utopias* vol.1, 84).

This is not a scenario which is thus recognizably "utopian" in the
sense in which Davis has described it, any more than Jonathan Swift's
famously satirical description of the land of the Houyhnhnmns in
Gulliver's Travels (1726) is. In Kirkby's *The Capacity and Extent of
the Human Understanding; Exemplified in the Extraordinary Case of
Automathes*, following the natural life is a central theme. Occasionally
symbols of the pursuit of wealth in Europe, such as gold, are described
as abundant in primitive societies, even agricultural implements being
made of them – see *The Voyages, Travels, and Wonderful Discoveries
of Capt. John Holmesby*. In such texts there is little contest with a
malevolent natural order, and usually none at all with the human
passions within or hostile fellow-creatures without. But it is characteristic of the more realistic *utopian* genre as such – where scarcity,
sin, crime, and malevolence are controlled rather than wished away –
that such desires are not habitually described as evolving spontan-
eously or rooted in some superior natural order. They are rather the
product of regulation and, it should again be emphasized, folk-
memory of sumptuary regulation makes such propositions vastly less
unrealistic than would appear the case if they were proposed today. (A
male child's uniform of baseball hat, trainers, and T-shirt notwithstanding.) Institutional regulation is thus the rule throughout most
eighteenth- and nineteenth-century British utopias, commonly in
combination with some predominant social ideal enforcing the restraint of consumption. In *A Description of New Athens in Terra
Australis Incognita* (1720), one of the first English-language texts set
in this location, wages and prices are fixed, and a quasi-religious
ideology of equality and brotherhood prevails. In the *Travels of
Hildebrand Bowman*, the dire warning is issued that "your nation is
following exactly the steps of all rich and powerful kingdoms; luxury
has got in among you, and will soon destroy you," as evidenced
particularly in the manners and mores of women; such licentiousness
must be curbed (*Modern British Utopias* vol.4, 50). The logic of

regulation could be carried as far as complete national economic regulation, such as is proposed in Hodgson's *The Commonwealth of Reason*, where a "Committee of Agriculture, Trade and Provisions" ensures that every district has a proper supply of all necessaries at a regulated price.

Clothing and ornamentation were particularly important in an age where style had become all the rage. One of the clearest examples of overt prohibition of this type in a utopian text is in Burgh's *Account ... of the Cessares*:

> the senate is enjoined to establish sumptuary laws, and carefully to guard against the first introduction of all sorts of luxury: and to prohibit all those arts and trades, which minister only to idleness and pride, and the unnecessary refinements and embellishments of life, which are the certain fore-runners of the ruin of every state. And though it is very commendable to be neat and cleanly in our apparel, yet nothing is more contrary to a wise and rational conduct, than to lay out too much thought and expence upon it; and a frequent change of fashions shews a vain and trifling mind. The senate have therefore regulated every one's dress according to their age and sex: it is plain, decent and becoming, but no diamonds or jewels, no gold or silver lace, or other finery are allowed of, lest pride and vanity, the love of shew and pomp should steal in among us by imperceptible degrees (*Utopias of the British Enlightenment* 117).

In *An Account of an Expedition to the Interior of New Holland*, which describes a European colony evolved after 300 years of settlement, there is a condemnation of excessive bodily ornamentation where the mere demonstration of superfluity is intended, but nonetheless luxuries are permitted where their functionality is evident, such that we see:

> handsome and costly gold brooches and buckles, buttons made of jewels, embroidered garments, inlaid tables, and other such ornamental articles; but you will see no article that is merely an ornament. A gold brooch or button served as a fastening, not better indeed, but as well, as an iron or brass one. Its beauty is superfluous, but it is not itself superfluous, and destitute of all ostensible use So, also, a silver goblet serves to drink out of, and an embroidered gown to cover one, no less than plain ones (*Modern British Utopias* vol.7, 290).

In other accounts, a competition to demonstrate dress is recognized, but it is channeled into socially harmless functions. In *The Island of Content*, for instance, we are told that:

> neither is any Person here distinguish'd by their Dress, because every Body has the Liberty, without the least Expence, of chusing such Apparel as shall best humour their own Fancy; for which Reason our very Women here are wholly innocent of Pride, not at all regarding superficial Ornaments, endeavouring only to excel each other in Vertue, Modesty, Eloquence, Musick, and such like Female Graces, that are Ornaments to the Mind, as well as to the Body (*Utopias of the British Enlightenment* 8).

With respect to cookery, simplicity also prevails in the *Account of ... New Holland*, and social *morés* inhibit any development towards luxury:

> the cookery among the higher classes is for the most part plain and simple, and the few who have refined much upon the luxuries of the table are exposed to something of the same sort of contemptuous ridicule that the being called a dandy incurs among us (*Modern British Utopias* vol.7, 269).

Accoutrements, then, were an important facet of the simplicity of manners as such; with gambling, bawdiness, drunkenness, cruelty to animals (a theme developed in Burgh's *Cessares*, which condemns all sports which have "the least tendency to render the mind cruel," and in Erskine's *Armata*), the development of theater as a mode of improving character (suggested in *A Dream of Reform*), and the control of other vices, they could be controlled if Utopia were to remain balanced (*Utopias of the British Enlightenment* 112).

The fact that many such texts describe distant settlements well removed from the snares and temptations of European urbanity was, of course, crucial to their capacity to restrain the development of luxuries which had not yet achieved widespread circulation. In *New Britain*, the maintenance of small-scale communities, individual and martial virtue, the preservation of social equality, and an inhibition of the desire for power are all intimately intertwined:

> we consider it wise to live upon the spot where our necessaries of life are produced; and not to congregate in great cities, and thus have to fetch them

from a distance. We by this, prevent a few from rising into improper consequence, and the many from sinking into servility; the inevitable result of their different employments in such large collections of men; which appear to us to be large masses of human corruption. We also thus prevent that degradation of moral character, which would be alike despicable in those who would be so unjust as to grasp at more than what is needful of property or power, and in those who would be mean enough to submit to servility, or to the privation of any part of their just and equal rights. We read attentively the histories of other nations; and we consider that we have discovered the true source of all their misfortunes, collectively and individually, to be, the love of unreasonable wealth and power. Be not then surprised that we most determinedly avoid in ourselves, and prevent in others, these, as the greatest evils, which the people of other countries eagerly pursue as their greatest good. (*Modern British Utopias* vol.6, 174).

Many such texts rely, however, on fixed sets of rules for the regulation of property which usually invoke some variation on republican theories of an agrarian law, or limitation of landownership, or some variation of community of property or collective landholding. Such ideals, while common in eighteenth-century republican tracts – such as Macaulay's *Short Sketch of A Democratical Form of Government*, which emphasizes "the fixing the Agrarian on the proper balance," with an equal division of property among heirs, and a bias towards popular ownership, unless the example of Rome is to be followed in Britain – are particularly pronounced in the period commencing with the French Revolution, notably in the works of Spence, in Lithgow's *Equality*, in the Godwinian *An Essay on Civil Government* (1793), in Northmore's *Memoirs of Planetes*, and in Hodgson's *The Commonwealth of Reason*. In most such texts, such as Forrest's *A Dream of Reform*, crime is described as still existing, but much reduced, there being "few vicious people" in the reformed society, although private property still requires protection from those who remain. However, the greater social equality which prevails as the characteristic utopian trope inhibits the propensity to crime in nearly all fictional ideal societies. Even in the relatively modest *Armata*, income is limited to a sum of £30,000 per annum, beyond which all labor is for the common good and landownership is also restricted to 3,000 acres. Such regulations spread "property over a large portion of the community: in fact, enables every industrious man to possess a small piece of land sufficiently large to hold a cottage, and a garden for rearing his own vegetables and flowers" (*Modern British Utopias* vol.6). Vice, in *A Dream of Reform*, is confessedly not eliminated, but its causes are described as essentially economic, with the systematic cure being as such:

> by enabling every man to earn a sufficiency to maintain a family in respect-ability; by superiority of moral education; by throwing open many businesses to single women, which are filled in other countries by males, such as shopwomen to linen-drapers, mercers, haberdashers, and so forth; by making them wood-engravers, ornament designers, portrait painters, writers, &c., but more es-pecially by placing woman in her proper sphere in society, as the companion instead of the servant of man; and by our wealthier classes taking the initiative in cultivating a healthier and higher tone of morality amongst the female portion of our community (*Modern British Utopias* vol.8, 434–5).

Conclusion

The problem of utopian restraint is characteristically solved in the genre during this period by a combination of explicit regulation, laws and customs, and an ideology which reinforces and underpins such regulations. This sense of commonalty or "community" (to take a cen-tral form of generic self-identification in nineteenth-century Owenite socialism) is usually described as inhibiting the development of desire and of self-interest. The people in *Gaudentio di Lucca*, for instance, are described as "the freest and yet strictest People in the world, the whole Nation [...] being more like one universal regular College, or Community, than any Thing else" (*Modern British Utopias* vol.1, 358–9). Their morals are underpinned by a religion whose basis is the belief that those who debase themselves by succumbing to undue passions will find that animal souls enter into the human – an in-teresting variation on various primitive beliefs. This view, we are told:

> is instill'd into them so early, and with so much care, that it is of very great Benefit to keep them within the bounds of Reason. [...] This makes them all be always watchful, and upon their guard against their own Passions, not to be

surprized by such a merciless Enemy. [...] The fear of being abandon'd to the Slavery of these brutal Souls is so deeply imprinted in them from their Infancy, that they impute the temperance and regularity of their Lives to, and think it in a great Measure owing to this Doctrine (*Modern British Utopias* vol.1, 358–9).

Many similar schemes could be detailed from this period in which a communal ideal is linked or more deeply wedded to some form of religious ideal – such as Owen's "New Religion" in order to offer a more substantive metaphysical basis for communalism. Although my concerns here have been with how the maintenance of order was conceived in eighteenth- and early nineteenth-century utopianism, I think it is worth recalling that the characteristic association of totalitarianism with twentieth-century dystopianism, and the consequent dismissal of the utopian form as invariably engendering some form of police state (see Talmon) does force us to reconsider how order functions by being internalized in the utopian genre, but largely externalized in reality. Just why this occurred is answerable in various ways, but it is worth recalling that many modern utopias willingly paid a high price for the maintenance of order. In *The Island of Content*, for instance, all learning beyond reading and writing is abjured as hostile to public order.

Developments to 1900

Finally, a few words on how these issues develop in the later nineteenth century. Utopias after 1850 introduce several unsettling elements into the problems I have thus far explored. The impact of Charles Darwin's *Origin of Species* (1859) and the debate which grew around it were by the end of the century linked to a distinctively *fin de siécle* feeling of decadence and decline. Yet, such was the intensity of the commitment to reform that this was, in terms of the numbers of texts written on both sides of the Atlantic, much the most utopian age of the modern period. And the revival of socialism lent much utopian writing a solid theoretical bent lacking in many earlier nineteenth-century works.

Thematically, the idea of passion and its containment was given a dramatic twist by post-Darwinian developments. By the mid-1870s, the notion of species degeneration was becoming a widely, and hotly, debated topic, with Darwin's cousin, Francis Galton, proposing the new science of eugenics in order to regulate and improve human offspring. The perfectibility of the body had been a constant theme in utopian writing from Plato onwards, and it was taken up widely by utopian writers in the last third of the century. It is central in works like Anthony Trollope's *The Fixed Period* (1882), which is based around the idea of euthanasia at age sixty-seven and a half in order to remove the pressure of population.

In all of these texts it is, of course, sexual passion and its consequences which loom centrally in modern thought. Intertwined with this theme is that of democratic versus élite rule, the imminent domination of society by scientific and technical innovation, and the increasing freedom of women. Within a generation, much of the traditional content of utopianism would branch off into science fiction and, as often as not, scientific dystopianism. As the destructive power of technology seemed increasing to outweigh its constructive potential, the political optimism which reached a crescendo with the Bolshevik Revolution gave way, in turn, to the enormity of totalitarian horror under Josef Stalin and Adolf Hitler.

As in the earlier period, the utopian genre of the late nineteenth century not merely reflects but bends these themes prismatically through its own historically-formed agenda. The imagined futures of the late Victorians are pervaded with anxieties about degenerating races and revolutions that eventuate in dictatorship or successful collectivist utopias that destroy individualism by merging it in a "great all-engulfing collectivism," as expressed, for example, in James Ingleton's *The History of a Social State. A.D. 2000* (1887). Catastrophist images like that portrayed in Richard Jefferies's *After London* (1885), which inspired Morris, displace earlier concerns with the corruption of manners. Racial wars pit white against "Yellow" and "Black," sometimes resulting in the victory of the former – for instance, in William Deslisle Hay's *Three Hundred Years Hence* (1881). There are some ideal societies of the more traditional type, notably Edgard Bulwer Lytton's *The Coming Race* (1872), in which a land is discovered whose inhabitants possess a great scientific power and who have abolished coercion, crime, poverty, and war, while retaining private property.

And the moral of the story? If I commenced my academic career as a Marxist of sorts, I have ended up as a "utopian": that is, in my terms, someone who persists in believing that human life can be improved immeasurably, but not to perfectibility; someone who thus disdains the search for perfection as an essentially theological enterprise doomed to failure; someone who does not wish to eliminate the causes of human conflict, but to adjudicate rationally amongst desiring people.

Works Cited

Claeys, Gregory. *Citizens and Saints: Politics and Anti-Politics in Early British Socialism.* Cambridge: Cambridge University Press, 1989.

—— *Machinery, Money and the Millennium: From Moral Economy to Socialism.* Princeton: Princeton University Press, 1987.

—— (ed.). *Modern British Utopias.* 8 Vols. London: Pickering and Chatto, 1997.

—— (ed.). *Restoration and Augustan British Utopias.* Syracuse: Syracuse University Press, 2000.

—— (ed.). *Utopias of the British Enlightenment.* Cambridge: Cambridge University Press, 1994.

Davis, J.C. *Utopia and the Ideal Society. A Study of English Utopian Writing 1516–1700.* Cambridge: Cambridge University Press, 1981.

de Mandeville, Bernard. *The Fable of the Bees, or Private Vices, Publick Benefits.* 1714. 3 February 2005 <http://oll.libertyfund.org/ToC/0014.php>.

Godwin, William. *Enquiry Concerning Political Justice.* London: G.G.J. and J. Robinson, 1793.

Harrison, John F.C. *Quest for the New Moral World: Robert Owen and the Owenites in Britain and America.* New York: Charles Scribner's Sons, 1969.

Lithgow, John. *Equality; Or, A History of Lithconia.* 1802. Philadelphia: Liberal Union, 1827.

Talmon, Jacob L. *Utopianism and Politics.* London: Conservative Political Centre, 1957.

PHILLIP E. WEGNER

Here or Nowhere: Utopia, Modernity, and Totality

One of our charges in this volume is to discuss something of our own intellectual history – what brought us into utopian studies in the first place, as well as some of the problems and questions in our various disciplinary specialties that continue to most interest us within what I like to think of more generally as the utopian studies *problematic*: that is, "not a set of propositions about reality, but a set of categories in terms of which reality is analyzed and interrogated, and a set of 'contested' categories at that" (Jameson, "Science Versus Ideology" 283). In this vein, I thought I would begin by offering a distinction, one that is by no means original to me. Any investigation of the question of Utopia within literary and cultural studies needs first to distinguish between utopia as a hermeneutic, that is as an interpretive schema, and utopia as a particular literary genre (no matter how broadly or narrowly the latter is defined).

My own intellectual and scholarly interests in Utopia really begin with the former. While in graduate school at Duke University in the late 1980s and early 1990s, I became a student of Fredric Jameson. One of Jameson's contributions to utopian studies has been his insistence on the presence in every form of cultural production of utopian hope or, what Jameson's own intellectual model, Ernst Bloch, calls "anticipatory illumination"; and he has elaborated a hermeneutic sensitive to Utopia's operations in a vast range of different kinds of texts. From the most exalted monuments of modern literature to the detritus of mass culture, from free market ideologies to religious fundamentalisms, we can find, Jameson argues, in all cultural work the signs, figures, or formal traces of the deeply human drive toward a radically other, utterly transformed, and redeemed collective existence. Indeed, we might say that this drive to recover the utopian dimension of all culture represents a fundamental *axiom* of Jameson's intellectual program. It is interesting to note in this regard that his formulation of a utopian hermeneutic quite often takes the form of the axiomatic "all": what Jameson himself has described as (following the lead of the historian R.G. Collingwood) "absolute presuppositions" or, in other words, "the 'code' in terms of which [...] thinking is done," "categories" that "are also 'operations'" ("Science Versus Ideology" 288). To give only a few examples:

> works of mass culture cannot be ideological without at one and the same time being implicitly or explicitly Utopian as well: they cannot manipulate unless they offer some genuine shred of content as a fantasy bribe to the public about to be manipulated (*Signatures* 29).

Or:

> all contemporary works of art – whether those of high culture and modernism or of mass culture and commercial culture – have as their underlying impulse – albeit in what is often distorted and repressed unconscious form – our deepest fantasies about the nature of social life, both as we live it now, and as we feel in our bones it ought rather to be lived (*Signatures* 34).

Or finally, "all ideology in the strongest sense [...] is in its very nature Utopian" (*Political Unconscious* 289).

Rather than restricting our interpretive freedoms, such axioms become productive of new and original interpretations of overly familiar works, for they force us as readers to push our analyses further, often with quite unexpected results, most especially in the case of those texts where such a utopian horizon or impulse may not be so readily apparent. The axiom then functions something like the much-maligned urban and architectural grid as it is re-imagined for us by Rem Koolhaas in his "retroactive manifesto," *Delirious New York*; or, to take two cases more relevant to the Irish context, as in the various organizing schemas – chapters of the *Odyssey*, colors, organs, art, technique – of James Joyce's *Ulysses*; or of the closures for IRA prisoners of the Maze prison regime as these are described by Allan Feldman in his underappreciated *Formations of Violence: The Narrative of the Body and Political Terror in Northern Ireland*. It is the fundamental insight of Jameson, Koolhaas, Joyce, Feldman, and others that it is only by working within such strict closures that we can break with our exhausted habits and truly introduce something new, or even utopian, into the world.

A similar hermeneutic approach to Utopia is also developed in the work of Louis Marin, whose *Utopiques: jeux d'espace* was also introduced to me by Jameson through his 1977 *Diacritics* review essay. Marin locates two specific narrative operations in all utopian texts (although his primary object of study is Thomas More's *Utopia*), operations he calls "neutralization" and "figuration." The first describes the way the utopian text produces its image of "an other world" through a careful working upon the raw materials of the historical situation from which it emerges. Neutralization refers to what other scholars of Utopia such as Darko Suvin have called the critical "estranging" work performed by these texts; or what Jameson describes as a "point by point negation or canceling" of the historical and ideological context from within which the particular utopia emerges, it being understood that this context itself is also "constructed" by the utopian text. Such an indispensable critical operation is, however, only a first step, clearing the stage for the productive creative operation that Marin calls utopian figuration. Marin argues that the neutralization, deconstruction, or deterritorialization of the ideological parameters of one social situation opens up the space for the construction of something new, the contours of this latter receiving one of its first elaborations in the neutral space represented by the utopia. The utopian text thereby maps the place of an imminent and concrete future, forming *within* the horizons of its present this emerging history and serving as what Marin calls the "absent referent" of the form (*Utopics* 196). This process of utopian figuration represents a schematizing or "pre-conceptual" way of thinking, taking the form in the utopian text of the "speaking picture" or narrative elaboration of the utopian society. Marin describes such an operation as pre-conceptual – but this is better understood as pre-theoretical – because while crucial aspects of a newly emergent social reality are present in the utopian figure, the relationship between these elements, which are dispersed in the textual mapping, cannot yet be articulated. That is, the utopia presents a narrative picture of history-in-formation rather than the theoretical description of a fully formed historical situation.

Marin offers a powerful, and to my mind indispensable, tool for the reading of any utopian fiction. And while his emphasis is primarily on the classical literary utopias, he too offers an approach that can be applied to many texts. Indeed, my initial doctoral research project was to have been an investigation of the dialectic of neutralization and figuration in works that would not readily be thought of as part of the utopian genre. The one residual of this early project is my essay on Rudyard Kipling's *Kim*, wherein I argued that Kipling produces a specific utopian figure of India through the careful neutralization of a series of "disorders" plaguing his present: the inefficacies of contemporary British rule, the events of the 1857 uprising, the emerging power of the Indian National Congress, and, indirectly, anti-colonial struggles, including that of the Irish – Kimball O'Hara, "Kim Rishti Ke" or "Kim of the Rishti," is, after all, of Irish descent (*Kim* 134).

My encounter with Marin's work did, however, bring me closer to the genre of the utopian narrative proper. As I began to delve further into this rich tradition (also teaching, while a graduate student, an introductory literature seminar on utopian fictions from More to Ursula K. Le Guin and Margaret Atwood), I began to realize that an investigation of utopian literature would serve as an ideal site for exploring a series of more general problematics in which I was deeply interested. First, I recognized that utopias offered what were almost ideal laboratory conditions for the exploration of some of the central questions of literary *genre*. The utopian narrative is one of those relatively rare forms in that it has an explicit and locatable moment of birth, with, of course, More's *Utopia*. Crucially, this is not to say that there were not earlier forms of imagining ideal communities; and, indeed, More drew inspiration from some of them. However, the "evental site" – to use Alain Badiou's productive concept – that is More's work changes these practices forever and utterly transforms how we read precursor works as well. And yet, as with any such event, it is not really true that it is More's work itself that gives rise to the genre; rather, the establishment of the genre as genre occurs with those first readers of the text who looked back to it as a model for a particular literary and cognitive practice – readers who may very well have included More himself (and the unique compositional history of *Utopia* needs to be kept in mind here, wherein Book Two, outlining the structures of life in Utopia, is written before Book One, wherein we see a number of other small scale utopian narratives).

This is a process Gary Saul Morson calls "re-authoring":

> in an important sense, it is really the *second* work of a genre that creates the genre by defining conventions and *topoi* for the class. Read in the context of the second and subsequent works, the style of the first becomes the grammar of the class, and its idiosyncratic themes and rhetorical devices are rediscovered as the motifs and tropes of a tradition (75).

In other words, it is an act of repetition that establishes the "historical necessity" of the founding case; or, as Slavoj Žižek argues:

> the crucial point here is the changed symbolic status of an event: when it erupts for the first time it is experienced as a contingent trauma, as an intrusion of a certain non-symbolized Real; only through repetition is this event recognized in its symbolic necessity – it finds its place in the symbolic network; it is realized in the symbolic order (61).

Thus, in terms of a narration of the birth of a genre, the original intentions of the author as she sets out to accomplish a specific textual performance become less significant: far more important, from the perspective of the later institutionality of the genre, are what the subsequent readers take it to mean. Moreover, similar acts of re-authoring are performed on any works that only now, in historical revision, are "recognized" as genetic predecessors of the newly established genre, Plato's *Republic* being the classic case of such a re-authoring in the institution of the narrative utopia. Something similar happens in the twentieth century to the narrative utopia itself, as it is now "recognized" as both one of the roots of science fiction (sf), and, as Suvin notes, "retroactively, one of its forms. [...] Utopian fiction is the sociopolitical subgenre of SF" (38).

My reading of the genre of utopia also highlighted some of the problems raised by classical taxonomic or structural approaches to questions of genre. Such approaches are open to the same criticism that V.N. Volosinov levels against the Saussurean model of *langue*: the system, whether it be the inner structure of language or the formal rules of generic behavior, is "merely an abstraction," one that ignores the place of the specific performance, the speech act or the individual text, in a number of different overlapping and interwoven contexts (67). I argue instead that genre needs to be understood as akin to other collective institutions – languages, cultures, nations, classes, bureaucracies, corporations, and so forth – in that it too possesses what Martin Heidegger names *Da-sein* (being-in-the-world). As with the particular embodiments of these other institutional forms, the works composing any genre make palpable, in the course of their narrative realization, a self-interpreting "awareness" of what it means to be part of this institution and its history. Such a self-interpretation becomes evident both in the ways each participant in the generic institution engages with the possibilities and potentialities of its predecessors – the existence or being-in-the-world of the individual text placed in a background of shared social practices that are sometimes referred to by the abstraction "generic conventions" – and also in its particular remaking of the institution in response to the desires and interests of its unique historical context. Thus, in a manner reminiscent of Heidegger's phenomenological analysis, this approach to genre means that we set aside the impossible goal of describing definitively the set of necessary and sufficient conditions for membership in the genre – which would be nothing less than a quest after ontological *essences* – and instead explore how such a critical "self-awareness" itself defines the genre's *existence*. And this in turn will enable us to bring into focus the ways the various works making up the generic institution of the narrative utopia engage simultaneously in a number of what Mikhail Bakhtin describes as *dialogic* relationships: with the traditions of utopian writing that both precede and follow them; with the broader literary and intellectual presents they inhabit; with their variously situated readers; and finally, with the concerns of the larger cultural and social realities in which they first appear.

Indeed, Michael McKeon argues that any genre takes root and becomes productive when and where it does precisely because of its ability to formulate, in ways no already existing forms can do, the concerns of its particular historical situation: "the ideological status of genre, like that of all conceptual categories, lies in its explanatory and problem-'solving' capacities" (20). This then leads into the second set of problems that I found that utopian narrative so effectively brought into focus: the genre serves as a marvelous way of thinking about the histories and processes of western *modernity* and *modernization*, the traumatic upheavals and sometimes violent dissolutions of traditional and older organizations of social and cultural life (a process so marvelously captured in Karl Marx's much-cited phrase from *The Communist Manifesto*: "all that is solid melts into air"), and the long revolution of creative destruction and ultimate recomposition of the social body that begins, not coincidentally, in the very moment that also witnesses the birth of the genre of utopia. Utopia as a form, I argue, *thinks* spatially – as do works in the larger and older genre of the romance from which it arises and in the genre of sf, in whose formation the utopian narrative will play an indispensable role. It is my contention that the performative dimensions of the utopia make it closer to something like an architectural drawing – a mapping, itinerary, or script – than what we think of as literature or political theory. It is this spatial thinking that then enables us to highlight the ways modernity and modernization themselves unfold through a process of spatial transformations: enclosure and clearance, voyages of discovery and conquest, colonization, migration, wide-scale civilian mobilizations for warfare, urbanization, disciplinarity, and so forth. Indeed, in a claim whose significance will become evident moment-arily, I argue that these processes of spatial transformation provided the basis for a new thinking of time and history, one that is evident in the genre as well.

Now it is along these lines that I believe one of my more useful contributions to the study of literary utopias develops. I argue in *Imaginary Communities* that, again beginning with More's work, the narrative utopia offered a central site wherein people began to think of themselves as communities in wholly new ways – as members, as citizens, or as parts of what Benedict Anderson calls the "imagined community" of the modern nation-state. And it is here that we see the significant pedagogical dimensions of this form, what E.P. Thompson called the utopia's work of "the education of desire." Following the lead of Žižek and Étienne Balibar, I suggest that modernity can best be understood in terms of a "constitutive contradiction," of a reflux movement between, on the one hand, a series of universalizing ten-dencies (the evacuation of the content from previously existing cult-ural heterogeneities; the dissolution of older particular hierarchies, roles, and systems of value in order to re-present every element within the new structure as exchangeable with any other: as commodity, as exchange value, as the money form, as juridico-political subject, and so forth) and, on the other, the emergence of new kinds of particularization – a process, in short, of what Gilles Deleuze and Felix Guattari describe as the de- and re-territorializations of social desire. Thus, in addition to the abstracting and universalizing tendencies of modernity so effectively articulated by Marin, what we see suddenly exploding forth in More's work is a radically new and deeply spatialized kind of political, social, and cultural formation – that of the modern nation-state.

More's figuration of the spatial form of the nation-state occurs during Hythloday's narration of the "birth" of Utopia:

> as the report goes and as the appearance of the ground shows, the island once was not surrounded by sea. But Utopus, who as conqueror gave the island its name [...] ordered the excavation of fifteen miles on the side where the land was connected with the continent and caused the sea to flow around the land (113).

By digging the trench that creates the insular space (*Utopia Insula* in More's Latin original), Utopus marks a *border* where there had previously existed only an indistinct *frontier* between "neighboring peoples," a disjunctive act of territorial inclusion as well as exclusion that Anthony Giddens defines as a crucial dimension of the subsequent spatial practices of the modern nation-state.

Granted, in its original moment of emergence there are competing forms of spatio-communal state formation: Balibar identifies, for example, "the form of empire, and, most importantly, that of the transnational politic-commercial complex, centered on one or more cities" (89). To this latter especially, we might also locate corresponding competitor "utopian" forms, Tommaso Campanella's *La città del sole* offering one preeminent example. However, More's fiction, just as the nation-state form itself, wins out over these various competitors and establishes the central line of an institutional *Da-sein* that will continue on into our own present. Indeed, the utopia is so successful in its work that in subsequent centuries, the nation-state becomes the "naturalized" scale of communal identification, a way of mediating between our particular individual experiences in the world and the emergent abstract and economic and political structures we always already inhabit. Thus, whatever else the nation-state may be, it is a form of what Jameson has theorized as "cognitive mapping" (and it is perhaps no coincidence that some of Jameson's earliest reflections on this concept of cognitive mapping occur in his essay on Marin's work). And it is this form of thinking that we then see at work in all of the great utopian texts, from Francis Bacon's early reply to More's work, *The New Atlantis,* to Edward Bellamy's globally influential work of the late-nineteenth century, *Looking Backward.*

However, as we approach the twentieth century, a crisis emerges in the form, as the sense becomes more and more evident of the insufficiency of this older way of thinking ourselves for a newly emerging social, economic, and political global reality. Twentieth-century utopias then register this crisis in a variety of ways, and it is the goal of most of *Imaginary Communities* to trace out these responses in some of the most significant "utopian" texts of the twentieth century: most centrally, though I do touch on a wide range of other texts, Jack London's *The Iron Heel*, Alexander Bogdanov's *Red Star*, Yevgeny Zamyatin's *We*, George Orwell's *Nineteen Eighty-Four*, and Ursula K. Le Guin's *The Dispossessed*.[1]

What all of this suggests is something I was perhaps a bit less sure about making explicit in my book, but which I would like to stress now – namely, the deep relationship between Utopia and the concept of *totality*. While the particular scale of this totality goes through a series of historical transformations, it always remains a conceptualization of a particular *world* – and I do mean for the Heideggerean resonances of the term to be here as well – as a fundamentally closed whole. It thus should come as no real surprise that utopian thought in general, and the genre of utopia in particular,

---

1   I recognize that I am conceiving of the utopian genre quite broadly here, to include what has been distinguished as eutopian, dystopian, and anti-utopian works – as for example, in the work of Sargent. Such an approach is enabled by the Heideggerean institutional definition of the genre that I offered above: for what marks all of these works is the way that they engage in a self-reflexive dialogue with a chain of predecessor texts that ultimately extend all the way back to More's founding fiction.

fell into such disfavor in the heyday of postmodern thought (and whether such a moment continues into our present is a question I will address below), as totality itself became one of its most stigmatized concepts. For example, Jean-François Lyotard concludes *The Post-modern Condition*, a text that became a touchstone for postmodern thought, with the rallying cry, "let us wage a war on totality" (82). Indeed, as Jameson and others have pointed out, in much of post-modern thought both Utopia and totality became inseparably linked to the political concept of totalitarianism, and, in this way, to the political catastrophes of the last century.

And yet, to dispense in this way with the concept of totality, and along with it Utopia, does in fact have some significant political consequences. The price to be paid for jettisoning the concept of totality becomes evident in the instance of an interesting, and largely forgotten, exchange that took place in the middle of the nineteenth century between Marx and the author of one of the century's most influential utopian texts, Étienne Cabet. A fascinating figure in his own right, Cabet was born on the eve of the French Revolution; he was trained as a lawyer and became a staunch opponent of the restoration monarchy. As a reward for his work as a leading member of the Insurrectionary Committee in the July 1830 revolution, he was briefly awarded the post of Procurer-General for Corsica, before being elected in 1831 as a representative in the Chamber of Deputies. How-ever, ever the true revolutionary, Cabet became increasingly dis-enchanted with Louis Philippe's government and, in 1833, launched the radical democratic and socialist newspaper, *Le Populaire.* Faced with the prospect of a two-year prison term as a result of his con-demnation by the government, he moved to England in 1834 and remained there for the next five years. While in exile, he encountered the utopian socialism of Robert Owen and, more importantly, read More's *Utopia.* These two events had a decisive influence on the rest of his life. Upon his return to France, he published his best-known work, the long utopian narrative, *Voyage en Icarie*, whose vision drew greatly upon More. This utopia was a tremendous success, and it led to Cabet becoming the leader of a utopian socialist political movement whose membership at its peak was said to number 400,000. As the decade progressed, however, Cabet became increasingly frustrated by both the slow pace of change in France and the intense governmental persecution of his followers. In the May 1847 issue of *Le Populaire*, he issued an appeal, under the title of "Allons en Icarie!," for as many of his followers as were willing to join him for a voyage to the United States where they would form a colony based on the principles he had outlined in his utopian text. A small group did depart for Texas in early February 1848 – ironically, only weeks before the fall of Louis Phillippe's government.[2] After a series of fiascos, in part brought on by crooked land dealings and in part by their utter lack of preparations for the harsh conditions of rural Texas, the initial colony was soon abandoned. It would exist in a fitful state for a number of years in a few other locations, including Nauvoo, Illinois, the former settlement of the Mormons. However, Cabet, becoming increasingly inflexible and intolerant in his own views, was purged from the community a few years later and died in St. Louis in 1856 an embittered man.

It was upon first learning of his initial plans that Marx writes an open letter to Cabet, begging him to reconsider his plans. After outlining both the troubling effects such a project would have on the European communist movement ("It would encourage thousands of discouraged communists to leave our cause. [...] The proletariat would probably suffer in misery that much longer as a consequence") and the various hardships the ill-prepared communitarians would face, Marx concludes:

> moreover, we have not yet mentioned the persecution to which the Icarians, if they wished to remain in contact with the outside society, would probably, indeed nearly certainly, be exposed in America. [...] Brothers, remain in the fight for our old Europe, work and struggle here, because it is only in Europe where there already exists all the elements for the establishment of a community of wealth, and this community will be established here or it will be nowhere (quoted in Marin, *Utopics* 277–8).

2   One of the most poignant stories of the whole incident is the following: a faster ship left France at the end of the month, and passed the colonists in transit, reaching New Orleans days before them. When the colonists arrived at the end of March, they heard the booming of heavy artillery, which they assumed was intended to greet them. Alas, the festivities were in celebration of the fall of the French government. A number of the colonists immediately turned around and headed back to France, further undermining the strength of the settlers' party.

By prophetically pointing toward the direct assault upon and ultimate incorporation of the (Icarian) community by *la société extérieure*, the capitalist order, Marx also emphasizes that the formation of the nowhere (the utopian community, *nulle part*, a term often used as a synonym for utopia), can occur only through the transformation of the *totality* of the world that already exists. In effect, Marx short-circuits Cabet's vision of a spatial "delinking" from the totality of the present, pointing out its anti-utopian consequences; and he replaces it with a vision of the realization of utopia located in time, one that comes about only through direct human praxis. In Marx's terms, "no where" becomes reinscribed as "now here." This notion is then echoed in the celebrated closing lines of Marx and Friedrich Engels's contemporaneous work, *The Communist Manifesto*, which state:

> the Communists disdain to conceal their views and aims. They openly declare that their ends can be attained only by the forcible overthrow of *all existing* social conditions. Let the ruling classes tremble at a Communistic revolution. The proletarians have nothing to lose but their chains. They have a *world* to win (*Reader* 500, emphasis added).

And it would be this vision of a struggle between the bourgeoisie and the proletariat for a world, now expanded to a global horizon, as necessary precursor to the formation of communist utopia that would also be in effect a few years later in Marx's notebook manuscript, *Grundrisse*.

If Marx's vision of the process of the incorporation of the exterior by the interior unfolds in a prophetic register, by the time we get to our present it is a process that has been completed; or at least this is the argument of Michael Hardt and Antonio Negri. They contend:

> the spatial configuration of inside and outside itself, however, seems to us a general and foundational characteristic of modern thought. In the passage from modern to postmodern and from imperialism to Empire there is progressively less distinction between inside and outside (186–7).

It is this collapse of the distinction between inside and outside that, for Hardt and Negri too, inaugurates a new revolutionary temporality in our present. The opposition that both Marx and Hardt and Negri set into play – between what we might call alternative spaces (utopian enclaves) and a revolutionary utopian temporality (the totality trans-formed) – is one that is also staged in the greatest utopian fictions: for these, again from More's founding work onward, are never about the establishment of a community somewhere outside of the dominant order, but rather fundamentally concerned with the transformation of the world, or totality, that already exists – that is, with the birth, or winning, of a new *world*. More's *Utopia*, although represented as located somewhere in contemporary space, is quite evidently also a vision of an England transformed, an England imagined for the first time in More's work in the form of the totality of the modern nation-state.[3] The staging of the closure of space offered in utopian fiction then becomes a way of inaugurating an original modern sense of temporality, for which the supreme event is that of *revolution:* the rupture or break located in time between what are in fact two different worlds. Conversely, I would suggest, narratives of temporal closure – from Francis Fukuyama's "end of history" to Margaret Thatcher's infamous mantra of TINA ("there is no alternative") to the now oft-trumpeted global victory of capitalism – legitimate an opening up of space, grounding neo-imperialist projects such as the U.S. occupation of Iraq in the name of the spread of democracy. Might then we not suggest that one of Utopia's central goals is "the education of our desire" for the supreme project of human praxis, that of revolution?

It is precisely this notion of revolution that becomes all but unimaginable within postmodern theory, with its privileging of micro-politics, small group identity, language games, local struggles, and reactive tactics. The most interesting question that all of this raises for me is whether such description still holds for us, two decades or more after the publication of many of the classic works of postmodern theory. The 1990s (a period that I locate between the "event" of the November 1989 fall of the Berlin Wall and the September 2001 destruction of NYC's World Trade Center; the second "event" re-peating the first, in a way not unlike the process outlined above in terms of a genre's history) appear in this light to have been a form of what Žižek describes as the "place 'between two deaths,' a place of

---

3   It is for this reason among others that More later distances himself from the dangerous claims of his text, ultimately denouncing it altogether.

sublime beauty as well as terrifying monsters," a place of openness, instability, experimentation, opportunity, and the insecurity that comes from the lack of a stable identity – a place, in other words, wherein history might have moved in any number of possible different directions (135).

It is in *this* moment then that we witness a number of important linked developments that take us beyond postmodernism. I want to focus briefly on three of them. First, the 1990s sees the emergence of a new kind of counter-globalization political movement, whose moments of crystallization bear the names Seattle, Genoa, Quebec City, and Porto Alegre.[4] Second, there occurs the articulation of a series of original and influential "universalizing" theoretical projects (Hardt and Negri's, but also Žižek's, Jameson's, Badiou's, and Judith Butler's later work, to name only a few of the most prominent examples), all of which marked an authentic "negation of the negation," a post-postmodernism, or movement beyond the paralyses of the postmodern and a rebirth of the radical transformative energies of the modern itself.

Finally, there is in this decade a resurgence once again of utopian imaginings, including Kim Stanley Robinson's *Pacific Edge* (1990) and *Mars* trilogy (1992–1996), Joe Haldeman's *Forever Peace* (1997), Toni Morrison's *Paradise* (1997), and Ken MacLeod's "Fall Revolution" quartet (1995–1999). These works differ from many of their predecessors in the genre in that they focus less upon the utopian worlds and more on the processes, the political actions and decisions, what Georg Lukács characterized as the *Augenblick*, by which their new worlds come into being. This too might suggest another way to read Tom Moylan's analysis of what he and others call the "critical dystopia," a form which holds open the place of the political in the

---

4   Indeed, a collection of discussions from the World Social Forum in the last
     location bears the title, *Another World Is Possible*; and in their foreword to that
     volume, Hardt and Negri bear out its utopian aspirations: "The World Social
     Forum at Porto Alegre has already become a myth, one of those positive myths
     that define our political compass. It is the representation of a new democratic
     cosmopolitanism, a new anti-capitalist transnationalism, a new intellectual
     nomadism, a great movement of the multitude" (xvi). See also Fitting and Zaki
     in this volume.

dim closures of the postmodern.[5] The sequence of texts that Moylan examines in the latter part of *Scraps of the Untainted Sky* – Robinson's *The Gold Coast*; Marge Piercy's *He, She and It*; and Octavia E. Butler's *Parable of the Sower* and *Parable of the Talents* – might then be rewritten as offering an effective narrative of the various moments in the transition from one situation to the next, culminating as I argue elsewhere in the reemergence of a figure of revolution in Butler's most recent fiction (see "We're Family").

In this way too, the repetition of the end of the Cold War that occurs on 11 September 2001 should be understood as marking the beginning of a full-scale conservative counter-offensive, an attempt to strangle in the cradle these resurgent radical energies and impose on the global totality a new truly post-Cold War order.[6] The ultimate success of such a counter-offensive thus becomes the fundamental political question of our moment – and to cite Walter Benjamin's timely reminder in another parallel situation, *"even the dead* will not be safe from the enemy if he is victorious. And this enemy has never ceased to be victorious" (391).

In conclusion, I am suggesting that there has always been a deep link between the figure of utopia, the concept of totality, and the project of revolution. What these texts remind us of then is the fundamental need in our present, with the full realization of a new kind of global reality, to re-invent Utopia as much as we need to re-imagine our collective belonging to a truly global community, something that in both cases involves far more than a simple expansion of old concepts to a newer, bigger level. In short, what is called globalization should never be thought of as simply a newer/bigger/faster capitalism

5   The negative dialectics of Theodor Adorno, the conspiracy fictions of Philip K. Dick, and the eventual conclusions of Alfred Bester's two great novels play a similar role in the parallel situation of the 1950s.

6   The three moments involved in the historical trajectory I am tracing here – the Cold War imaginary, the end of the Cold War in the early 1990s and the opening of the indeterminate "place between two deaths," and the imposition of a new symbolic order on September 11th – are evident in the dystopian (or is it utopian?) *Terminator* trilogy. Similarly, it may be the interruption of September 11th that accounts for the complete failure of the last two *Matrix* films to fulfill the utopian and radical promise of the first film.

– we need to keep in mind the fundamental dialectical principle that quantitative changes always produce qualitative differences. And it is to both of these projects I would like to conclude that the rich tradition of utopian fictions still has a tremendous amount to contribute.

Works Cited

Anderson, Benedict. *Imagined Communities: Reflections on the Origin and Spread of Nationalism*. 2nd edn. New York: Verso, 1991.

Balibar, Étienne, and Immanuel Wallerstein. *Race, Nation, Class: Ambiguous Identities*. Trans. Chris Turner. New York: Verso, 1992.

Benjamin, Walter. "On the Concept of History." *Selected Writings*, Vol.4, 1938–1940. Cambridge, Massachusetts: Harvard University Press, 2003. 389–400.

Hardt, Michael, and Antonio Negri. *Empire*. Cambridge, Massachusetts: Harvard University Press, 2000.

—— "Foreword." *Another World Is Possible: Popular Alternatives to Globalization at the World Social Forum*. Ed. William F. Fisher and Thomas Ponniah. New York: Zed, 2003.

Jameson, Fredric. "Of Islands and Trenches: Neutralization and the Production of Utopian Discourse." *The Ideologies of Theory, Essays 1971–1986*. 2 Vols. Minneapolis: University of Minnesota Press, 1988. 75–101.

—— *The Political Unconscious: Narrative as a Socially Symbolic Act*. Ithaca: Cornell University Press, 1981.

—— *Postmodernism: Or, the Cultural Logic of Late Capitalism*. Durham: Duke University Press, 1990.

—— "Science Versus Ideology." *Humanities in Society* 6.2 (1983): 283–302.

—— *Signatures of the Visible*. New York: Routledge, 1990.

Kipling, Rudyard. *Kim*. New York: Penguin, 1987.

Lukács, Georg. *A Defence of History and Class Consciousness: Tailism and the Dialectic*. Trans. Esther Leslie. New York: Verso, 2000.

Lyotard, Jean François. *The Postmodern Condition*. Trans. Geoff Bennington and Brian Massumi. Minneapolis: University of Minnesota Press, 1984.

Marin, Louis. *Utopics: The Semiological Play of Textual Spaces*. Trans. Robert A. Vollrath. Atlantic Highlands: Humanities Press International, 1984.

Marx, Karl, and Friedrich Engels. "Manifesto of the Communist Party." *The Marx-Engels Reader*. Ed. Robert C. Tucker. New York: Norton, 1978. 469–500.

McKeon, Michael. *The Origins of the English Novel, 1600–1740*. Baltimore: Johns Hopkins University Press, 1987.

More, Thomas. *Utopia*. Ed. Edward Surtz and J.H. Hexter. Vol.4 of *The Yale Edition of the Complete Works of St. Thomas More*. Ed. Louis L. Martz. New Haven: Yale University Press, 1965.

Morson, Gary Saul. *The Boundaries of Genre: Dostoevsky's* Diary of a Writer *and the Traditions of Literary Utopia*. Austin: University of Texas Press, 1981.

Moylan, Tom. *Scraps of the Untainted Sky: Science Fiction, Utopia, Dystopia*. Boulder: Westview, 2000.

Sargent, Lyman Tower. "The Three Faces of Utopianism Revisited." *Utopian Studies* 5.1 (1994): 1–37.

Suvin, Darko. "Science Fiction and Utopian Fiction: Degrees of Kinship." *Positions and Presuppositions in Science Fiction*. Kent: Kent State University Press, 1988.

Thompson, E.P. *William Morris: Romantic to Revolutionary*. New York: Pantheon, 1977.

Volosinov, V.N. *Marxism and the Philosophy of Language*. Trans. Ladislav Matejka and I.R. Titunik. Cambridge, Massachusetts: Harvard University Press, 1986.

Wegner, Phillip E. "Horizons, Figures, and Machines: The Dialectic of Utopia in the Work of Fredric Jameson." *Utopian Studies* 9.2 (1998): 58–73.

—— *Imaginary Communities: Utopia, the Nation, and the Spatial Histories of Modernity*. Berkeley: University of California Press, 2002.

—— "'Life as He Would Have It:' The Invention of India in Kipling's *Kim*." *Cultural Critique* 26 (1994): 129–59.

—— "'We're Family': Monstrous Kinships, Fidelity, and the Event in *Buffy the Vampire Slayer* and Octavia Butler's *Parable* Novels." *Living Between Two Deaths: Periodizing U.S. Culture, 1989–2001*. Durham: Duke University Press, forthcoming.

Žižek, Slavoj. *The Sublime Object of Ideology*. New York: Verso, 1989.

KENNETH M. ROEMER

More Aliens Transforming Utopia: The Futures of Reader Response and Utopian Studies

Reading Utopia

My entry into the academic world of utopian studies was quite mundane, even marginal – quite literally in the margins. In a senior United States history course the professor returned an important exam. I received a high A. In the margin next to one essay he had written a few complimentary comments about my notion that the American penchant for perceiving the U.S. as utopia helped to explain some of the best and worst qualities of American culture. Those few marginal comments reinforced my interest in the U.S.-Utopia connection. The next grand step in my progress toward utopography was less marginal but inappropriately practical for a field marked by visionary perspectives. My Ph.D. fellowship money lasted three years and my wife was pregnant; I had approximately nine months to conceive of, research, and write a dissertation and get a job. I was still interested in the America-as-utopia syndrome and American literature. At that time the only book that combined the two – Vernon Louis Parrington, Jr.'s *American Dreams* – indicated that there were only about forty literary utopias published during the heyday of American utopian literature (1888–1900). The University of Pennsylvania, the New York Public, and the National Library of Congress libraries were all within walking or driving distance for me. I could read those forty books and complete my dissertation (which would help me get a job) while still a fellow and before my wife gave birth.

In other words, if Lyman Tower Sargent's extensive bibliographies of utopian literature had existed in 1969, I might not have pursued utopian studies. As it turned out, my "new discoveries" of utopian titles (I finally stopped at 160) almost undermined my practical plan. I am glad I persisted. I finished on time (our daughter was born the day I completed final revisions), I got a job, and the 1970s were an exciting time to be in the field. I recall one Modern Language Association panel that was so packed that we worried about the fire marshal halting the session; the Society for Utopian Studies was established in North America; exciting feminist and ecotopian fictions and new and old writings by Norman O. Brown, Herbert Marcuse, and Charles Reich inspired debate inside and outside academe; reviews of academic books in the field (including weighty tomes like Frank and Fritzie Manuel's *Utopian Thought in the Western World*) appeared in the *Times Literary Supplement* and other widely distributed periodicals; intentional communities, urban and rural, spread across America; anti-war movements helped to bring about the end of the Vietnam War and, in conjunction with continuing women's and civil rights movements, revive visionary hopes raised in the 1960s for a grand and more egalitarian America. Certainly "America as utopia" was no longer a marginal matter.

In the first years of the twenty-first century, Utopia seems to have retreated to the margins. Certainly in the academic world utopian studies is more established than ever before (see Roemer, *Utopian Audiences* 1–2), and thousands of visitors saw the impact of utopian thinking while attending the marvelous international exhibit, *Utopia: The Search for the Ideal Society in the Western World* in 2000 and 2001 at the Bibliothèque Nationale in Paris and the New York Public Library. But the 9/11 tragedy, the ongoing war in Iraq, the slow and uncertain climb out of economic recession, and the bitter divisions of the 2004 presidential campaign all tended to dampen (if not crush) utopian visions of America as utopia. I certainly cannot offer any Pollyanna-ish answers to these challenges. But the topic of this collection – the emphasis on how each contributor's own scholarship reflects utopian method and vision – does raise a potentially useful question: can utopian visions and methods still help us to meet such daunting challenges?

My response to this question is "marginal" in the sense that my own study of American literary utopias may seem trivial in light of the immensity of the problems of the twenty-first century. But the spectrum of utopian visions gathered together by fifteen scholars and five authors of utopias (Edward Bellamy, B.F. Skinner, Robert Rimmer, Thomas M. Disch, Ursula K. Le Guin) in my second book, *America as Utopia*, does offer relevant insights, especially into the beneficial and destructive effects of the long history of the exceptionalist, go-it-alone, "City Upon a Hill" concept of America. This concept was first fully articulated by John Winthrop in his sermon "A Model of Christian Charity" in 1630 (before he had ever set eyes on the "new" world) and revived most recently in Ronald Reagan's rhetoric, which was re-revived during his funeral services in 2004 and by George W. Bush in campaign speeches.[1]

My other three books suggest the relevance of utopian methods or methods inspired by utopian literature. The little course textbook, *Build Your Own Utopia*, was inspired by a freshman composition class in which I asked students to imagine they had unlimited support and could create a utopian Arlington, Texas. One of the brightest students in the class, a thirty-six-year-old grandmother, was perplexed: "What if I believe Arlington, Texas, is utopia?" she asked. The other students chuckled at her comment, but their papers, in which they offered superficial modifications to the present (including a winning season for the local baseball team and bigger parking lots), demonstrated that their "method" of perceiving reality was woefully lacking in its capacity to measure the present and past by contrasting them to imaginings of alternatives (arising out of the present's potentialities) to their realities. My response was not unlike, though much less sophisticated than, the Imaginary Reconstruction of Society (IROS) method described by Ruth Levitas in her essay in this book. Utilizing an approach to teaching (Guided Design) devised by engineers at West Virginia University, I planned a course around several hypothetical problems: for example, create one "ideal" individual, imagine a family structure that would answer the needs of a free love intentional community burdened with too many undisciplined children, and design an ideal community living situation for students at our university. To address these hypothetical problems, the students drew upon assigned utopian literature readings, other relevant

---

1   In honor of bipartisan fairness, it should be noted that John Kerry can also be related to this utopian vision, since he is a distant relative of John Winthrop.

readings, life experiences, and (in more recent classes) the internet. The Guided Design approach navigates small group discussions through stages of defining the problems, gathering information, and evaluating possible solutions by judging their value "against" the criteria indicated by the defined problems (Roemer, "Using Utopia" 2–5). One of my goals was to "produce" citizens who could evaluate private and public issues by enhancing their knowledge of the past and present with an ability to perceive alternatives that would improve their lives and their society.

My first and most recent studies of Utopia deal less with enactments of utopian method and more with the need to develop methods inspired by a desire to use the literature as a cultural index and by the nature and reception of utopian literature. In *The Obsolete Necessity: America in Utopian Writings, 1888–1900*, I attempted to use American literary utopias as indices to American attitudes. I could not claim a "representative sample," since most of the authors were white, male, and middle-aged (about fifty years old), but the authors' geographical distribution was fairly representative, and they represented an important leadership group, middle- to upper-class professionals and businessmen (9–11). To "weigh the evidence," I devised a method that baffled a *Times Literary Supplement* reviewer (see Smith), but it is a method that is still useful today. For each attitude examined (e.g., concepts of history, the individual, technology, the family), I evaluated three types of indices: a "content" analyses of the entire sample; examinations of the most popular works (e.g., *Looking Backward* and *In His Steps*); and of the most complex works, which were sometimes written by well-known authors like Mark Twain or William Dean Howells, but often by obscure authors, such as the Rabbi Solomon Schindler (Roemer, *Obsolete Necessity* 11–14).

One advantage of this method is that it helps to avoid simplistic generalities that reduce utopian literature to a set of monolithic viewpoints. Take for example the relationship between technological advances and utopia in late-nineteenth-century American utopias (see Segal; and Roemer, *Obsolete Necessity* 110–18). Although there were a few authors – notably Robert Grimshaw, an engineer; Simon Newcomb, an astronomer; and Chauncey Thomas, a master mechanic – who envisioned utopias dominated by technology, a content analysis reveals a broad consensus that depicts technological advance, not as the ultimate goal of Utopia, but certainly as a crucial and exciting means to achieve utopian goals: if technological advances were developed and administered by the right people (those who promoted cooperation, equal opportunity, efficiency, and good health), then the advances would indeed help usher in America as utopia. Examination of the most popular utopia, *Looking Backward*, reinforces this consensus: Dr Leete's descriptions of the future include high-speed trains, pneumatic-tube deliveries, home-cleaning devices, advanced public kitchens, the equivalent of radio, and the famous automatic sidewalk umbrellas. These and other developments help to ensure that all the utopians have the opportunity to experience fine music, lectures, and sermons; clean homes and dining areas; high-quality goods and freedom from sniffles caused by wet feet. Furthermore the emphases on efficiency, opportunity, health, and cleanliness reflect important American Victorian values. Hence, if we restricted our view to the "average" or "consensus" viewpoint and to one popular work, we would conclude that the utopian literature embraced an American pro-technology vision of the future.

Adding other popular utopias and at lest one obscure but perceptive work to the discussion complicates this consensus picture. In the tremendously popular partial utopia *In His Steps*, Charles M. Sheldon places little emphasis on technology. Possibly more relevant, in Twain's popular, powerful eutopian-dystopian *Connecticut Yankee*, we discover a complex, ambivalent, even tortured view of technological advance. As many critics have noted, Hank's "factories" and inventions do promote opportunity, efficiency, and health; but they also magnify and extend his narrow pro-Yankee ideologies; so that by the end of his stay in the land of King Arthur the horrific carnage caused by his volcanic technological miracles cause inefficacy and waste (factories blown up), inequality (obviously the knights are victims of discrimination), disease, and mass death. In a much more obscure, but also insightful work, *The Land of the Changing Sun*, Will N. Harben gives the depiction of technological advance a distinctly Orwellian turn as the rulers use technology to monitor and control the population (Roemer, "1984 in 1894"). *Connecticut Yankee* and *The Land of the Changing Sun*, especially the first, go beyond consensus warnings about technology in the wrong hands to dramatize intrinsic dangers associated with technological developments.

My point in these brief comments on technology is that complementing the content-consensus analyses and examination of one popular work with discussion of another popular work and an obscure but insightful dystopia helps us to avoid hasty generalities about connections between popular utopian and Victorian values. Certainly this is not an astoundingly original observation. But considering the repeated tendency to make reductionist generalities about utopian viewpoints and about connections between the literature and its culture, my three-level method does provide a useful "check and balance" against simplistic portraits of utopian literature.

In my most recent book, *Utopian Audiences: How Readers Locate Nowhere*, I argue that utopian literature is a fascinating site for the expansion of reader-response and reception methodologies. There have been thousands of essays and books about literary utopias, their authors, and their historical periods; but surprisingly few studies of the readers of utopias (either as theoretical constructs or actual readers) who made meaning out of these strange texts and, in several celebrated cases (e.g., Thomas More, Bellamy, Skinner), used their interpretations to change parts of their worlds.[2] I say "surprisingly" because the diversity of the literature and its hybrid nature (combining, among other genres, manifesto, treatise, argument by dialogue, and narratives of travel, romance, and mystery) invite such a rich variety of responses (19–29), and because there is so much "documented evidence" of reading experiences – e.g., reviews, marginalia, letters, sequels, prequels, book-length fictional responses, illustrations, and material about the founding of intentional communities, reform movements, and grand projects directly or indirectly inspired by literary utopias (30–68). The method that I developed is eclectic. Focusing on

---

2   The one book that focuses on reader-response criticism (especially the implied reader) is Ruppert's. Morson's is a provocative study of the intersections of genre and reading. Besides my articles, several of which were revised for inclusion in *Utopian Audiences*, those by Cornet, Fitting, Khanna, Pfaelzer, Shor, and Widdicombe all made important contributions to reader-response interpretations of utopian literature.

America's most influential literary utopia, Bellamy's *Looking Backward*, I begin with broad cultural perspectives examining the historical events, key attitudes (e.g., about technology), worldviews (e.g., Christian millennialism), and concepts of reading (especially the belief that reading could transform lives) that led to the social construction of readers ready to perceive literary utopias as vehicles for social and personal change (71–89). I then move to a particular reading competence (the knowledge of conventions of the sentimental romance) that facilitated entry into Bellamy's utopia (90–116), and then to analyses of implied readers (117–28). The rest of the book examines the responses of "real" readers: the first reader (the author, 128–36), professional readers (reviewers, 139–68), and a sample of 733 late-twentieth-century readers, dubbed "aliens" because the text was in many ways foreign to them (169–224). I hoped that this eclectic approach would offer a more complete view of the readers' roles in utopian literature than a methodology that emphasized one critical viewpoint.

Except for the brief conclusion, the remainder of this essay will view *Utopian Audiences* as a launch point for further studies of the personal and social roles of readers of literary utopias. I will begin with a catalogue of possibilities and then focus on an issue that cuts across most of my chapters: *book power*, the belief that reading a book can transform readers and their societies. This issue is central to our understanding of the nature and function of utopian literature. I will conclude with brief speculations about the impact of emphasizing the readers' roles in the history (and future) of utopian literature.

I will begin my catalogue with possibilities for text-based reader-response studies of implied and "competent" readers, and then move on to the reception implications of the physical characteristics of the books (illustrations in particular) and translations into other media (films, opera, World's Fair exhibitions). I will conclude this section with the focus on actual readers, either those acting out Utopia in communities or reform programs or those represented by surveys and readers' analyses of associations that gave meaning to the utopian texts they read. As the word "catalogue" indicates, each receives only brief notice. I intend to ask questions and provoke interest, rather than provide "definitive" research projects.

Before *Utopian Audiences*, the one book that consistently emphasized a reader-response approach to utopian literature was Peter Ruppert's *Reader in a Strange Land*. Like the few other reader-response utopian studies of the 1970s and 1980s, including those by Robert J. Cornet, Peter Fitting, Jean Pfalezer, Lee Cullen Khanna, and Gary Saul Morson, the emphasis was on textual constructions of implied or competent readers. This is not surprising. As Robert Scholes has noted about speculative fiction, "whole worlds inhabited by sentient creatures take dimensions of development that no mind can encompass; no writer can invent an entire world" (188). Many of the resulting "indeterminacies" or "gaps," to use Wolfgang Iser's terms, invite readers to project meaning into the text. One significant example of this process that I began to explore in *Utopian Audiences* was the relationship among narrator, fictional narratee, the implied initial readers, and later real readers (125–6). In *Looking Backward*, in an attempt to explain the huge gaps in the historical knowledge about the instability of the past to his (fictional) twentieth-century readers, Julian West used the analogy of a stagecoach riding over bumpy ground. The violent motion of the coach tossed the rich as well as the poor from the coach. The implied readers in 1888 might begin reading with smugness, since they knew much more about the nineteenth century than the fictional twentieth-century readers. But the analogy can startle their smugness, because it invites a defamiliarization, a new perception of their era as a chaotic one. One hundred years later, readers in my sample had a different perspective, since to them a stagecoach evoked romantic visions of the Old West, making the narrator's analogy a nostalgic or quaint invitation rather than a provocative defamiliarizing one. Since utopian narrators typically engage in similar multi-level invitations to fictional narratees and implied readers (from More's Hythloday to H.G. Wells's multiple voices in *A Modern Utopia* to Le Guin's complex Pandora in *Always Coming Home*), there are numerous possibilities for similar studies that could potentially suggest how the eyewitness tellers of utopian tales engage readers, and how that engagement can change over time.

Studies of the narratee often imply assumptions about "competent" fictional or real readers. In *Utopian Audiences*, I argued that to be a competent reader of *Looking Backward* in the nineteenth century, a person had to be familiar with, among other concepts, Christian millennialism, the basics of an American historiography that embraced a "City-on-the-Hill" identity, and the reading conventions of popular genres such as the sentimental romance (71–113). It would be interesting to explore cross-cultural, trans-historical competency studies. For instance, what are the implications of the different types of competencies needed by sixteenth-century Chinese readers to be responsible readers/viewers of Wen Zhengming's painted scroll of an idyllic landscape that concludes with Wan Wei's eighth-century poem version of Tao Qian's ancient prose poem depicting the "Peach Blossom Spring" (see Atkinson)?

Mention of Zhengming's scroll opens a particularly fascinating possibility for reception studies: multi-media texts and texts transformed into other media. One of the first readers/interpreters of a utopian text is the illustrator (*Utopian Audiences* 37–60). Typically the illustrator will attempt to create visual correspondences to the text; but which scenes s(he) selects and how they are rendered can invite interpretations that can transform or even contradict the text. For example, the only fully illustrated American edition of *Looking Backward* (1941, illustrated by Elise Cavanna) includes a substantial number of line drawings whose intimate simplicity are reminiscent of Picasso's *The Love of Jupiter and Semele* (1931). Cavanna's drawings could be viewed as the first feminist reading of Bellamy's masculine utopia (*Utopian Audiences* 45–50). Dan Beard goes many steps further by radically transforming the horrifying ending of Mark Twain's utopian-dystopian *Connecticut Yankee*. Instead of depicting the death and destruction that culminates in Hank Morgan's visit to Arthurian England, Beard drew a utopic scene: Hank reunited with his sixth-century wife and child, triumphing over Father Time and Death. And Twain fully approved of Beard's illustrations (44–6). Are there other examples of illustrators modifying or radically changing the message of the text? How do these transformations relate to publishing history and authorial reputation?[3] Other important questions

---

3   In the advertising prospectus and publisher's announcement for *Connecticut Yankee*, the illustrations and Twain's reputation as a humorist were featured prominently (Twain 523–41).

and hypotheses about illustrated utopian texts could be explored in a
variety of experiments: for example, give three different groups, three
different editions of More's *Utopia*, each with a different frontispiece
depiction of the island of Utopia. Do these different initial glimpses
yield different readings? Have two groups read an illustrated and an
unillustrated version of any literary utopia? Do different readings
result? What are the implications?

Or what about more radical transformations – when a utopian or
dystopian text comes accompanied with an audiotape (the first edition
of Le Guin's *Always Coming Home*) or when the text becomes a play
(the dramatic version of George Orwell's *Animal Farm*) or a film (the
famous 1984 film version of Orwell's *Nineteen Eighty-Four*) or even
an opera (Poul Ruder's adaptation of Margaret Atwood's *The Handmaid's Tale*)? Or what are the implications of transforming the
technological utopias examined by Howard Segal in *Technological
Utopianism in American Culture* into World's Fair exhibitions such as
the 1939 General Electric Futurama? Or transforming the whole of
western utopian history into a grand exhibit such as the Bibliothèque
Nationale and New York Public Library's *Search for the Ideal
Society*? We can consider many layers of readers: the composers,
playwrights, directors, librettists, set and exhibit designers, curators,
and corporate funding agencies as reader/interpreters, and, of course,
the listeners and viewers as multi-media readers. Media transformation studies are particularly important because, as I will argue later,
the power of the book to transform lives may well have been eclipsed
by the power of other media.

The remainder of this catalogue will focus on "real" readers. This
emphasis is offered as a corrective to the decades of reader-response
criticism that emphasized theoretical constructs of readers; or if they
did suggest an actual reader, it was often the critic posing as the
competent, ideal, or clever reader (*Utopian Audiences* 3, 6). In particular, I will focus on the author as the first reader, those who "act
out" the text in intentional communities and reform movements, surveys of readers, and discussions of readers' analyses of how association between the texts and previous experiences and belief systems
helped them to give meaning to the texts.

In *Utopian Audiences*, I examined Bellamy as the first reader of a book that was transformed several times during the composition and publication stages as he read and re-read what he wrote (128–36). For example, in the first of his two essays on composing *Looking Backward*, Bellamy recalls reading his in-process draft of a fantasy set in A.D. 3000 and realizing that an element of the fantasy, the Industrial Army, could be a real means of transforming society. This reading inspired him to change the manuscript radically, bringing the time setting closer to the present and reshaping his utopia more as a blueprint than a thought experiment or fantasy ("How I Came to Write" 1–4). This trend continued through further rereadings and revisions, including his sequel *Equality*. Although it is common knowledge among specialists that utopists have often reread/reshaped their utopias (e.g., Aldous Huxley, Charlotte Perkins Gilman, Ernest Callenbach), there is no comprehensive study of this phenomenon and its publishing, aesthetic, psychological, political, and cultural implications.

Similarly there is no comprehensive study of another well-known phenomenon – the "acting out" of a select number of popular literary utopias – studies that would, for example, build upon Hilke Kuhlmann's "The Reception of *Walden Two* in Intentional Communities in North America," which investigates the selectivity of readings/applications (e.g., with the exception of a Mexican community, the tendency to omit Skinner's child-rearing models). There is also a need for application-reception studies with extended historical and cross-cultural scopes. For instance, there have been detailed studies of Bellamy Clubs and Nationalism (see, for example, Howe, Lipow, MacNair); but there needs to be more attention paid to the extended impact of *Looking Backward* at least through the New Deal, when key figures influenced by Bellamy held power – such as Bellamy's biographer, Arthur E. Morgan, who directed the Tennessee Valley Authority (Segal 238, n.81). Although there is at least one published and one unpublished cross-cultural reception study of *Looking Backward* (see Bowman, Toth) and a few more specialized studies, especially those focusing on New Zealand (see Shor; and, with a broader scope than Bellamy's influence, Sargisson and Sargent), we need more comparative studies of how different cultural, political, and environmental forces shape the reception and application of literary utopias.

Utopian Audiences offers the first extensive surveys of readers of a literary utopia. My sample, collected from 1983 to 1997, included 733 readers from seven states and four countries.[4] The size of the sample is fairly impressive: most of the readers were employed at least part-time; the gender balance was fairly representative (female: fifty-eight percent, male: forty-two percent); and there was some racial diversity (Asian American, Asian, African American, Hispanic, and American Indian readers made up almost twenty-five percent of the sample). However, for the U.S., the geographic representation was skewed toward Texas and the Midwest (sixty-three percent); only twenty percent of the sample were married; and, despite a broad age range (sixteen to eighty-nine), the average age was only twenty-three, reflecting the dominance of college students (233–7). Obviously there is a need for larger and more representative samples in future work (see below).

My tentative findings invite further questions and verification. I speculated that the hybrid nature of a utopian text would produce reading responses that represented more of a mix of types of responses than responses to "realistic" fictions. The readers' descriptions of associations they used to give meaning to *Looking Backward* (I termed these influences "transformational associations") supported my hypothesis. The transformational associations typically took the form of a hierarchy of mixed types – general beliefs/attitudes; specific personal (non-academic) experiences; reading/viewing tastes; immediate circumstances; academic experiences. The associations for realistic

---

4   The states were Texas, Minnesota, New York, Kentucky, Maryland, Massachusetts, and California; the countries were the United States, Canada, Japan, and Austria (see *Utopian Audiences* 233–7). More than two-thirds of the readers came from two large state schools, The University of Texas at Arlington and the University of Minnesota. A substantial number came from New York (fifty-one). All the readers from California were from a retirement home. The international samples were small: Japan (twenty), Canada (eight), Austria (one). As I noted earlier, I labeled them "aliens" – a term borrowed from Robert Escarpit (78, 81) – because they were often so far removed from the worldviews that guided Bellamy and his original readers (175–7).

fiction were limited primarily to specific personal experiences. But how well do my expectations hold up for other utopian and non-utopian works? For example, the hierarchy was quite different (a greater emphasis on reading taste) when students read a complex critical utopia, Le Guin's *Always Coming Home*. Also, the representations of the hierarchies took the form of verbal constructs with hazy borders (e.g., where does a specific experience end and a general attitude begin?). Possibly brain-imaging experiments that map electrical pulses and trans-synapse chemical reactions could offer meaningful and more precise definitions of the intellectual and emotional energies drawn upon while reading a utopia.

I would also like to see verification of several significant patterns I discovered using the surveys and descriptions of transformational associations. Is it true that having experienced poverty or a move from one country or one culture to another constitute two of the most powerful past experiences that facilitate engagement with a utopian text? Is it true that the influence of particular types of immediate interpretive communities (e.g., the nature of a classroom culture) and particular work experiences can "overpower" expected gender responses?

Only five readers in my sample indicated that their substantial wealth influenced their responses to Bellamy's utopia. On the other hand, more than one hundred, mostly from the University of Texas at Arlington (UTA) and the University of Minnesota samples, identified short and extended periods of poverty as crucial associations. Some of these experiences were as short as one Rensselaer Polytechnic Institute student's experience living in a tent for three months because his family could not afford a house. Others seemed endless. One UTA mother recalled her childhood growing up with fourteen brothers and sisters. She wore flower-sack dresses through her teens and did not visit a grocery store until she was twelve: "There were things there that I didn't know existed." Whether the poverty experiences were short or long, they typically enabled these readers to empathize with the nineteenth-century poor described by Julian West and Dr. Leete and to sympathize strongly with the emphases on equality of opportunity in Bellamy's utopia. These responses were strong enough to overpower aversions that these readers might have to what they per-

ceived as Bellamy's secular humanism (many of these readers identified themselves as ardent believers in Christianity).

Whereas experiencing poverty allowed readers to engage in
portraits of particular types of people (the poor) and with egalitarian
outlooks, experiencing a cultural or national change impacted the entire reading process. Readers' memories of these changes provided
personalized paradigms of the comparative modes of perception that
are so essential to engagement in a utopian reading experience. In
effect, these readers said that we can read utopias with intensity and
sympathy because we have already seen their world in terms of
layered comparisons before. Depending on the specific cross-cultural
experience, the responses might be positive or negative. For example,
several of the students attending UTA, Hood College, and the University of Minnesota had lived in countries governed by various forms
of socialism or strong centralized governments – West Germany, Fin-
land, Honduras, for example. The former two associations created
powerful positive biases towards Bellamy's utopia; the latter, a negative response. Living in Taiwan during the Tienamen Square massacre
and reading *Looking Backward* within view of the extremes of wealth
and poverty in Cancun, Mexico, set up strong criticisms of Bellamy's
authoritarianism for the former and great enthusiasm for Bellamy's
egalitarianism for the latter. The positive or negative nature of the
responses varied dramatically depending on the specific international
experience. But the intensity of engagement suggested that cross-
cultural experiences greatly facilitated readers' willingness to engage
actively with a utopian text.

I also encouraged examination of the influence of more
immediate circumstances: is it true, for instance, that the influence of
particular types of immediate interpretive communities (e.g., the
nature of a classroom culture) and particular work experiences can
"overpower" expected gender responses? This may indeed be the case,
as suggested by three sub-samples of all women readers – at a
women's college with a respected feminist professor (the readers
responses concentrated on women's issues); at a coed college with a
respected male professor, much more interested in religious than
women's issues (only one student commented on women's issues);
and in the case of a physically strong African American's "overlook-

ing" of Dr Leete's derogatory comments on the physical inferiority of women because she was so impressed with career equality in Bellamy's utopia that contrasted so strikingly with the prejudice she experienced as a female construction worker (207–11). Then there is the age variable. Is it true, as my sample suggested, that older readers process the utopian texts differently than younger readers, not only placing more emphasis on a richer network of associations with past experiences but highlighting the influences of particular watershed experiences they have defined (200–3)? This is a particularly important question, since the implementation of utopian ideas is typically carried out by readers in positions of influence, which in most cultures means citizens over forty years old.

Of course the answers to all these questions depend on further studies based on larger and more representative samples than my group of "alien" readers. Expanding the sample by placing surveys on a website or by utilizing the "reviews" contributed to Amazon.com have potential, but these approaches cannot guarantee that the readers have read the book or are telling the truth about their backgrounds. A better, though time-consuming, method involves using surveys and interviews with reading groups (I used only one), following the lead of classic reader-response studies like Janice Radway's *Reading the Romance*.

Even more promising would be tapping into a recent U.S. phenomenon, the "One Book, One Community" craze: a community selects a specific title as the focus of a series of community gatherings in public libraries and schools (usually including the author). A recent segment of *Studio 360*, a National Public Radio program, focused on Utopia (see "Utopia"). "One Book, One Community" was featured because one of the titles frequently selected is Lois Lowrey's *The Giver*, a young adult dystopia often included in junior high and high school curricula. If a researcher could convince a community to select *The Giver* and get permission to use surveys and interviews of readers and tapes of the gatherings, s(he) would have a fascinating resource for reception studies with a much greater age diversity than my sample.

Book Power

All the possibilities outlined in my "catalogue" should contribute to our understanding of how readers give meaning to utopian literature. One other possibility deserves more than a paragraph overview: the evolving phenomenon of book power – the assumption that reading a utopia can transform perceptions, lives, and whole societies. I say evolving because there has been a fundamental change in the power of book power, since the days when, for example, hundreds of thousands of people read *Looking Backward*, which inspired significant numbers to change themselves and their conditions in the United States and other countries.

As I argued in *Utopian Audiences*, a convergence of forces helped enhance the power of book reading experiences in America during the late nineteenth century: increasing literacy rates, improved means of producing and distributing books (which helped to reduce prices), and advances in eyeglasses and lighting systems that facilitated reading for longer hours (80–9). Furthermore, print culture did not have to compete with film, radio, television, and the internet. Recently David Bleich has suggested another factor. Throughout the nineteenth century, print culture was more closely aligned with oral culture. The importance of oratory in secular and religious realms was not seen as a competitor with the printed word but as an enhancer, as if the power of the spoken word could be heard/seen though the printed word (288–9). Hence it is not surprising that Bellamy and other utopists included long sermons or speeches in their narratives.

Possibly the most significant shaping force was what John L. Thomas, in *Alternative America*, has called the "community of moral discourse" (91). Thomas and other scholars of nineteenth-century American culture have emphasized "the symbolic community of the printed word" and a concurrent "belief in the power of print [that] was almost unlimited in Victorian America" (Sicherman 142). This faith was reflected in the numbers and impact of manuals – "child-rearing manuals, books on household management, etiquette books, even joke books to tell people how to be funny" (Howe 527). And certainly sentimental and religious reform novels – Harriet Beecher Stowe's *Uncle Tom's Cabin* and T.S. Arthur's *Ten Nights in a Barroom* – are prime examples of books that transformed lives. Barbara Sicherman has observed that some contemporary reviewers even "maintained that the novel had replaced the sermon as the principle shaper of character" (143). Combine this attitude with economic and social instability and the great divide between the rich and the poor, broadcast in bestsellers such as Henry George's *Progress and Poverty*, and it is not difficult to imagine why a form of literature grounded in stark contrasts and offering hopes of stability and a radiant future could change lives.

Certainly during the second half of the twentieth century and the opening of the twenty-first there is still evidence of book power. Obvious instances are the Bible and the Koran, as well as works such as Tim LaHaye's apocalyptic "Left Behind" series, which has influenced so many on the Christian Right in the U.S., and Salman Rushdie's *Satanic Verses*, whose power was reflected in efforts to suppress the novel and kill its author. Self-help books, ranging from Robert Atkin's diet manuals to Alain de Botton's popular *How Proust Can Change Your Life*, change bodies and minds, and reception theorists demonstrate how romance novels and confessional magazine romances impact the lives of women readers (see Radway; Greer). Beyond the bibliographies of most American scholars, there are recent authors and titles that offer striking examples of book power: for example, the novelist Orhan Pamuk, whom Margaret Atwood calls "the equivalent of rock star, guru, diagnostic specialist and political pundit" in Turkey (1); and *Rukhname*, a collection of "moral and ethical commandments" by the President of Turkmenistan, Saparmurat Niyazov. Drawing upon the authority of the author's Stalinesque powers and the Koran, *Rukhname* may, within a more limited sphere, exert more power than Mao's *Little Red Book* did (see "Church Confiscated"). Closer to home and to utopian studies, I can recall the power of Rachel Carson's *Silent Spring* that helped to inspire ecological movements and the Green Party; *Walden Two* that, as previously noted, inspired the formation of intentional communities; and Rimmer's *Harrad Experiment* that possibly facilitated co-ed rooming in colleges (though I know of no studies demonstrating that).

But when we focus more intently on utopian literature, it is also clear that there has been a decline in the power of books to transform lives. There are no reform clubs or political parties inspired by Le Guin, Marge Piercy, Samuel R. Delany, Octavia E. Butler, or Kim Stanley Robinson; and the reviews and essays written about their utopias lack the sense of dire warnings or ecstatic hopes about the impact of reading utopias that characterized the reviews of late-nineteenth-century American utopias (*Utopian Audiences* 141, 145–6, 160–1). The responses my readers made to questions about reading utopias also suggest the decline. Although a majority (ninety-seven percent) believed that Bellamy hoped to change social systems and/or change individual reader's feelings and thoughts, only forty percent believed that reading *Looking Backward* had changed their view of society and only twenty-five percent believed that the reading had changed their self concepts (*Utopian Audiences* 216, 252–3).

Authors of literary utopias and scholars have offered plausible explanations for the decline of utopian book power. At least as early as 1973 in "The Ones Who Walk Away from Omelas" and as recently as 15 August 2004 on the "Utopias" segment of the National Public Radio Radio program *Studio 360*, Le Guin emphasized how skeptical modern readers were about Utopia. Twentieth-century Americans had been disappointed (New Deal, War on Poverty), frightened (Soviet communism), and repulsed (Nazism and Stalinism) by well-known and sometimes well-intentioned attempts to realize utopian ideals. Long before Le Guin's time, powerful dystopias by Yevgeny Zamyatin, Huxley, and Orwell had merged the images of totalitarian regimes and Utopia in the popular mind. An awareness of the incredible diversities of national and global worldviews, further complicated old-style utopianizing. Even the optimistic "Omelas" narrator's enumeration of the wonders of utopia is tinged with tongue-in-cheek skepticism and an admission that only the reader can imagine his or her utopia:

> central heating, subway trains, washing machines, and all kinds of marvelous devices not yet invented here, floating light sources, fuelless power, a cure for the common cold. Or they could have none of that: it doesn't matter. As you like it (2).

Considering all the forces undermining belief in our ability to imagine Utopia as a "perfect" world, it is not surprising that the literary utopias most often admired by critics and scholars are complex and ambiguous. In other words, they are the types of books unlikely to spawn large-scale activist groups.

General forces reshaping and decentering the power of authors and print culture also help to explain the decline of utopian book power. In a review of a Graham Greene biography, Paul Theroux writes of a time "when writers were powerful, priestlike, remote and elusive" replaced by a present when publishers are "corporate middle-brow monsters" who can "bully writers into the open, [...] invisible[,] they were more powerful for seeming forever elsewhere" (1, 10). Bleich argues that the disconnect between the printed and spoken word – the loss of the living performative sense of words on a page – has undercut the book's ability to be a "force in society" (290). Bleich's emphasis on the disconnect between different forms of expression can be related to an obvious decentering: today, the book competes against radio, film, television, the internet, and mixtures of all of the above. Fredric Jameson also claims that traditional utopias do not move people today because their requisite audience has vanished: "a certain type of reader, whom we must imagine just as addicted to the bloodless forecasts of a Cabet or a Bellamy as we ourselves may be to J.R.R. Tolkien, *The Godfather*, *Ragtime*, or detective stories" (2).

A provocative site for the study of the convergence of many of the forces that created utopian book power in the late nineteenth century and the decline of that power today can be found in an arena rarely discussed in utopian studies: the American phenomenon of Oprah Winfrey. One of the most publicized projects of Oprah's multi-media empire was the Oprah's Book Club segment of her popular television show. In "That, My Dear, Is Called Reading," Rona Kaufman offers a fascinating study of the first year of the Book Club (September 1996–August 1997) plus one later show concentrating on Toni Morrison's *Paradise*. Oprah stressed "reading as a transformative [...] act" (224). Hence, there is an obvious relation between her goal and the general issue of book power and the specific reactions of my 733 readers who believed that reading *Looking Backward* did not affect their self-images. Oprah wanted more than to "get America reading again." She wanted readers who, like many of Bellamy's initial readers, would be transformed by what they read.

As described by Kaufman, Oprah followed a basic format for the Book Club. She selected a book and gave her viewers a month to read it. She invited readers to write letters describing their responses to the book. From the thousands of letter writers, she choose "four or so" to come to Chicago "for the in-person book club, which would include Oprah and the author." The actual television presentation typically included a videotaped biography of the author and highlights of the club meeting, plus Oprah interviewing the author (224).

Oprah used this basic format for all the books during the first year. But for the one book after this year that can easily be placed in the utopian literature tradition, Morrison's *Paradise*, she changed the format. The setting was Princeton University, where Morrison is a professor. The meeting was more like a classroom experience. Morrison adopted a role similar to that of contemporary reviewers of *Looking Backward* who assumed that readers needed guidance with a difficult book, since it could challenge their views of society and self. Another connection to my study was that, like all utopias, *Paradise* is a complex hybrid – in this case a combination of historical, ethnic, and feminist fiction, with strong utopian and dystopian elements. The small band of 158 freedmen who established the all-black Oklahoma town of Ruby in the late nineteenth century had lofty goals of "self-sufficiency, pride, and mutual support." They created a community free of crime where "no one goes hungry" (Allen 6). But the brutal attacks on the nearby broken-down convent that takes in women drifters highlight the tragic flaws of isolated static concepts of Utopia.

Compared to the other books previously selected which invited primarily "emotive" responses, *Paradise*, like most utopias, invited greater varieties of responses, and its "cognitive estrangement" called for cognitive responses.[5] Hence, in the Morrison segment, there was

---

5 The books Kaufman mentions as selected for the first year were Maya Angelou's *Heart of a Woman*, Jacquelyn Mitchard's *Deep End of the Ocean*, Jane Hamilton's *The Book of Ruth*, Wally Lamb's *She's Come Undone*, and Toni Morrison's *Song of Solomon* (224).

less of an outpouring of emotional transformational responses. To quote Kaufman, "ultimately, what made the *Paradise* meeting different from the *Song of Solomon* meeting was not that one text was necessarily more difficult than the other but that the personal never took over the stage" (244–5). One way to read the *Paradise*-Oprah phenomenon is as a confirmation of what I discovered in my sample and what Jameson and Le Guin propose about vanished and skeptical readers of utopian literature. Even in the midst of an influential celebrity's attempt to reestablish a transformational sense of book power, there is evidence of resistance to perceiving a utopian literature reading experience as an act of personal transformation. My brief presentation of this case is an invitation for further study. Transcripts of Oprah's Book Club shows are available. Reviewing videotape of the *Paradise* segment and gaining access to the *Paradise* letters (if they still exist) and comparing the transcripts, tapes, and letters from this program to the other Book Club sessions would offer fascinating opportunities to discuss the evolution of transformative book power and to evaluate how readers make meaning of utopian and non-utopian works. This archival work can be supplemented by two recent studies, Cecelia Konchar Farr's *Reading Oprah* and Kathleen Rooney's *Reading with Oprah*.

New Directions

What, therefore, are the implications of placing the reader at the forefront for the study of utopian literature? What are the implications of focusing on narrator/narratee relationships, on cross-cultural reading competences, on the effects of illustrations, on the impact of transformations from print to another media, on "real" readers (whether they be the author, reviewers, students, reading clubs, website respondents, participants in "One Book, One Community" programs, or Oprah's letter writers and television audiences), or on the many other possibilities posed by reader-response and receptions studies?

One obvious implication is that students of utopian literature will be studying different types of "texts" and "evidence" from different theoretical perspectives. Instead of focusing exclusively on utopian texts, authors' lives, and political, economic, intellectual, and socio-historical contexts, they will emphasize the histories of reading conventions, literacy, publication contexts, and the types of documents, surveys, and culture studies suggested by the examples enumerated here and in *Utopian Audiences.* There will be parallel theoretical shifts toward the types of methods advocated in well-known collections such as Jane Tompkin's *Reader-Response Criticism: From Formalism to Post-Structuralism,* Susan R. Suleiman and Inge Crosman's *The Reader in the Text: Essays on Audience and Interpretation,* James L. Machor and Philip Goldstein's *Reception Study: From Literary Theory to Cultural Studies,* and Patrocinio P. Schweickart and Elizabeth A. Flynn's *Reading Sites: Social Difference and Reader Response.* If scholars undertake extensive national and international surveys of readers, there will have to be more collaborative research, in undertakings such as the Genre Evolution Project (described in the special issue of *PMLA* on science fiction in May 2004) or the project on Irish utopian literature conducted at the University of Limerick's Ralahine Centre for Utopian Studies.

How we define utopian literature and how we conceptualize the history of that literature will also change. In *Utopian Audiences,* I offered the following working definition, which combines concepts articulated by Darko Suvin, Sargent, Jameson, and others with a strong emphasis on the role of the reader:

> a fairly detailed narrative description of an imaginary culture – a fiction that invites readers to experience vicariously an alternative reality that critiques theirs by opening cognitive and affective spaces that encourage the readers to perceive the realities and potentialities of their culture in new ways. If the author or reader perceives the imaginary culture as being significantly better than the present, then the work is a eutopia, or in the popular usage, a utopia; if significantly worse, it is a dystopia (65).

The redefinition of utopian historiography and hermeneutics from a reader-response perspective is a challenging undertaking that will require collaborative efforts. Instead of using initial publication dates as the foundations of a chronological history, the dates when the readers made the book most influential would guide a multi-level literary-cultural history. In some cases, the traditional linear and the more complex readers' histories would overlap, at least temporarily. For example, since it only took a year for *Looking Backward* to begin its surge to popularity and influence, it could still be defined as an expression of late-nineteenth-century utopianism. But it could also be argued that, in terms of influencing the lives of readers capable of actually reshaping society on a grand scale, it was not until the New Deal – when readers strongly influenced by Bellamy, such as Arthur Morgan, were in positions of power – that *Looking Backward* reached its full meaning and impact. Hence, *Looking Backward* should be studied as much or more during the 1930s. This repositioning, or multi-positioning would challenge the notion that utopian literature in America reached its peak in the late nineteenth- and early twentieth-centuries and that there was, in comparison, a scant amount of utopian literature in America during the 1930s. In terms of number of titles and initial publication dates, the old theory is valid; in terms of recognizing the impact on readers who acted out their interpretations of Bellamy's ideas on a large scale, the old theory is less valid.

Two other obvious examples that could provoke new concepts of the history of utopian literature would be Gilman's *Herland* and Skinner's *Walden Two*. *Herland* had a small reading audience in its magazine form in 1915, but after book publication in 1978, it became a key text in the feminist utopian canon (similar cases could be made for other rediscovered feminist utopias, although many of the texts anthologized in Carol Farley Kessler's *Daring to Dream* are still known primarily by utopian scholars). *Walden Two*'s impact in the late 1940s and early 1950s was small (though it did receive press, sometimes scathing press) compared to its impact in the 1960s and 1970s when the triumphs of behaviorist psychology and the search for alternative lifestyles made the book more believable and more desirable. We would still have to view these and other utopian texts at their places of historical entry – still have to consider the social construction, authorial composition processes, and the initial receptions. But we would also have to re-examine them in light of later, often more significant receptions.

New forms of "evidence," different theoretical orientations, reader-oriented definitions, and multi-dimensional historiographies would make our scholarly lives more complex, and messier. If a significant number of utopias need to be considered several times as they re-enter history through the powers of readers (just imagine how many times Plato and More reenter), then Sargent's bibliography of 5,000 plus utopias in English will rise to the tens of thousands. Add to this the multiple responses of all those readers "vicariously experiencing" each re-entry in its illustrated or non-illustrated, print, film, or opera versions, and we are surrounded by hundreds of thousands of utopias – and that's not counting one blossom of a Chinese utopian peach tree.

Highlighting the reader transforms the study of utopian literature into a disturbingly complex matrix of encounters and re-encounters. But steps in that murky direction open up worlds of provocative investigations as limitless as our ability to imagine the imaginings of readers. Placing readers at the forefront of utopian studies will also help us to understand more fully and accurately what the noplaces of Utopia have done, do, and will do to the someplaces of our world.

Works Cited

Allen, Brooke. "The Promised Land." Rev. of *Paradise*, by Toni Morrison. *New York Times Book Review* 11 January 1998: 6–7.

Arthur, T.S. *Ten Nights in a Bar-Room.* Philadelphia: Lippincott, 1855.

Atkinson, Alan. "Visions of Peach Blossom Spring: Artistic Recreations of a Fourth-Century Chinese Utopia." Society for Utopian Studies Conference. San Antonio, 12 November 1999.

Atwood, Margaret. "Headscarves to Die for." Rev. of *Snow*, by Orhan Pamuk. *New York Times Book Review* 15 August 2004: 1+

Bellamy, Edward. *Equality.* New York: Appleton, 1897.

—— "How I Came to Write Looking Backward." *Nationalist* May 1889: 1–4.

—— *Looking Backward, 2000–1887.* 1888. Ed. John Thomas. Cambridge, Massachusetts: Belknap-Harvard University Press, 1967.

Bleich, David. "What Literature is 'Ours.'" Schweickart and Flynn. 286–313.

Bowman, Sylvia, *et al. Bellamy Abroad: An American Prophet's Influence.* New York: Twayne, 1962.

Carson, Rachel. *Silent Spring.* Boston: Houghton Mifflin, 1962.

"Church Confiscated in Turkmenistan." *Voice of the Martyrs.* 6 March 2003 <http://www.vom.com.au/news/article.esp?artID+%7BEB1874FF-6E61-47BC-B7D41231DB0157D>.

Cornet, Robert J. "Rhetorical Strategies in *Looking Backward.*" *Markham Review* 4.3 (1974): 53–8.

Escarpit, Robert. *Sociology of Literature.* Trans. Ernest Pick. Planesville: Lake Erie College Press, 1965.

de Botton, Alain. *How Proust Can Change Your Life.* New York: Pantheon, 1997.

Farr, Cecilia Konchar. *Reading Oprah: How Oprah's Book Club Changed the Way America Reads.* Albany: State University of New York Press, 2005.

Fitting, Peter. "Positioning and Closure: On the 'Reading Effect' of Contemporary Utopian Fiction." *Utopian Studies.* Vol.1. Ed. Gorman Beauchamp and Kenneth M. Roemer. Washington: University Press of America, 1978. 23–36.

George, Henry. *Progress and Poverty: An Inquiry* [...]. 1879. New York: Modern Library-Random House, n.d.

Gilman, Charlotte Perkins. *Herland.* 1915. New York: Pantheon, 1979.

Greer, Jane. "'Some of their stories are like my life, I guess': Working-Class Women Readers and Confessional Magazines." Schweickart and Flynn. 135–65.

Grimshaw, Robert. *Fifty Years Hence; or What May Be in 1943...* New York: Practical, 1892.

The Handmaid's Tale. By Poul Ruders. English libretto by Paul Bentley. Dir. Phyllida Lloyd. Cond. Richard Bradshaw. Hummingbird Centre for the Performing Arts, Toronto. 9 October 2004.

Harben, Will N. *The Land of the Changing Sun.* New York: Merriam, 1894.

Howe, Ron. "Reconsidering Bellamy in the Year 2000." *Revisiting the Legacy of Edward Bellamy (1850–1898), American Author and Social Reformer.* Ed. Toby Widdicombe and Herman Preiser. Lewiston: Mellen, 2002. 417–32.

Jameson, Frederic. "Of Islands and Trenches: Neutralization and the Production of Utopian Discourse." *Diacritics* 7.2 (1977): 2–21.

Kaufman, Rona. "'That, my dear, is called reading': Oprah's Book Club and the Construction of a Readership." Schweickart and Flynn. 221–55.

Kessler, Carol Farley. *Daring to Dream: Utopian Stories of United States Women, 1836–1919.* Syracuse: Syracuse University Press, 1995.

Khanna, Lee Cullen. "The Reader in *Looking Backward.*" *Journal of General Education* 33 (1981): 69–79.

—— "Text as Tactic: *Looking Backward* and the Power of the Word." *Looking Backward,* 1988–1888. Ed. Daphne Patai. Amherst: University of Massachusetts Press, 1988. 37–50.

Kuhlmann Hilke. "The Reception of *Walden Two* in Intentional Communities in North America." Diss. Albert Ludwigs University zu Freiburg, 1999–2000.

Le Guin, Ursula K. *Always Coming Home.* New York: Harper & Row, 1985.

—— "The Ones Who Walk Away from Omelas (Variations on a Theme by Henry James)." 1973. *Utopian Studies* 2 (1991): 1–5.

Lipow, Arthur. *Authoritarian Socialism in America: Edward Bellamy and the Nationalist Movement.* Berkeley: University of California Press, 1982.

Lowrey, Lois. *The Giver.* New York: Bantam Doubleday Dell, 1993.

Machor, James L., and Philip Goldstein, (eds.). *Reception Study: From Literary Theory to Cultural Studies.* New York: Routledge, 2001.

MacNair, Everett. *Edward Bellamy and the Nationalist Movement, 1889 to 1894.* Milwaukee: Fitzgerald, 1975.

Manuel, Frank, and Fritzie Manuel. *Utopian Thought in the Western World.* Cambridge, Massachusetts: Belknap-Harvard University Press, 1979.

More, Thomas. *Utopia: A New Translation, Backgrounds, Criticism.* Ed. and trans. Robert M. Adams. New York: Norton, 1975.

Morrison, Toni. *Paradise.* New York: Knopf, 1998.

Morson, Gary Saul. *The Boundaries of Genre. Dostoevsky's* Diary of a Writer *and the Traditions of Literary Utopia.* Austin: University of Texas Press, 1981.

Newcomb, Simon. *His Wisdom the Defender.* New York: Harper & Brothers, 1900.

Orwell, George. *Nineteen Eighty-Four.* London: Secker & Warburg, 1949.

Parrington, Vernon Louis, Jr. *American Dreams: A Study of American Utopias.* Providence: Brown University Press, 1947.

Pfaelzer, Jean. "Immanence, Interdeterminance, and the Utopian Pun in *Looking Backward.*" *Looking Backward, 1988–1888.* Ed. Daphne Patai. Amherst: University of Massachusetts Press, 1988. 51–67.

Rabkin, Eric S. "Science Fiction and the Future of Criticism." *PMLA* 119 (2004): 457–73.

Radway, Janice. *Reading the Romance: Women, Patriarchy, and Popular Literature.* Chapel Hill: University of North Carolina Press, 1991.

Rimmer, Robert. *The Harrad Experiment.* 1966. Buffalo: Prometheus. 1990.

Roemer, Kenneth M. "1984 in 1894: Harben's *Land of the Changing Sun.*" *Mississippi Quarterly* 26 (1972–1973): 29–42.

—— *Build Your Own Utopia: An Interdisciplinary Course in Utopian Speculation.* Washington: University Press of America, 1981.

—— *The Obsolete Necessity: America in Utopian Literature, 1888–1900.* Kent: Kent State University Press, 1976.

—— "Using Utopia to Teach the 80s: A Case for Guided Design." *World Future Society Bulletin* 14.4 (1980): 1–5.

—— *Utopian Audiences: How Readers Locate Nowhere.* Amherst: University of Massachusetts Press. 2003.

—— (ed.). *America as Utopia.* New York: Burt Franklin, 1981.

Rooney, Kathleen. *Reading with Oprah: The Book Club that Changed America.* Fayetteville: University of Arkansas Press, 2005.

Ruppert, Peter. *Reader in a Strange Land: The Activity of Reading Literary Utopias.* Athens: University of Georgia Press, 1986.

Rushdie, Salman. *Satanic Verses.* New York: Viking, 1989.

Sargisson, Lucy, and Lyman Tower Sargent. *Living in Utopia: New Zealand's Intentional Communities.* Burlington: Ashgate, 2004.

Sargent, Lyman Tower. *British and American Utopian Literature, 1516–1975: An Annotated Bibliography.* Boston: G.K. Hall, 1979.

—— *British and American Utopian Literature, 1516–1985.* New York: Garland, 1988.

—— "The Three Faces of Utopianism Revisited." *Utopian Studies* 5.1 (1994): 1–37.

Schaer, Roland, Gregory Claeys, and Lyman Tower Sargent (eds.). *Utopia: The Search for the Ideal Society in the Western World.* New York: Oxford University Press, 2000.

Schweickart, Patrocinio P., and Elizabeth A. Flynn (eds.). *Reading Sites: Social Difference and Reader Response.* New York: MLA, 2004.

Segal, Howard P. *Technological Utopianism in American Culture.* Chicago: University of Chicago Press, 1985.

Sheldon, Charles M. *In His Steps. "What Would Jesus Do?"* Chicago: Advance, 1897.

Shor, Francis. "The Ideological Matrix of Reform in Late Nineteenth-Century America and New Zealand: Reading Edward Bellamy's *Looking Backward.*" *Prospects* 17 (1992): 29–58.

Sicherman, Barbara. "Reading and Middle-Class Identity in Victorian America." *Reading Acts: U.S. Readers' Interactions with Literature, 1800–1950.* Ed. Barbara Ryan and Amy M. Thomas. Knoxville: University of Tennessee Press, 2002. 137–60.

Smith, D.B. "Blueprints for Paradise." *Times Literary Supplement* 10 September 1976: 1112.

Stowe, Harriet Beecher. *Uncle Tom's Cabin.* 1852. Columbus: Merrill, 1969.

Suleiman, Susan R. *The Reader in the Text: Essays on Audience and Interpretation.* Princeton: Princeton University Press, 1980.

Suvin, Darko. "Defining the Literary Genre of Utopia." *Metamorphoses of Science Fiction: On the Poetics and History of a Literary Genre.* New Haven: Yale University Press, 1979. 37–62.

Theroux, Paul. "Damned Old Graham Green." Rev. of *The Life of Graham Green,* Vol.3, by Norman Sherry. *New York Times Book Review* 17 October 2004: 1+

Thomas, Chauncey. *The Crystal Button.* Boston: Houghton Mifflin, 1891.

Thomas, John. *Alternative America: Henry George, Edward Bellamy, Henry Demarist Lloyd, and the Adversary Tradition.* Cambridge, Massachusetts: Belknap-Harvard, 1983.

Tompkins, Jane (ed.). *Reader-Response Criticism: From Formalism to Post-Structuralism.* Baltimore: Johns Hopkins University Press, 1980.

Toth, Csaba. "The Transatlantic Dialogue: 19th-Century American Utopianism and Europe." Diss. University of Minnesota, 1992.

Twain, Mark. *A Connecticut Yankee in King Arthur's Court.* 1899. Ed. Bernard L. Stein. Berkeley: University of California Press, 1979.

"Utopia." *Studio 360.* National Public Radio. WNYC. 15 August 2004.

Wells, H.G. *A Modern Utopia.* 1905. Lincoln: University of Nebraska Press, 1967.

RAFFAELLA BACCOLINI

Finding Utopia in Dystopia: Feminism, Memory, Nostalgia, and Hope

> Tengo nostalgia de un país que no existe todavía en el mapa.[1]
>
> Eduardo Galeano, *Días y noches de amor y de guerra*

In this essay, I will trace some of the ways in which feminism – and feminist literary and cultural theory, in particular – intersects with utopian studies.[2] In so doing I am going to foreground issues of cultural and geographical diversity; but also, in a perspective informed by gender, I will look at how Utopia and desire intersect with memory, nostalgia, and genre. Thus, I will link questions of location and positionality with issues like desire, an essential component of utopian literature, as well as nostalgia; for it is desire for change, for a better place, and a better life, that moves Utopia, and it is desire for a lost place and a lost time that informs nostalgia. It is widely accepted today that whenever we receive or produce culture we do so from a certain position and that such location influences the ways we theorize about and read the world (see Rich, "Notes"; Haraway). As an Italian woman who did her graduate work in the U.S. in the 1980s, and who specialized in American "high" modernist poetry, my approach to utopian studies has been shaped by my cultural and biographical

---

1   "I am nostalgic for a country that does not exist yet on the map." Unless otherwise cited, translations are mine.

2   I am grateful to Giuseppe Lusignani and Bruna Conconi, with whom I have discussed Italian terrorism; Patrick Leech, Sam Whitsitt, and Rita Monticelli, who have read and discussed parts of this essay; and Breda Gray, Sinead McDermott, Bríona Nic Dhiarmada, Cinta Ramblado, and Liam Bannon for sharing their ideas on memory. My thanks also to the audiences in Limerick and Galway – and to Tom Moylan and Hoda Zaki, in particular – who, in the winter 2004, asked me very stimulating questions.

circumstances as well as by my geography. It is therefore a hybrid approach that combines these geographical and historical circumstances with other issues like desire and interest. In particular, my interest in feminist theory and in writings by women has intersected with the desire, naïve or romantic as it may seem, to contribute to the transformation of society. It is an approach that has foregrounded from the very beginning issues of genre writing as they intersect with gender and the deconstruction of high and low culture. Such an approach, however, has and must also come to terms with the political and cultural circumstances that characterize this recent turn of the century.

"Intellectual Biography": Or, How I Came to Work on Dystopia

> Non si ricordano i giorni, si ricordano gli attimi.[3]
> Cesare Pavese, *Il mestiere di vivere*

I consider myself a "child of conflict" – to borrow the words that the Ekumenical Envoy, Tong Ov, uses to describe the Terran Observer Sutty in Ursula K. Le Guin's novel, *The Telling* (26). Born in 1960, I have no direct recollection of nor nostalgia for the struggles and atmosphere of 1968; rather, I belong to the generation of the 1970s, a generation marked, like the rest of my country, by the "years of lead" (*anni di piombo*) – which refers to the attacks from the extreme left by the Brigate Rosse (Red Brigades), that between 1976 and 1980 killed almost 100 people, and the bombings by extreme-right terrorists and state apparatuses, that from 1969 on killed many more people. While I do not remember the rallies of the late 1960s, I cannot forget the black and white pictures of the fascist bombs in Piazza Fontana in Milan (12 December 1969). I do remember the "heavy" atmosphere of the daily tolls on the news at night when the country was informed of how

3   "We do not remember days, we remember moments."

many people had been injured or killed during terrorist actions. Such a biography accounts, I think, for some of the reasons why I am more drawn to dystopian than to utopian literature. Dystopia speaks to me more than the utopias of the 1960s and early 1970s. And this is one of the reasons why I have become interested in the recent production of dystopian science fiction (sf). To a certain extent, this is also one of the elements that shapes my approach to utopian studies. In the past few years, I have been studying dystopian literature in its formal and thematic features, while trying to look for other modes of articulating horizons of hope.[4] I have come to believe that contemporary sf production, in its themes and in its formal aspects, is an example of a new oppositional and resisting form of writing, one that maintains a utopian horizon *within* the pages of dystopian sf *in* these very dark times.

Starting with the conservative reaction of the 1980s, Utopia has been under attack. At the same time, however, it has been co-opted. Often, in these unquestionably anti-utopian times, Utopia has been conflated with materialist satisfaction and thus has been commodified and devalued. In a society where consumerism and instant pleasure have come to represent the contemporary modality of happiness, Utopia has, apparently, become an outmoded value. And yet, the pursuit of individual happiness, which is none other than material success, corresponds to what Darko Suvin has called the "Disneyfication strategy" (194) – a notion and a practice that former Italian prime minister, Silvio Berlusconi, fully embraced. For these reasons, in my approach I try to find ways to highlight the transgressive and radical nature of some of the literature being written today, as we need to develop a critical perspective that can point us toward action and change. And I have come to believe that we need to move away from

---

4 This also resting on Sargent's and others' distinction between anti-utopia and dystopia. "Dystopia or negative utopia: a non-existent society described in considerable detail and normally located in time and space that the author intended a contemporaneous reader to view as considerably worse than the society in which the reader lived. [...] Anti-utopia: a non-existent society described in considerable detail and normally located in time and space that the author intended a contemporaneous reader to view as a criticism of utopianism or some particular eutopia" (Sargent 9).

the mere pursuit of happiness to recover Utopia – hence my interest in memory and nostalgia, as I think, and as I will try to argue, that a constant awareness of a "slight suffering" is the necessary condition of Utopia (one lesson, I would say, that Joanna Russ had already pointed us to in the powerful story "When It Changed"). Since one of the functions of memory – and of memorializing in particular – is a certain kind of catharsis, I argue that we need to keep remembering and that one of the things that makes memory and possibly nostalgia relevant for Utopia is that we must keep feeling uncomfortable.

But there is also another way in which I consider myself a "child of conflict": a conflict resulting from the encounter/clash between cultures, the Italian-European, on the one hand, and the North-American, on the other, leaving me in a situation that has prompted me to wrestle with issues like nostalgia, memory, and desire. I believe we are, in a sense, what we write and what we choose to read. I need stories that speak to me. There is a statement by Marge Piercy that I find striking for both its simplicity and lucidity:

> When I was a child, I first noticed that neither history as I was taught it nor the stories I was told seemed to lead to me. I began to fix them. I have been at it ever since. To me it is an important task to situate ourselves in the time line so that we may be active in history. We require a past that leads to us. After any revolution, history is rewritten, not just out of partisan zeal, but because the past has changed. Similarly, what we imagine we are working toward does a lot to define what we will consider doable action aimed at producing the future we want and preventing the future we fear (1–2).

The way we position ourselves toward the past can take at least two possible directions: through idealization in order to reproduce a seam-less, perfect picture of the past, or through desire, gaps, and pain in order to critically understand the past and change it. My framework borrows directly from feminism and from the concept of re-vision as formulated by Adrienne Rich.[5] But while acknowledging this debt, I

---

5   "Re-vision – the act of looking back, of seeing with fresh eyes, of entering an
     old text from a new critical direction – is for us more than a chapter in cultural
     history: it is an act of survival. Until we can understand the assumptions in
     which we are drenched we cannot know ourselves. And this drive to self-
     knowledge, for woman, is more than a search for identity: it is part of her

will also try to include nostalgia, traditionally seen as regressive even in most feminist criticism, as a concept that can be of use to Utopia.

Gender and Genre

> Words and eggs must be handled with care.
> Once broken they are impossible
> things to repair.
> Anne Sexton, "Words"

Most women's utopian literature has addressed particular, gendered concerns, and today, through a series of strategies and features, it has renovated the traditionally oppositional nature of the genre. In particular, I have found the discourse of genre and its deconstruction and appropriation by women writers particularly fruitful.[6] An analysis of women's approach to the sf genre is what allows us to recognize, in the new production of some women writers, a subversive and oppositional strategy against hegemonic ideology. As feminist scholars,

refusal of the self-destructiveness of male-dominated society. A radical critique of literature, feminist in its impulse, would take the work first of all as a clue to how we live, how we have been living, how we have been led to imagine ourselves, how our language has trapped as well as liberated us; and how we can begin to see – and therefore live – afresh. [...] We need to know the writing of the past, and know it differently than we have ever known it; not to pass on a tradition but to break its hold over us" (Rich, "When We Dead Awaken" 35).

6 My initial interest in women's intervention on genre writing developed from my work on the American poet H.D. At that time, having read Margaret Atwood's novel *The Handmaid's Tale* and having seen some negative reviews she received – mostly accusing her of having written a novel that did not fit the dystopian genre – I started studying the convention of utopian and dystopian literature. What most reviewers seemed to imply is that since Atwood's novel is similar to Orwell's *Nineteen Eighty-Four* but does not follow entirely the traditional conventions of the dystopian genre, it cannot be considered a proper, successful dystopia and needs to be labeled differently. This led some critics to consider Atwood's novel a failure, rather than an experiment with the dystopian genre (see Baccolini, "Breaking the Boundaries").

therefore, we may want to question the very notion of genre, boundaries, and exclusionary politics – notions and practices that have traditionally proved detrimental for women – and investigate instead the intersection of gender and generic fiction. The ways in which gender enters into and is constructed by the form of genre have some bearing on, in turn, the creation of new critical texts.

Genres, with their set rules, conventions, and expectations, have been traditionally one of the measures against which to judge a work's, and a writer's, greatness. Genres are "essentially literary institutions, or social contracts between a writer and a specific public, whose function is to specify the *proper* use of a particular cultural artifact" (Jameson, *Political Unconscious* 106, emphasis added). Far from being mere aesthetic markers, however, genres are "drenched in ideologies" (Schenck 282); and an analysis of a single work in relation to the genre it belongs to also allows us to understand that work as a product of the historical and literary times in which it was written. Genres are then culturally constructed and rest on the binary between what is *normal* and what is *deviant* – a notion that feminist criticism has deconstructed since it consigns feminine practice to the pole of deviation and inferiority. Feminist reappropriations of generic fiction can therefore become a radical and oppositional practice.[7]

The intersection of gender and genre in sf has opened up the creation of new, subversive, and oppositional literary forms. Sf is already regarded as a potentially subversive genre, often a "degraded product – held at bay, and yet rich in themes and obsessions which are repressed in high culture" (Angenot, quoted in Parrinder 46). In its developments, then, sf has come to represent a form of counternarrative to hegemonic discourse. In its extrapolation of the present, sf has the potential to envision different worlds that can work, at least, as purely imaginative constructs, or at most, as critical explorations of our society. Sf has then the potential, through estrangement and cog-

---

7   The use of generic fiction as a form of political resistance by women has been
     studied, among others, by Anne Cranny-Francis, and much sf research by
     women scholars has investigated the ways in which gender informs sf. See the
     work of Joanna Russ, Marleen Barr, Sarah Lefanu, Lee Cullen Khanna, Carol
     Farley Kessler, to cite only a few.

nitive mapping, to move its readers to see the differences of an else-where and, in turn, to think critically about one's own world and, possibly, to act upon it to change it. Thus, women's sf novels have contributed to the exploration and subsequent dismantling of certainties and universalist assumptions – those damaging stereotypes – about gendered identities; and they have done so by addressing, in a dialectical engagement with tradition, themes such as the representation of women and their bodies, reproduction and sexuality, and language and its relation to identity.

But genres change in relation to the times; and our times, characterized by a general shift to the Right in the 1980s and 1990s, have produced what myself, Tom Moylan, and a series of other scholars have addressed as a "dystopian turn" in Anglo-American sf (see Baccolini and Moylan). There is still writing in these decidedly anti-utopian times, but the writing is mostly *about* these dark times, to paraphrase Bertolt Brecht's famous lines.[8] After the revival of Utopia in the 1960s and 1970s, the appearance, in the 1980s, of the cynical cyberpunk sf foreclosed any real subversive critique of the conservative society. Sf's oppositional and critical potential was subsequently recovered and renovated in the production of a number of writers – mostly women, like Octavia E. Butler, Marge Piercy, and Ursula K. Le Guin – whose turn to dystopia recovered Utopia. Especially by the 1990s, this kind of dystopian writing, critical and ambiguous and mainly produced by feminist writers, had become the preferred form for an expression of struggle and resistance.

As I have argued in "Gender and Genre in the Feminist Critical Dystopias," dystopia is traditionally a bleak, depressing genre with no space for hope within the story, where utopia(n hope) is maintained *outside* the story: it is only if we consider dystopia as a warning that we as readers can hope to escape such a pessimistic future. This option is not granted, for example, to the protagonists of George Orwell's classical dystopia, *Nineteen Eighty-Four*, who are crushed by the totalitarian society. Conversely, recent novels such as Margaret Atwood's *The Handmaid's Tale*, Le Guin's *The Telling*, or Butler's

---

8   "In the dark times / Will there also be singing? / Yes, there will also be singing / About the dark times" (Woolrich online).

Parable series allow readers and protagonists to hope by resisting closure: the ambiguous, open endings of these novels maintain the utopian impulse *within* the work. In fact, by rejecting the traditional subjugation of the individual at the end of the novel, the critical dystopia opens a space of contestation and opposition for those groups – women and other "ex-centric" subjects whose subject position is not contemplated by hegemonic discourse – for whom subjectivity has yet to be attained (Baccolini, "Gender and Genre" 18).

Another factor that makes these novels sites of resistance and oppositional texts is their blurring of different genre conventions. Drawing on the feminist criticism of universalist assumptions, singularity, and neutral and objective knowledge, and acknowledging the importance of difference, multiplicity and complexity, situated knowledges, as well as hybridity, recent dystopian sf by women resists genre purity in favor of an impure or hybrid text which renovates dystopian sf by making it politically and formally oppositional. In *Kindred*, for example, Butler revises the conventions of the time travel story and creates a novel that is both sf and neo-slave narrative. While Atwood employs the conventions of the diary and the epistolary novel in *The Handmaid's Tale*, Le Guin combines a political fable with storytelling for her most recent novel of cultural contact. Thus, it is the very notion of an "*impure* genre, with permeable borders which allow contamination from other genres, that represents resistance to a hegemonic ideology and renovates the resisting nature of sf" (Baccolini, "Gender and Genre" 18).

Memory, Forgetting, and Utopia

> The struggle of man against power is the struggle of memory against forgetting.
> Milan Kundera, *The Books of Laughter and Forgetting*

On a more thematic level, in most of these novels, resistance is maintained through the recovery of history and literacy, together with individual and collective memory. But while the last twenty years have seen a profusion of studies on memory (with regard to slavery, the Holocaust, colonialism, trauma, heritage, nationalism), we can also agree with Pierre Nora that "we speak so much of memory because there is so little of it left" (7). Moreover, the sustained efforts to study memory from a gendered perspective (see Lourie, Stanton, and Vicinus; and, more recently, Hirsch and Smith) have been few. With the exception of Vincent Geoghegan's studies on the relationship between memory and Utopia, such an intersection has been largely ignored. Despite the fact that, as Gayle Greene says, "memory is especially important to anyone who cares about change, for forgetting dooms us to repetition; and it is of particular importance to feminists," the importance of memory in utopian studies has not been adequately underlined (291). I think, instead, that an emancipatory notion of memory is fundamental to our discussion of Utopia.

The very notion of memory, however, calls for a reflection on forgetting (see Baccolini, "Sometime"). Forgetting is a necessary and vital part of memory. According to Greek mythology, Lethe is a female divinity whose mother is Eris, the goddess of strife and discord (Theoi Project on line). Lethe, the goddess of forgetfulness and oblivion, is associated with night and is opposed to Mnemosyne, the goddess of memory associated with light. Lethe is also the river of forgetfulness: we drink of the waters of Lethe so that once we are born, by forgetting our past life we make room for our new life and all the emotions, thoughts, and actions that will determine the quality of that life to come. The river Lethe is also connected with death and the Underworld, where the shades of the dead had to let go of their earthly lives by drinking from its waters. Forgetting, then, can bring relief from the painful memories of life at the same time that it can lead to sleep (Lethe, night), as Paul Valéry once wrote that "to go to sleep is to forget" (quoted in Weinrich 5). But dreams, as we know, are also associated with memory and imagination: in our dreams we remember and transform people and events from our lives (Baccolini, "Sometime" online).

For many, forgetting continues to be seen as necessary. Marc Augé, for example, claims that it is indispensable: we need to know how to forget in order to taste the present; we need to forget the recent past to recover the more distant past (11). Paul Ricoeur focuses the last part of *Memory, History, Forgetting* on the need of forgetting as a condition for the possibility of remembering, asking whether there can be something like happy forgetting in parallel to happy memory (589–646). For both, and since Friedrich Nietzsche who also concluded his reflection on the use and abuse of history and the past with the recommendation, "learn to forget," an "active forgetting" (Nietzsche) is necessary to open up the possibility of the future. Like plants in a garden, memories must be selected and pruned to help new memories to bloom and grow (Augé 29). It is clear that for Augé and others, forgetting does not really mean the loss of memory *tout court*, but rather the possibility of movement and change against an official, sometimes rigid, prescribed memory. Without forgetting, there could be no memory. Forgetting, thus, serves as imagination, to maintain memory and the curiosity for the past alive (Baccolini, "Sometime" online).

Despite these reflections, I remain uncomfortable with the idea of forgetting. One way to approach this discomfort is to see whether there are different kinds of forgetting in the same way that there are different kinds of memories: i.e., if oblivion can be of use, or whether there is such a thing like a "critical" or "radical forgetting." Psychoanalysis provides one such distinction, between what Harald Weinrich has called "'unpacified' [...] and 'pacified' forgetting" (136): i.e., the retrieval of the repressed before and after the cure. According to Sigmund Freud, forgetting and memory have to do with the avoidance of displeasure: whatever one finds unpleasant or embarrassing is repressed and forgotten, as in the case of traumas. Valéry provides another distinction between different kinds of forgetting: he distinguishes between "forgetting that results in mere loss [...] [and] a kind of forgetting that has positive effects." Forgetting then becomes what we need "to differentiate quotidian and trivial memories from memories that serve life" (Weinrich 145). Similarly, Ricoeur distinguishes between complete forgetting and a kind of forgetting that he calls "kept in reserve." Whereas complete forgetting threatens to destroy memory traces once and for all, forgetting that is kept in reserve allows memories, temporarily forgotten, to be retrieved (626). In this sense, forgetting suggests that the persistence of memory is not consciously perceptible and that we actually forget less than we think or fear we will (Baccolini, "Sometime" online).

But my sense of unease with forgetting has to do, most of all, with the fact that the very notions of oblivion and memory also call into question other issues, such as ethics and identity. The vital notion of "active forgetting" clashes with the choice of what can be forgotten, what must not be forgotten, and who makes the decision. In fact, what renders forgetting problematic is the issue of positionality. While these various claims are compelling, they sound "intellectual," or abstract and unconvincing, when placed next to the vexing call to "forgive and forget" that people who have gone through traumas, losses, and conflicts experience. Similarly, another reason why the idea of forgetting is disturbing is that memory and forgetting have always been and still are profoundly associated with the idea of identity. In *The Ethics of Memory*, Avishai Margalit states that "who we are depends on our not forgetting things that happened and that are important in our lives" (208). To go back to Greek mythology, memory is inextricably linked with imagination and identity. Mnemosyne, the goddess of memory, is the mother of the muses and the patroness of intellectual and artistic efforts; and she grants the power to tell about present, past, and future, so that memory becomes, in a sense, the source of creativity. Conversely, to be bereft of memory is equivalent to losing oneself (Baccolini, "Memory and Historical Reconciliation" 131–2). Thus, the link between memory, imagination, and identity is a founding element of western culture, and frequently recurs in much literature, including the utopian tradition. In a poem called "Transcendental Etude," Adrienne Rich underlines the condition of loss in women's lives, where the lack of remembering becomes a fragmentation of one's body and a displacement: "But in fact we were always like this, / rootless, dismembered: knowing it makes the difference" (75). The past and the knowledge of it, then, become an aspect of memory that can be empowering.

Western discourses about memory have been characterized by the attempt to identify and distinguish different kinds of memories. According to western philosophical tradition, for example, we move from a simpler *recall* to the more profound and unsettling *recognition* of Plato, Aristotle, Aquinas, and Augustine – two types of memories

of which the second involves judgment and leads to knowledge (see
Yates 1–81). Such distinction has continued throughout the centuries,
maintaining a difference between a less valuable memory, like habits
that tended to hinder individual growth, and a highly functional
memory that is instrumental for an understanding of the present and
the future alike. The division between, as I have argued, anti-utopian,
or conservative, and utopian, or progressive, features of memory (see
Baccolini, "Memory and Historical Reconciliation") may also prove
useful if applied to nostalgia.[9]

In my work on memory and Utopia, I have tried to review some
of the most relevant discussions of the utopian value of memory,
starting with Ernst Bloch, who distinguishes between "*anamnesis*
(recollection) [and] *anagnorisis* (recognition)" (Geoghegan 58).
Whereas, recollection is conservative and precludes new knowledge,
since all knowledge lies in the past, *anagnorisis* "involves recognition": here "memory traces are reactivated in the present, but there is
never simple correspondence between past and present, because of all
the intervening novelty. The power of the past resides in its complicated relationship of similarity/dissimilarity to the present" (Geoghegan 58). Bloch's value for a utopian theory of memory lies in his
recognition of the importance of memory as a repository of experience
and value. In order for memory and history not to hinder progress or
Utopia, there has to be room for novelty in memory and history must
not be cyclical (Geoghegan 59). Memory is therefore necessary to an
understanding of oneself and of the past, but also of the present and
the future alike, and acquires thus a social dimension (Baccolini,
"Memory and Historical Reconciliation" 118).

Whereas, forgetting is often associated with loss and disem-
powerment, memory is connected with emancipation. Remembrance,
for Theodor Adorno, is an act of resistance against "the advancing
bourgeois society [that] liquidates Memory, Time, Recollection as
irrational leftovers of the past" (quoted in Marcuse 99); whereas for

---

9   Geoghegan has best explored the relationship between memory and utopianism.
     In his study, he says that for many people "memory has a built-in utopian
     function" (54). However, even though desire is a fundamental component of
     Utopia, not all desires automatically fit the notion of Utopia.

Herbert Marcuse it is perceived as dangerous and subversive because, as "a mode of dissociation from the given facts, [...] [it] breaks, for short moments, the omnipresent power of the given facts" (98). Memory, then, helps to break hegemonic historical discourse, the master narratives that have erased our historical memory so that it becomes hard to distinguish between past and present (Baccolini, "Memory and Historical Reconciliation" 118).

Finally, in Walter Benjamin's "Theses on the Philosophy of History," memory is associated with hope and thus has a redemptive power: "To articulate the past historically does not mean to recognize it 'the way it really was' [...] It means to seize hold of a memory as it flashes up at a moment of danger" (VI 247). For Benjamin, memory is important, "for every image of the past that is not recognized by the present as one of its own concerns" – and thus is not remembered – "threatens to disappear irretrievably" (V 247). Thus, a society that is incapable of recollection, recognition, and remembrance is without hope for the future, as it shows no concern for the often silenced histories of the oppressed, the marginalized, the dispossessed. As Benjamin reminds us, "it is only for the sake of those without hope that hope is given to us" (quoted in Marcuse 257). Historical amnesia therefore leads us toward Anti-Utopia and creates a false sense of the past as a better time. By leaving out "embarrassing" memories of an unjust past, official commemorations offer a sanitized version of history and thus extend injustice into the future and foreclose the possibility for change (Baccolini, "Memory and Historical Reconciliation" 118–19).

My reflection on memory and Utopia stresses the importance to distinguish, then, between a conservative, or anti-utopian, and a progressive, or utopian, use of memory – the latter acquiring also a social and ethical dimension. Choice, responsibility, and action are linked to memory and knowledge of the past for Rich, who claims them as fundamental for resistance and change: "If it is the present that calls us to activism, it is history that must nourish our choices and commitment" ("Resisting Amnesia" 152). She also stresses our responsibility and accountability in the choices we make: "Historical responsibility has, after all, to do with action" (145). By choosing to remember, we show ourselves capable of taking responsibility for our actions and being accountable; whereas by choosing to ignore or forget what was or what we did ultimately means that we avoid responsibility and thus risk political paralysis (Baccolini, "Memory and Historical Reconciliation" 119).

Thus, I have argued that the utopian value of memory rests in nurturing a culture of memory and sustaining a theory of remembrance. These actions, therefore, become important elements of a political, utopian praxis of change, action, and empowerment: indeed, our reconstructions of the past shape our present and future. Memory, then, to be of use for Utopia, needs to disassociate itself from its traditional link to the metaphor of storage and identify itself as a process. As Utopia is a process, so memory needs to be perceived as a process, not fixed, or reachable, but in progress (Baccolini, "Memory and Historical Reconciliation" 117–20).

Nostalgia and Utopia

> Nostalgia is the desire for desire.
> Susan Stewart, *On Longing*

Nostalgia, on the other hand, has traditionally been viewed as a type of conservative or regressive memory. Compared to memory, it is a more "recent" concept, as it was first introduced in 1688 by a Swiss medical student, Johannes Hofer, to describe the pain experienced by Swiss mercenaries for being away from home. Coined by Hofer from the Greek, it links pain (*algos*) with return (*nostos*) and stands for the painful desire to return home.[10] Originally a medical notion, nostalgia started to lose its medical associations in the nineteenth century and became, in the twentieth, more of a general condition, often comparable but not exactly like regret, *mal du pays*, *rimpianto*, *saudade* (Prete 10). What made this transition possible was a movement from

---

10   His list of symptoms includes despondency, depression, lack of appetite, bouts of weeping, and even death.

space (home) to time (past), as noted by the philosopher Immanuel Kant (Hutcheon online). Kant noticed that people who did return home were usually disappointed and, thus, cured: their desire was not simply to return home, it was not directed to a place or a thing that could be recovered, but to the home of their youth, hence toward a time that is irretrievable (Kant, quoted in Prete 66). Because of the irretrievability of the past, nostalgia, from a curable medical disease, morphed into an incurable general condition. However, though universalized, nostalgia is culturally and historically specific and works differently in very different contexts, as I hope the examples I have chosen will show.

Despite the fact that nostalgia is very much an aspect of memory – it is the memory of home, its scent, of a time gone – it has often been seen as antithetical to memory.[11] Feminist studies on nostalgia and memory have stressed this contrast between the two, partly because feminists have little to be nostalgic for. If for David Lowenthal the past is a foreign country, for women it has often been an inhospitable one. For Greene, for example:

> nostalgia and remembering are in some sense antithetical, since nostalgia is a forgetting, merely regressive, whereas memory may look back in order to move forward and transform disabling fictions to enabling fictions, altering our relation to the present and future (298).

Likewise, for Rich, while memory is linked with connectedness and historical responsibility (to re-membering), "Historical amnesia *is* starvation of the imagination; nostalgia is the imagination's sugar rush, leaving depression and emptiness in its wake" ("Resisting Amnesia" 145). For Janice Doane and Devon Hodges, finally, nostalgia is not "just a sentiment but also a rhetorical practice" that, in the writings of social and literary critics as well as of 1980s novelists, serves to reinstate traditional values against the gains of the feminist movement (3).

---

11   Nostalgia is, in fact, an aspect of memory, where both happiness and sadness are associated with the act of remembering. The memory of something good from the past makes us yearn for that past, but the realization that the past is irrecoverable makes us sad.

Even reflections about nostalgia in a non-specifically gendered perspective often point to its backward, even reactionary nature. In short, nostalgia seems to be antithetical to progress: for Charles Maier, "nostalgia is to memory as kitsch is to art" (quoted in Boym xiv); or, according to Michael Kammen, it is "essentially history without guilt" (quoted in Boym xiv). As Svetlana Boym sums up, seen in this perspective, nostalgia "is an abdication of personal responsibility, a guilt-free homecoming, an ethical and aesthetic failure" (xiv). Nostalgia, then, is characterized by loss, lack, and inauthenticity. For Nicholas Dames, "authentic memory" – if there is one – is "exactly what is nonnostalgic" (74). "By the narrative process of nostalgic reconstruction," says Susan Stewart, "the present is denied and the past takes on an authenticity of being" (23).

A first reappraisal of nostalgia comes early on from Fredric Jameson, as he claims, in "Walter Benjamin or Nostalgia," that nostalgia potentially offers a "revolutionary stimulus" provided that it is a nostalgia conscious of itself:

> But if nostalgia as a political motivation is most frequently associated with Fascism, there is no reason why a nostalgia conscious of itself, a lucid and remorseless dissatisfaction with the present on grounds of some remembered plenitude, cannot furnish as adequate a revolutionary stimulus as any other (*Marxism and Form* 82).

Among critics, Vladimir Jankélévitch and Antonio Prete refuse to give nostalgia a fixed political connotation. Boym also distinguishes nostalgia along the same lines that characterize the discourse on memory and sees a restorative and a reflective nostalgia, of which the second is preferable. While restorative nostalgia emphasizes *nostos* and "proposes to rebuild the lost home and patch up the memory gaps," reflective nostalgia thrives on *algia*, on "longing and loss, the imperfect process of remembrance" (41) and reveals that "longing and critical thinking are not opposed to one another, as affective memories do not absolve one from compassion, judgment or critical reflection" (49–50). For Mary Jacobus: "Feminist nostalgia looks back not only to what feminism desires but to what it desires different, now" (138). Similarly, Therese Lichtenstein argues that a critical, progressive nostalgia uses the past "in a dialectical way – to change and illuminate present conditions and both individual and class consciousness in a way that might lead to political action and social change" (217).

And yet, if there have been recent attempts to recuperate nostalgia on the part of feminists and others, to my knowledge none of these explicitly link nostalgia to the field of utopian studies, as none look at its potential utopian dimension.[12] Nostalgia, nevertheless, shares with Utopia some important features. Both are informed by desire: it is desire for a better change that moves Utopia, and it is desire for a lost place and a lost time that characterizes nostalgia. In addition, nostalgia and utopian tradition are connected through displacement: while a utopia leaves its readers/visitors displaced, suspended between the knowledge of their society and the discovery of the new one, nostalgia similarly evokes displacement, the loss of a place or a time, in those who experience it. Nostalgia, then, can be seen as the refusal to let go of the past in its attempt to recover the irretrievable and to open a space for the possible. The combination of desire and estrangement and the presence of a slight suffering, all informed by a re-visionist approach, can turn nostalgia to a critical

---

12   See in particular, the work by Boym, McDermott, Probyn, and Rubenstein, as excellent studies that attempt to recuperate nostalgia. Boym's extensive study of nostalgia questions its existing definitions in order to find its lost political potential. Through the analysis of Jane Smiley's *A Thousand Acres*, McDermott also points to a critical nostalgia – "a mode of engagement with the past [that] has a number of political advantages" (404). It functions as a "means of defiance," "a mode of critique," and a possibility to break with the past (404–5). Probyn shows us that, far from being reassuring, the use of nostalgia and of the past can be dislocating and can thus unfix the present (114). For Rubenstein, nostalgia may have a liberating or compensatory dimension: evoking nostalgia or longing is a way to enable characters and readers "to confront, mourn, and figuratively revise their relation to something that has been lost, whether in the world or in themselves. [...] Narratives that engage notions of home, loss and/or nostalgia [can] confront the past in order to 'fix' it" (6). For comments on the use of nostalgia and the different awareness about the past in classical and feminist, critical dystopias, see Baccolini, "Journeying" and "Memory and Historical Reconciliation." In critical dystopias, nostalgia can have a progressive value, provided that its cure, to return home, is not considered its solution. Feminist, critical dystopias, in fact, have shown that there cannot be return if there is awareness and knowledge of the past, since home is a place that has never been as it was and past is the root of our present.

reexamination of the past and present and thus render it as an important stimulus for a desire for change. In this sense, there can be a connection between the "never more" of nostalgia and the "Not Yet" of Utopia: the desire for something irretrievable that can only begin to find its realization in what is still to be accomplished. To this extent, some critics have attempted to point to a connection between nostalgia and the dream of a better future: "Without nostalgia for the past, there can exist no authentic dream of the future" (Loewy and Sayre 3). Or, according to Boym, "nostalgia itself has a utopian dimension, only it is no longer directed toward the future" (xiv). The critic who has come closest to an articulation of nostalgia and Utopia is perhaps Elspeth Probyn, who defines nostalgia "not as a guarantee of memory but precisely as an errant logic that always goes astray"(103). Following Jankélévitch, she argues that nostalgia "becomes a variant of a method that has as its purpose the turning around of things, of rendering the real as the inside-out of past and present" (117). She urges us to use nostalgia in the telling of our stories "with the *fervor of the possible*, not the implacability of truth-telling" (116, emphasis added). These efforts, however, have not been followed by a sustained analysis of how nostalgia can actually work within dystopian nor utopian texts.[13]

---

13   Indeed, even my own studies on memory in dystopia tend to see nostalgia as
      regressive, but mostly in classical – hence male – dystopias like Orwell's,
      where Winston's dream of the Golden Country, an idealized past, fails to see
      the imperfections of that past and the connections between the seemingly
      "perfect past" and the dystopian present. Conversely, in a novel like Atwood's
      The Handmaid's Tale, nostalgia is recovered as the desire for what could have
      been. See Baccolini, "Journeying."

Memory, Critical Nostalgia, and Imagination

> When you happen to be trapped powerless behind
> walls, stuck in a dead-end harem [...] you dream of es-
> cape. And magic flourishes when you spell that dream
> and make the frontiers vanish. Dreams can change
> your life, and eventually the world. Liberation starts
> with images dancing in your little head, and you can
> translate those images in words.
> Fatima Mernissi, *Dreams of Trespass*

I would like to give here only brief examples of how nostalgia can work in four very different works that I would call – stretching the term a little, perhaps – critical dystopias. They are very different by geography, culture, time, and genre: one is Joanna Russ's 1972 sf short story "When It Changed," a story of cultural contact that marks the end of a separatist utopia; one is the film *Men with Guns* (released in 1997) by independent director John Sayles, a story of "ordinary" violence in an unnamed Central American country; and the last two are the memoir of an Italian terrorist, Anna Laura Braghetti, called *Il prigioniero* (1998) on the 1978 kidnapping of Aldo Moro, and the film based on this book, *Buongiorno, notte* (2003), by the Italian director Marco Bellocchio. In all these works, nostalgia functions as some- thing radical, especially in anti-utopian times. It triggers a journey of critical recognition that takes different shapes: it is the physical journey through the horrors of his country for the protagonist of Sayles's movie, a doctor in search of his students; it becomes a journey of memory for Braghetti, who mostly relives the fifty-five days of the kidnapping, and a journey of memory and resistance for Janet, the protagonist of Russ's story.

Nostalgia is linked with resistance and hope in Russ's "When It Changed," a narrative that describes a separatist utopia and its coming to an end. The narrative opens on a distant planet where an Earth colony has changed its name to "Whileaway" from the original "For- a-while," after half of its population (the men) died because of a plague. The remaining half, the women, has survived for six-hundred years by developing a technique of reproduction that does not require men's genes. The all-female population has formed a "necessarily," or what would be considered to be a separatist, lesbian utopia if men were still around. It is a community that seems somewhat pastoral and agrarian, despite the acceptance of personal violence and anger. Things are fine until Earth men (as males) come back with the intention to return things to "normality." Badly in need of new, fresh, and healthy genes for their dying population back home, the men disguise their own lack and their attempt at recolonization and correction of what they consider Whileway's unnatural ways as a magnanimous gesture toward the women that will bring them "trade, exchange of ideas, education" (415). But the colonizing, homophobic, and misogynist nature of their actions is revealed in one of the men's speeches: "But Whileaway is still missing something. [...] You know it intellectually, of course. There is only half a species here. Men must come back to Whileaway" (415).

And so, as the narrator Janet sarcastically tells us at the end, "men are coming to Whileaway. When one culture has the big guns and the other has none, there is a certain predictability about the outcome" (415). The somewhat frustrating ending – women's resigned acceptance of the invasion without a fight – invites readers to resist in at least a couple of ways. The story asks us to be "resisting readers" in the sense that Judith Fetterley meant when she articulated her theory. We are asked to resist the identification with the men's point of view and the acceptance of the traditional values that are associated with them. Whatever our sexual preference may be (and especially in the case of heterosexual readers), we are invited to refuse a normative, compulsory heterosexuality that would justify the men's actions. By resisting traditional values, we readers create new possibilities for the female characters we read about.[14] Second, the story and its frustrating ending invite readers to resist by foregoing, for the time being, action

---

14   This strategy also completes what Russ has started at the beginning of the story: it takes the "average" reader a couple of pages to realize that the first person narrator who speaks of a wife is a woman herself. Heterosexuality being the norm, it is taken for granted that the couple we read about is formed by a woman and a man. Such a "certainty" is criticized by Russ with her displacing, disorienting opening that shows and asks of us to be resisting readers.

and to develop instead our resistance against the men's invasion with memory, awareness, critical nostalgia, and deferral.[15] Together, these invitations form the necessary elements of hope. Thus, against the desire to see the men be wiped away as in a regular Hollywood movie where the bad guys are punished and the good guys win, we readers are invited to follow Janet in her last thoughts that are pervaded by nostalgia and are governed by the act of remembering and by the choice of deferral of action to a better time:

> I will remember all my life those four people I first met who were muscled like bulls and who made me – if only for a moment – feel small. A neurotic reaction, Katy [her wife] says. I remember everything that happened that night; I remember Yuki's [her daughter] excitement in the car, I remember Katy's sobbing when we got home as if her heart would break, I remember her lovemaking, a little peremptory as always, but wonderfully soothing and comforting. I remember prowling restlessly around the house after Katy fell asleep with one bare arm hung into a patch of light from the hall. The muscles of her forearms are like metal bars from all that driving and testing of her machines. Sometimes I dream about Katy's arms. I remember wandering into the nursery and picking up my wife's baby, dozing for a while with the poignant, amazing warmth of an infant in my lap, and finally returning to kitchen to find Yuriko fixing herself a late snack. My daughter eats like a Great Dane.
> "Yuki," I said, "do you think you could fall in love with a man?" and she whooped derisively. "With a ten-foot toad!" said my tactful child (415–16).

In this painful and nostalgic passage, Janet uses memory as an attempt to fix the good moment before it changes forever, before – as Benjamin suggests – that moment and that history, if not remembered, are lost forever. Memory thus becomes a way to preserve the past against the unavoidable changes that occur in life and that we cannot control. Yet, further, while nostalgia may initially offer itself as a regressive mourning for the past that was and cannot return, it could (if linked with deferral – as the postponement, until a better time, of pain and discomfort but also the space of the possible, where one comes to terms with the past, undoes it, and provides the possibility for change) become a vehicle for remembering and retelling that might lead, in time, to other, possibly more positive changes. It is, therefore, Janet's

---

15   On deferral as an alternative to forgetting, see Baccolini, "Sometime."

awareness and nostalgic memory of what she and the other women have created and accomplished that gives her the strength to accept changes as part of life and that in their retelling, in time, may inspire others to resist.

Memory and nostalgia allow Janet not only to remember what the women of Whileaway were like, but what they are and still can be. Against Janet's fear that with the invasion and the return of men, their "own achievements will dwindle away from what they were […] to the not-very-interesting curiosa of the human race, the oddities you read about in the back of the book, things to laugh at sometimes because they are so exotic, quaint but not impressive, charming but not useful," the knowledge and the memory of their lives, complete with the feelings, desires, and emotions attached to those lives (nostalgia) can represent a form of resistance and hope (416). In this light, the ending of the story suggests that changes are unavoidable, but also that their acceptance does not mean a refusal of resistance: "This, too, shall pass. All good things must come to an end. Take my life but don't take away the meaning of my life" (416). Thus, unavoidable changes need to be accepted as part of life cycle, but such an acceptance does not entail a forgetting of the past and what it means. Hope, then, may be deferred to a later time, but it is still there, as suggested by the presence of the nostalgic and hence potentially subversive memories as well as, in what seems an ironic critique of fairytales, by the daughter's refusal to imagine herself as interested in a "ten-foot toad." Russ's utopian message, moreover, rests in the acceptance and the awareness of a slight suffering as the necessary condition of Utopia.

John Sayles's movie is also pervaded by nostalgia, with characters who are haunted by their past. His protagonist, Humberto Fuentes, an aging doctor who has just lost his wife, decides to take a journey through his country in search of what he considers to be his "legacy": "The Alliance for Progress" or the "Ambassadors of Health," a somewhat liberal but patronizing government-sponsored program through which he trained a group of students to go work among the Indians in the poor villages. Fuentes, a man of science, is moved by nostalgia: filled with the loss of his wife, the longing for his students, and for a romantic, simplistic belief in progress. Challenged by his cynical son-in-law who doubts that his students are still working with the Indians, he nostalgically remembers lecturing to his students: "where you're going your principal enemies will be bacteria and ignorance"; as he pulls a photo of himself with his students off the wall, he sighs and says, "it was an excellent idea" (Sayles 10). This first instance of nostalgia looks uncritically to the past; but, as the film increasingly reveals the program to have been a failure, Fuentes finds out that all his students have indeed been killed by the men with guns, either the army or the guerrilla. This discovery initiates Fuentes's journey of knowledge and responsibility.

The man of science is in fact, as Bravo, a former student who has left the program and now sells drugs in the slums, tells him, "the most learned man [...] [a]nd the most ignorant" (Sayles 13). Fuentes's education and class have shielded him from truly knowing the horror and poverty of the remote areas of his country. But these factors only partially account for his ignorance; for his apparent innocence also grows out of willed ignorance: his not knowing or, more likely, his not believing in certain rumors – or, better his choosing not to know – allowed him to live without responsibility for his actions. This ignorance led him to get "people involved in things that got them killed" (Sayles in Smith 237). The doctor's journey then becomes an initiation into violence, poverty, and horror, as he learns that his legacy is very different from what he had imagined:

> You can never save a life. You make it longer, make it better, relieve pain – but everybody dies. I wanted to leave something in the world, something [...] Something practical. Something to be passed on from person to person. [...] And [...] ended up a total failure. [...] I should have warned them. [...] I should have known (Sayles 57–8).

As is typical of Sayles's movies, Fuentes's story crosses over into the lives of other people. His journey intersects with that of two American tourists who are better informed than he is. This device serves as a "thermometer to put up against Fuentes to see how he changed where they didn't have to," as the two are what Sayles calls "teflon tourists" (Sayles in Carson 227). Along the way, Fuentes picks up an unusual group of people: Rabbit, an abandoned kid born of a rape, who will act as a guide for the doctor; Domingo, a deserter who also served as a medic in the army; Padre Portillo, a former priest who has lost his faith; and Graciela, a young woman who has been raped and has since been mute.[16] For all of them, the journey becomes their possibility of redemption and a new start. Nostalgia, however, works only for the doctor; whereas for the others it is memory that activates the desire for change.[17] For Fuentes, a combination of nostalgia with its clash with reality triggers his search for Utopia. In their stop in Modelo, an army camp also ironically dubbed "Community of Hope," where people whose village was burned by the army are taken, they hear of Cerca del Cielo, a mythical place unknown to the army soldiers.

In the last part of the journey, the false and very imperfect utopias so far encountered (the Program, Modelo) are contrasted with a potentially authentic utopian community. But while rumors have it that Cerca del Cielo is a place where you can forget, Sayles is ready to show us that this is "not Paradise" (Sayles 97). Upon discovering that even the last of his students is dead, Fuentes bitterly but also peacefully reconciles himself with the legacy he leaves and with the painful knowledge he has acquired. His death precipitates his legacy, as Domingo, aided by Rabbit, is silently urged by Graciela, who hands him the doctor's bag, to carry on Fuentes's work in the community. But the film does not merely end on the important notion that nostalgia has brought awareness and responsibility to Dr. Fuentes and, consequently, to his unusual companions. Sayles's typical open ending allows a space for Utopia itself. Sayles's final shot shows us Graciela closely and nostalgically looking at Fuentes and walking away through the trees. As she steps into a clearing, she looks out at the open sky and at a distant mountain, and smiles, suggesting that the journey toward Utopia is a continuous struggle.

16   This is an element in Sayles's film that is consistent with utopian tradition: Rabbit acts as a guide for the doctor, but the doctor also acts as his own guide and a guide for the audience in this journey through a very concrete dystopia.

17   Another instance of nostalgia in the film is when two guerrilla boys ask Fuentes to tell them all the ice-cream flavors from the city store one of them once visited: this allows them to pretend to be having ice-cream and contrasts sharply with the situation. Here nostalgia acts as a powerful break from the violence and the rigidity of war.

My last example is from Italian culture, and deals with the issue of terrorism. It is not my intention here to analyze the utopian elements that, despite its outcome, could be present in terrorism. It is enough to say that terrorism can represent Utopia-gone-wrong, as its demand to live in a better world and not just to dream of it was accompanied by the violent methods employed. The experience of the Red Brigades (BR) (that lasted from 1969 to 1987) was "officially" declared over and defeated in 1987 in a series of "open letters" signed by some terrorists who refused, however, to disassociate themselves from or even reject the experience of terrorism as others had previously done (see 1985 document of *dissociati*, "Manifesto"). The kidnapping of Aldo Moro, President of the Christian Democratic Party, on 16 March 1978, represented a turning point for Italian terrorism. This attack on the "heart of the State" marked the highest point of their armed struggle, but also the beginning of the end. The government refused any negotiation with the terrorists (they were asking for the release of political prisoners; but at the end of the fifty-five days of Moro's captivity, they were ready to accept the exchange of Moro for just one terrorist); and the kidnapping ended, on 9 May, with the death of Moro.[18]

Anna Laura Braghetti's memoir is about those two months in 1978, but also much more: it recounts her two years of clandestine struggle until her arrest in 1980, and the almost twenty years in prison. Written together with the journalist Paola Tavella, *Il prigioniero* is one of a dozen books written by former terrorists. From the book,

---

18 We all remember where we were when a traumatic event occurs. For certain Italians of my generation, two such events were the kidnapping of Moro (16 March 1978) and the Bologna Railway Station bombing (2 August 1980). A recent event that seems to work in a similar way but in a larger geographical area is the World Trade Center attacks on 9/11; it has been said that this is an event that will change the world as we have known it, it is one of those instances that will be remembered by everyone, and that will mark our consciousness. And yet the film on 9/11 (*11'09''01*), shows us that we are all marked culturally and geographically, with the result that 9/11 means different things to Chilean exiles (who remember also their 9/11/1973), the women of Srebrenica who every 11th of every month remember the massacre of their husbands, or Afghan refugee children in Iran, who do not even have water or do not have any idea of what a tower looks like. Everyone has their own 9/11.

director Marco Bellocchio has made the film *Buongiorno, notte*, which does not want to be, however, a historical reconstruction of the Moro kidnapping. Rather, Bellocchio seems to tell his story, to use Probyn's words, "with the fervor of the possible, not the implacability of truth-telling" (116). To some extent, both memoir and film portray a sense of nostalgia for an irretrievable past: not in the sense, let me be clear, that the past remembered is slightly missed or yearned for, or that it is in fact a better past, but that it is a painful feeling for a past that cannot be changed and for the suffering that cannot be eased – a nostalgia, in other words, for what could have been. Toward the end of the memoir, Braghetti remembers her disagreement and discomfort with regard to the decision to kill Moro – a disagreement that only twenty years later she is able to express:

> I wasn't able then to support my idea politically [to free Moro]; to show how mirror-like, even terrifyingly similar, was the State's rigidity and our own. We should have turned sharply, we should have placed ourselves in another position, we should have been an alternative with what we did, from the start, to the decisions taken by the politicians. We should have represented another politics, if we wanted another world. We could have placed ourselves on a different level, we could have shown that we were better, and not follow the Christian Democrats', the Communist Party's, and the government's failure to retreat. Revolutionaries, I should have said, must be more far-sighted (181).[19]

The final pages of the book cannot imagine but only hint at the potentiality of a different world had Moro lived, offering a utopia of the imagination in the dystopia of the years of lead.

Similarly, the film employs what I would call a utopian ending. Chiara's (the character modeled after Braghetti) disagreement about killing Moro is but faintly articulated; rather, the film shows the young

19   The original text: "Non ero in grado, allora, di sostenere politicamente la mia posizione [liberare Moro]. Di mostrare quanto fossero speculari, simili in modo perfino impressionante, la rigidità dello Stato e la nostra. Noi avremmo dovuto fare uno scarto, metterci in un'altra posizione, essere un'alternativa nei fatti, fin da subito, alla scelta del Palazzo. Dovevamo essere un'altra politica, se volevamo un'altra società. Potevamo metterci su un altro piano, dimostrare che eravamo migliori, e non imitare l'incapacità di recedere della Dc, del Pci e del governo. I rivoluzionari, avrei dovuto dire, hanno il compito di essere più lungimiranti" (Braghetti 181).

woman leaving the door of the prisoner unlocked and going to bed. Her dream shows Moro leaving his prison while all four terrorists are asleep, and walking, free, at dawn through a deserted street in Rome. But the dream is only a dream: the scene is followed by the image of the three male terrorists who escort a blind-folded Moro to be executed. The film then rolls toward its end with the following sequences: the title of the movie, *Buongiorno, notte* (Goodmorning, night), in red script over the black screen that evokes the infamous five-pointed red star of the BR, followed by the real footage of Moro's funeral, showing the Pope and a great number of Italian politicians who were more or less responsible for the line of non-negotiation, and a final image. But two elements contribute to open up the utopian space in the film: the extremely effective use of music and the final shot. The dream and the funeral are accompanied by the introduction of the famous Pink Floyd's song, "Shine on You Crazy Diamond," with the crescendo of music (the drums) coinciding with the end of the dream and the realization of the death of the politician (and the appearance of the title). But as the images of the politicians of the time and of the Pope fade, so does the psychedelic, nostalgic (at least for me), and haunting music of Pink Floyd, to then be replaced, or nostalgically displaced by yet another sequence, accompanied by much lighter, and what I would call utopian, music of Schubert's Opus 94. The final image of Moro alive and free (the same image previously seen in Chiara's dream) breaks with the darkness of the film and those years and represents a return to life, a realization, even if only of the imagination, of moments of possibilities and of our desire to come out of that blackness. Thus, the film offers an artistic response of the imagination that politics has failed to give.

Memory, be it nostalgic or not, is, then, an important element for change. Whereas, in the classical dystopia, memory remains too often trapped in an individual, regressive nostalgia, critical dystopias show that a *culture of memory* – one that moves from the individual to the social and collective and one that can also include a critical nostalgia – must be part of a social project of hope. But the presence of utopian hope does not necessarily mean a consoling, happy ending. Rather, what I have called a slight suffering seems to be the precondition of hope. Awareness and responsibility are the conditions of the critical dystopia's citizens, and they are often triggered by the slight suffering that is typical of nostalgia. A sense of sadness accompanies the awareness and knowledge that the protagonists have attained, a sense of regret for a missed opportunity, for what a choice possibly entails and excludes. Instead of an easily compensatory and comforting happy ending, these critical dystopias' open endings leave their protagonists dealing with their choices and responsibilities – another radical element that contributes to the creation of the text's utopian horizon. Thus, such endings open dystopia to hopeful possibilities by cracking the image of the fixed past. Through memory and nostalgia it is possible to refuse to forget the past and find traces of Utopia in dystopia, or moments of possibilities. It is possible to look at the past critically and to yearn for a different past, now, and to desire a different future. It reminds us that it is necessary, to borrow the words of the American poet H.D., to remember the past always, but to remember it differently (31). It is in the acceptance of our responsibility and accountability, but accompanied by that sense of slight suffering, often worked through memory and even nostalgia, that we bring the past into a living relationship with the present and may thus begin to lay the foundations for a utopian change.

Works Cited

11'09''01. Dir. Samira Makhmalbaf, Claude Lelouch, Youssef Chahine, Danis Tanovic, Idrissa Ouedrago, Ken Loach, Alejandro González Iñárritu, Amos Gitai, Mira Nair, Sean Penn, Shohei Imamura. 2002.

Atwood, Margaret. *The Handmaid's Tale*. Boston: Houghton, 1985.

Baccolini, Raffaella. "Breaking the Boundaries: Gender, Genre, and Dystopia." *Per una definizione dell'utopia. Metodologie e discipline a confronto*. Ed. Nadia Minerva. Ravenna: Longo, 1992. 137–46.

—— "Gender and Genre in the Feminist Critical Dystopias of Katharine Burdekin, Margaret Atwood, and Octavia Butler." *Future Females, The Next Generation: New Voices and Velocities in Feminist Science Fiction Criticism*. Lanham: Rowman, 2000. 13–34.

—— "Journeying through the Dystopian Genre: Memory and Imagination in Burdekin, Orwell, Atwood, and Piercy." *Viaggi in Utopia.* Ed. Raffaella Baccolini, Vita Fortunati, Nadia Minerva. Ravenna: Longo, 1996. 343–57.

—— "Sometime, Between Memory and Forgetting." *mediAzioni. Online Journal of Interdisciplinary Studies on Languages and Cultures* 1 (2005). 24 May 2005 <http://www.mediazionionline.it/english/articoli/baccolini_english.htm>.

—— "'A useful knowledge of the present is rooted in the past': Memory and Historical Reconciliation in Ursula K. Le Guin's *The Telling.*" Baccolini and Moylan. 113–34.

Baccolini, Raffaella and Tom Moylan (eds.). *Dark Horizons: Science Fiction and the Dystopian Imagination.* New York: Routledge, 2003.

Benjamin, Walter. "Theses on the Philosophy of History." *Illuminations.* Trans. Harry Zohn. London: Fontana, 1992. 245–55.

Boym, Svetlana. *The Future of Nostalgia.* New York: Basic, 2001.

Braghetti, Anna Laura, and Paola Tavella. *Il prigioniero.* Milano: Feltrinelli, 2003.

Buongiorno, notte. Dir. Marco Bellocchio. 2003.

Butler, Octavia E. *Kindred.* 1979. London: Women's Press, 1995.

—— *Parable of the Sower.* New York: Warner, 1993.

Carson, Diane. "John Sayles: Filmmaker." *John Sayles: Interviews.* Ed. Diane Carson. Jackson: University Press of Mississippi, 1999. 223–34.

Cranny-Francis, Anne. *Feminist Fiction: Feminist Uses of Generic Fiction.* New York: St. Martin's Press, 1990.

Dames, Nicholas. *Amnesiac Selves: Nostalgia, Forgetting, and British Fiction, 1810–1870.* Oxford: Oxford University Press, 2001.

Doane, Janice, and Devon Hodges. *Nostalgia and Sexual Difference: The Resistance to Contemporary Feminism.* New York: Methuen, 1987.

Fetterley, Judith. *The Resisting Reader: A Feminist Approach to American Fiction.* Bloomington: Indiana University Press, 1978.

Galeano, Eduardo. *Días y noches de amor y de guerra.* 16 December 2005 <http://www.elortiba.org/galeano.html>.

Geoghegan, Vincent. "Remembering the Future." *Utopian Studies* 1.2 (1990): 52–68.

Greene, Gayle. "Feminist Fiction and the Uses of Memory." *Signs* 16.2 (1991): 290–321.

H.D. *By Avon River.* New York: Macmillan, 1949.

Haraway, Donna. "Situated Knowledges: The Science Question in Feminism and the Privilege of Partial Perspective." *Feminist Studies* 14 (1988): 575–99.

Hirsch, Marianne, and Valerie Smith (eds.). *Gender and Cultural Memory.* Spec. issue *Signs* 28.1 (2002).

Hutcheon, Linda. "Irony, Nostalgia, and the Postmodern." 3 February 2004 <http://www.library.utoronto.ca/utel/criticism/hutchinp.html>.

Hofer, Johannes. "Dissertazione medica sulla nostalgia." Trans. Alessandro Serra. Prete. 45–59.

Jacobus, Mary. "Freud's Menmonic: Women, Screen Memories, and Feminist Nostalgia." *Michigan Quarterly Review* 26.1 (1987): 117–39.

Jankélévitch, Vladimir. "La nostalgia." Trans. Alessandro Serra. Prete. 119–76.

Jameson, Fredric. *Marxism and Form*. Princeton: Princeton University Press, 1974.

—— *The Political Unconscious: Narrative as a Socially Symbolic Act*. Ithaca: Cornell University Press, 1981.

Kundera, Milan. *The Book of Laughter and Forgetting*. New York: Harper, 1999.

Le Guin, Ursula K. *The Telling*. New York: Harcourt, 2000.

Lichtenstein, Therese. *Behind Closed Doors. The Art of Hans Bellmer*. Berkeley: University of California Press, 2001.

Loewy, Michael, and Robert Sayre. *Révolte et Mélancolie*. Paris: Payot, 1992.

Lourie, Margaret A., Domna C. Stanton, and Martha Vinicius (eds.). *Women and Memory*. Spec. issue *Michigan Quarterly Review* 26.1 (1987).

Lowenthal, David. *The Past Is a Foreign Country*. Cambridge: Cambridge University Press, 1985.

"Manifesto dei detenuti politici." 18 gennaio 1985. 22 January 2004 <http://www. radioradicale.it/servlet/VideoPublisher?cmd=segnalaGoNew&livello=s7.2.4&fi le=uni_roberta_0_20030922154206.txt>.

Marcuse, Herbert. *One-Dimensional Man: Studies in the Ideology of Advanced Industrial Society*. Boston: Beacon Press, 1966.

Margalit, Avisham. *The Ethics of Memory*. Cambridge, Massachusetts: Harvard University Press, 2002.

McDermott, Sinead. "Memory, Nostalgia, and Gender in *A Thousand Acres*." *Signs* 28.1 (2002): 389–407.

Men with Guns. Dir. John Sayles. 1997.

Mernissi, Fatima. *Dreams of Trespass: Tales of a Harem Girlhood*. New York: Basic Books, 1994.

Nora, Pierre. "Between Memory and History: *Les Lieux de Mémoire*." *Representations* 26 (Spring 1989): 7–25.

Orwell, George. *Nineteen Eighty-Four*. New York: Harcourt, 1949.

Parrinder, Patrick. *Science Fiction: Its Criticism and Teaching*. London: Methuen, 1980.

Pavese, Cesare. *Il mestiere di vivere 1935–1950*. 1952. Torino: Einaudi, 2000.

Piercy, Marge. "Telling Stories About Stories." *Utopian Studies* 5 (1994): 1–3.

Prete, Antonio (ed.). *Nostalgia. Storia di un sentimento*. Milano: Cortina, 1996.

Probyn, Elspeth. "Suspended Beginnings: Of Childhood and Nostalgia." *Outside Belongings*. New York: Routledge, 1996. 93–123.

Rich, Adrienne. "Notes Toward a Politics of Location." *Blood, Bread, and Poetry: Selected Prose 1979–1985*. London: Virago, 1987. 210–31.

—— "Resisting Amnesia: History and Personal Life." *Blood, Bread, and Poetry: Selected Prose 1979–1985*. London: Virago, 1987. 136–55.

—— "Transcendental Etude." *The Dream of a Common Language: Poems 1974–1977*. New York: Norton, 1978. 72–7.

—— "When We Dead Awaken: Writing as Re-Vision." *On Lies, Secrets, and Silence.* New York: Norton, 1979. 31–49.

Rubenstein, Roberta. *Home Matters: Longing and Belonging, Nostalgia and Mourning in Women's Fiction.* New York: Palgrave, 2001.

Russ, Joanna. "When It Changed." *Science Fiction: The Science Fiction Research Association Anthology.* Ed. Patricia S. Warrick, Charles G. Waugh, and Martin H. Greenberg. New York: Harper Collins, 1988. 411–17.

Sargent, Lyman Tower. "The Three Faces of Utopianism Revisited." *Utopian Studies* 5.1 (1994): 1–37.

Sayles, John. *Men with Guns & Lone Star.* London: Faber and Faber, 1998.

Schenck, Celeste. "All of a Piece: Women's Poetry and Autobiography." *Life/Lines: Theorizing Women's Autobiography.* Ed. Bella Brodzki and Celeste Schenck. Ithaca: Cornell University Press, 1993. 281–305.

Sexton, Anne. *The Complete Poems.* Boston: Houghton Mifflin, 1981.

Smith, Gavin (ed.). *"Men With Guns." Sayles on Sayles.* London: Faber and Faber, 1998. 234–54.

Stewart, Susan. *On Longing.* Durham: Duke University Press, 1993.

Suvin, Darko. "Theses on Dystopia 2001." Baccolini and Moylan. 187–201.

Theoi Project. *A Guide to Greek Gods, Spirits and Monsters.* 11 March 2005. <http://www.theoi.com/index.htm>.

Weinrich, Harald. *Lethe: The Art and Critique of Forgetting.* Ithaca: Cornell University Press, 2004.

Woolrich, John. "Songs of War." *Guardian Unlimited* 3 February 2004 <http://www.guardian.co.uk/arts/fridayreview/story/0,12102,1004943,00.html>.

Yates, Frances A. *The Art of Memory.* Chicago: University of Chicago Press, 1966.

TOM MOYLAN

Realizing Better Futures, Strong Thought for Hard Times

> It was a good thing that Giacomo Paradisi had re-
> minded him not to be surprised. He kept careful hold
> of the knife, and put it down on the table before giving
> in to astonishment. Lyra was on her feet already,
> speechless, because there in the middle of the dusty
> little room was a window just like the one under the
> hornbeam trees: a gap in mid-air through which they
> could see another world.
> Philip Pullman, *The Subtle Knife*

> I have to cast my lot with those
> who age after age, perversely
> with no extraordinary power,
> reconstitute the world.
> Adrienne Rich, "Natural Resources"

Searching

It seems I have always lived between worlds, looking from one to another, finding ways to cut through the reality around me to see that other place that seemed to make more sense or at least be more interesting and maybe even satisfying. In that way, the method of Utopia, its double move of negation and anticipation, has been with me for a very long time.

I grew up finding my way across different cultures, different worlds. Son of Irish parents in Chicago, I lived between the Irish culture of my family and the new society of American promise in the postwar years of the 1940s and 1950s, happy in a nurturing home life yet often feeling it to be "old fashioned" when I went out and about in the city. Catholic, in an Irish immigrant way, I found a set of values and discipline (and repression) that gave me an alternative to an increasingly consumerist culture, even as that larger sphere offered an enticement not allowed by my parochial life. Working class, I found little in the sphere of the "rich" to interest me, and in fact I developed a nascent class antagonism as I saw my father patronized by his boss on the truck docks and stood there as the poor visitor as my dynamic and independent aunt was treated as a dutiful servant by the North Shore couple whose children she cared for. While my base in ethnicity, religion, and class gave me a secure sense of my self, I still looked outward to those other worlds as I found them to exceed all that I knew, thereby moving me to explore their ways, to consider their possibilities alongside the ones I knew so well. I came to see the stimulating differences in each of my new parallel worlds, realizing that each opened up the other for me, that each brought me to a world more intriguing or disturbing than the one at home.

This cultural tension gradually became more confrontational. That sense of committed difference that Catholicism gave me, that (still unformed) class anger I discovered, and that more distant sense of being of a people whose history had been one of occupation and dispossession segued into a more direct experience of assertion and contestation as I ventured out to the streets (as a child and later as that being called a "teenager"). In city parks, pizza parlors, and downtown avenues, I entered a newly named youth culture that rejected the mainstream conformist culture of the 1950s. In our all-too-innocent street gang baiting of the local police, in our clothing choice of blue jeans, combat boots, and black jackets, we stood for each other and against those who tried to tell us what to do. For me, especially, in what was becoming "our" own popular culture – of B-movies, comic books, and race, then rock, music – I discovered a standpoint from which I garnered a strength to be my "self" as I negotiated that mixture of old and new worlds. And yet, mainstream society also issued its own call to a strict loyalty and commitment as the official culture of anti-communism took hold. In the heroism proffered by re-run World War II movies, the new TV programming with series such as *I Led Three Lives* (featuring a "communist" who was an FBI spy and an "ordinary guy"), and the TV ads that sang the norms of democracy and liberty, my Catholic call to witness, to taking a moral stand in a valueless world, was given a very different invitation to a social, if not yet political, imperative to work for liberty and against oppression.

What enriched these various appeals to my knowledge and commitment was my proclivity to read. Growing up in a loving home but without books, I soaked up the book culture of Catholicism once I went to school, becoming both a "devout" Catholic as I read my way through liturgies and saints' lives and a "good" student as I eagerly entered the world of learning. Not able to afford books, and as a boy of my time, I bought hundreds of cheap comic books and immersed myself in the exploits of superheroes, the gore of horror, and the edginess of crime. And, I remember how in an early visit to the library I picked my first volume of Robert Heinlein off the shelf, and so had my mind turned forever by the usefully escapist literature of science fiction (sf). But my reading life took another turn when I was eleven years old. My Uncle John died, and my Aunt Catherine thought that I, as the studious lad, should be given his desk and books. As it happened, John was the only overtly political person in the family: a member of an elevator operator's union, he also attended what I later realized was a Trotskyist reading group; and what came down to me was his place of learning and his library. So, to my reading of saints' lives and sf, I added books such as Leon Trotsky's *History of the Russian Revolution* and Henry George's *Progress and Poverty*, along with an eight-volume atlas of the world. This infusion of history, political economy, and geography gave shape and depth to my ability to negotiate alternative, and oppositional, worlds.

For me, then, reading became a "subtle knife," that wondrous tool given to us in volume two of Philip Pullman's *Dark Materials* trilogy. Reading gave me a means to cut through the barriers between worlds and to step inside other places, and move back and forth as needed, emotionally or strategically. Devouring both religious and secular texts, I began to value a life of commitment, be it articulated in the religious language of vocation, the existential (popularly beatnik) language of freedom, or, eventually, the political language of activism. That this early understanding of such a life was for me wrapped up in Catholicism, anti-communism, a slightly more removed commitment to Irish freedom, and seasoned with the frisson of life in the city was but the throw of historical dice. That this amalgam led eventually to a secularity that embraced a materialist spirituality, a generous communism, and an advocacy for freedom won by all oppressed people was but the result of a series of subsequent steps.

By high school in the late 1950s, I had, through the Young Christian Students movement, grown from an abstract anti-communist stance into the anti-racist commitments of Chicago's Catholic Interracial Council, with its adult leaders who were already connected with the young Martin Luther King and the Southern Christian Leadership Conference, and shortly thereafter to what would be the Student Nonviolent Coordinating Committee. All this prepared me for work in my college years in the civil rights movement. From there, as a member of both the baby-boom and the 1960s generations, I entered the anti-war movement and then (as an eighteen-year old who had to make pressing decisions in what I would now call "choice" or "body" politics) the anti-draft movement, as I became a conscientious objector to the U.S. imperialist war. From there on, I affiliated with the New Left and in time with socialist-feminism, with people who saw activism as their way of life, in whatever ways they took it further into their personal and working lives. For me, that work life took me to graduate school and then to teaching in a community college. If reading was an engine of change on a personal level, my newly informed values and activism (which by this point can be named as political) led me to see teaching as a vehicle of socio-political challenge and transformation.

My purpose in recalling this trajectory in an essay on Utopia as vision and method is to offer an opening reflection that revisits my upbringing in terms of what I now would call a utopian imaginary, as I wandered, curiously and critically, between worlds – like a character in Pullman or like Shevek, the political activist and physicist in *The Dispossessed*, Ursula K. Le Guin's great utopian novel of the 1970s. National aspiration, spiritual witness, class anger, youth energy, intellectual hunger, and racial and gender solidarity fed what grew into a utopian proclivity and no doubt set me up for life as a member of what Fredric Jameson has named the "Party of Utopia," that long red line of those who will not settle for less than justice and freedom for everyone on an ecologically healthy earth, not via American imperialism or global capitalism but through the work of a collectively transformed and transforming humanity (*Archaeologies* epigraph). However, the more pressing question for this essay is how this proclivity grew into a developed problematic and a method, one that shaped my studies, my teaching, and my writing, as well as my life as a citizen, an intellectual, and activist.

Reading

> The object of study "writes" you as much as you "write" it. These moments [of new perspectives] force the researcher into a fresh humility, into an awareness of the limitations of one form of intellectual activity and its absolute dependence on these "others" [research subjects]. This is to say that our research cannot ever be wholly ours, nor should we want it to be, just as it is never the product of privatized theory.
> Angela McRobbie, "The Politics of Feminist Research: Between Talk, Text, and Action"

In his essay on the early days of the Birmingham cultural studies project, Stuart Hall described how he and his faculty colleagues would work with potential postgraduate students. As he put it:

> it was not possible to present the work of cultural studies as if it had no political consequences and no form of political engagement, because what we were inviting students to do was to do what we ourselves had done: to engage with some real problem out there in the dirty world, and to use the enormous advantage given to a tiny handful of us [...] who had the opportunity to go into universities and reflect on those problems, to spend that time usefully to try to understand how the world worked. [...] So, from the start we said: What are you interested in? What really bugs you about questions of culture and society now? What do you really think is a problem you don't understand out there in the terrible interconnection between culture and politics? [...]And then we will find a way of studying that seriously (13).

In this account, Hall identifies the very challenge that I faced as I stepped into graduate school in the mid 1960s. I knew that learning for me was more than scholarly understanding or aesthetic appreciation. For me, learning – as I had been given to understand from those diverse early influences – was a way to know the world critically and thus a way to help change that world for the betterment of all its people and not the privileged few. Leaving behind the study of medicine in my first year of college, I turned to literature, history, and philosophy; and so I looked for knowledge that would clarify what society was, how it worked, and how we could work to change it. Since I was studying at St. Mary's College in Minnesota, I learned these subjects with Christian Brothers and fellow students who were already affiliated not only with the progressive sensibility of the Second Vatican Council and existential philosophy, but also with the radical politics of the civil rights and anti-war movements (indeed, brothers and students at St. Mary's took up leadership roles in the non-violent anti-war actions of the Catholic Worker and the Catholic Left). And so, history, philosophy, and literary study on my campus were already in tune with the social and political world. In literature, especially, the interpretive frameworks of theological hermeneutics and the left populism of American studies gave me methods of social analysis that valued the aesthetic but did not stop at it.

However, in my Master's work at the University of Wisconsin-Milwaukee, the story was different. New Criticism reigned, and my MA studies did little to give me the critical paradigm and method that I looked for. Turning to work as a community college teacher after the MA, from 1968 on I searched for a critical problematic in my teaching, and it was then that I was asked by my students to take my personal love of sf into the classroom. As one of the generation that broke open the English curriculum to allow for studies of popular culture, I began to find another way of working with literary texts. And then, as I returned to doctoral studies in the early 1970s, Jack Zipes joined the faculty in Milwaukee; and, in his seminars (on Marxist criticism and on the fairy tale genre) and in my work with the first editorial collective of *New German Critique*, I studied the critical theory of the Frankfurt School. With a combination of an orthodox Marxism (learned from my activist life) and the Frankfurt problematic (learned in grad school), I began to work out a way to know the literary landscape in ways that went beyond the isolated form of the text, but took that form seriously in a broader historical approach.

And then I encountered the work of Jameson on the politics of form in his early books, especially *Marxism and Form*, and in his lectures at the July gatherings of the Marxist Literary Group (MLG). In the annual MLG Summer Institute of Culture and Society, I was able to work with Jameson but also with the likes of Stanley Arono- witz, Gayatri Spivak, Terry Eagleton, and others. Thus, what became a familiar matrix for many of us – German critical theory; French structuralism and post-structuralism; British cultural studies; Ameri- can New Left, anti-racist, and feminist/gay cultural critique; and third world liberation theory and criticism – gave me a more dynamic framework within which I could read literature in the context of the socio-political. With this framework, I was able in my Ph.D. work to find that "way," in Hall's sense, to work with sf, and then utopian fiction.

From this point, my sense of utopian aspiration began to find a more distinct method of producing and teaching critical, and trans- formative, knowledge. Central to this effort was my decision to let the object of my study – the history and form of sf and utopian fiction – shape my interpretive strategies. At the time, while teaching a graduate seminar at UW-Milwaukee's Center for Twentieth-Century Studies, research fellow and sf writer, Samuel R. Delany, argued forcefully that academic scholarship had to stop imposing the critical apparatus used in the study of "high" realist and modernist literature and to adopt a method that worked with the specificity of the sf form. Sf, he urged, had to be taken on its own terms, and thus we needed to look to the way sf writers, editors, fans, and now fans-become- scholars considered the sf genre. As Angela McRobbie would later put it, it was necessary to let the object of study shape the research, not the other way around.

Enriching this framework, the new writing by Darko Suvin on estrangement and cognition then became central to my evolving sense of form and method in sf studies; and Jameson added to this in both his general theory and his work on sf and Utopia. His review essay on Louis Marin's *Utopiques*, "Of Islands and Trenches," was a key text in the identification of Utopia's fundamentally negative quality. Rooted in the historical situation, Utopia's trajectory moves from its formal negation of that moment into the figuration of another possibility – a possibility, however, that is not attainable in the world as it is but one that pulls us into that not yet existent reality. Hence, Jameson made the first of several iterations that have recurred throughout his work: namely, that the "deepest subject" of the utopian text is precisely its impossibility in the world as it is. Only a revolutionary transformation can produce the future reality that Utopia, working as it does with the "raw material" of the material and ideological world, can only, ever, prefigure (*Archaeologies* 13). In addition, the 1976 special issue of *minnesota review* on "Marxism and Utopia," with Jameson's introduction ("To Reconsider the Relationship of Marxism to Utopia") and Suvin's essay ("'Utopian' and 'Scientific': Two Attributes for Socialism from Engels") reinforced my decision to focus on the new utopian strain of sf that had emerged in the oppositional movements and counter-cultures of the 1960s and 1970s.

Thus, I developed my work on the "critical utopia" in my first substantial effort to regard the political function of the utopian imagination as it informed a method of knowing and intervening in the world. My dissertation (directed by Zipes) led eventually to *Demand the Impossible: Science Fiction and the Utopian Imagination* in 1986. Therein, I argued that the new utopian sf of the period – by the likes of Joanna Russ, Marge Piercy, Ernest Callenbach, Le Guin, and Delany – revived and refunctioned the literary utopia. Influenced by postmodern attention to self-reflexive form, political engagement enriched by self-critical practice (e.g., feminist consciousness-raising, new left criticism-self-criticism), and a creative encounter with both anti-utopian critique and the utopian shadow of dystopian writing, these works (especially in the period between 1968 and 1976) offered a fresh approach to utopianism that emphasized its value as critical, negative phenomenon even as it explored – in the form of figurative, not prescriptive, thought experiments – versions of a post-revolutionary society as well as, and significantly so, the radical activism required for movement toward that transformation. As I put it then:

a central concern in the critical utopia is the awareness of the limitations of the utopian tradition, so that these texts reject Utopia as blueprint while preserving it as dream. Furthermore, the novels dwell on the conflict between the originary world and the utopian society opposed to it so that the process of social change is more directly articulated. Finally, the novels focus on the continuing presence of difference and imperfection within utopian society itself and thus render more recognizable and dynamic alternatives (*Demand* 10–11).

As it happened, my recognition in these works of a self-critical utopian method, and indeed of the figuration of a more open-ended utopian society of permanent revolution that develops through struggles deploying just such a self-critical process, was noted and worked with in both sf and utopian studies. Less attended to, however, was my argument that the critical utopias foreground a sharper focus on the nature and degree of political activism required for such practical and utopian transformations. My point was that in these works of a politically intense period the familiar organization of the literary utopia was reversed. Whereas, in more traditional utopian novels, the society is featured (with the visitor traveling through it and registering its wonders and differences from her or his homeland), in the critical utopias, "the primacy of societal alternative over character and plot [or the *iconic* over *discrete* registers] is reversed, and the alternative society and indeed the original society fall back as settings for the foregrounded political quest of the protagonist," a protagonist who is "part of the human collective in a time of deep historical change" (*Demand* 45).[1] Hence, the systemic alternative, while still formally and ideologically crucial, is approached by means of the political work required to produce that new society (and in achieved utopias to revitalize it); and so the ideological raw material and its figurative reworking centers more on the dynamics of the utopian process itself and "the ensuing strategy and tactics taken by a human subject once again able to carry on anti-hegemonic tasks aimed at bringing down the prevailing system [be it original or compromised utopia] and moving toward a radically different way of being" (*De-*

---

1   On the *discrete* and *iconic* registers of the sf/utopian text, and their relationship in critical utopias, see *Demand*, 36–8, 43–6, 46–50, and 210–13, especially.

mand 49). Thus, the critical utopia emerges as a "meditation on action rather than system" (*Demand* 49).

While in his important review and reconsideration of utopian theory, *Archaeologies of the Future*, Jameson rightly insists on separating the utopian project from any *immediate* connection with practical politics (most especially at times of focused revolutionary change), such imaginative explorations of the political process are nevertheless central to the utopian vocation (see *Archaeologies* 15). As he puts it, "politics is always with us," and it is Utopia's especial contribution to be able to foreground the political when it appears most "suspended" in "transitional periods" or most fulfilled in "post-revolutionary" ones (Jameson, "Politics of Utopia" 44, 43; *Archaeologies* 15–16). It is in such moments, in the "calm before [or after?] the storm," that Utopia's thought experiments on political possibilities can be most eloquent. That is, both in "periods of great social ferment" (e.g., the 1880s–1910s, the 1960s, the1990s, now?) that appear to be "rudderless, without any agency or direction" and in achieved, concrete utopias (e.g., the utopian societies imaginatively challenged by the critical utopian protagonists, or Bloch's actual dilemma with regard to the Soviet Union, as discussed below), the process of "utopian-creative free play" can feed and enliven the political imagination ("Politics of Utopia" 45–6).

Looking at the larger historical periodization, it does seem to be the case that Utopia's articulation of political challenges to, and transformations of, the hegemonic system became increasingly necessary, and evident, after the "victory" of capitalism in the late nineteenth century – as argued, for example, by Raymond Williams and Miguel Abensour as they traced the shift from systemic to heuristic utopias after the revolutions of 1848 (see Williams). Thus, from William Morris's chapters in *News from Nowhere* on "How the Change Came" through the (successful and defeated) struggles in the modern dsytopias to the existential and systemic political meditations in the critical utopias, the calling of the *political* has been brought to the fore. To be sure, Jameson is right to note that an indulgence in matters of practical politics in their own right has no place in the anticipatory utopian project: for, in times of outright revolution, there is, for that moment, little room for utopian speculation; and in times of growing tension caught in a "reality paralysis," such reductions tend to produce reformist plans and containing maneuvers ("Politics of Utopia" 44). However, at least since that historical/formal turn marked by Williams and Abensour, Utopia has told us, over and over, that *something* must indeed be done to begin to change a prevailing, apparently closed, system – to assert that not only can an alternative exist but that a political capacity exists to achieve it.

Politics in these utopias of capitalism are indeed "vexed," as Jameson puts it; not, however, because they are named and explored at the deeper, utopian, level of possibility and possibilities but because they have been – in so many instances by writers, theorists, activists, and readers alike – taken up, reductively, as immediate, practical steps (*Archaeologies* 205). The "registering apparatus" of utopian texts is certainly not a social inventor's how-to manual or cookbook of revolution but rather is a meditative expression (as text or lived social experiment) on the reality, the necessity, of collective political (as opposed to personal ethical) action (*Archaeologies* 13). Utopia – again, especially from Morris up through sf by the likes of Kim Stanley Robinson, Ken MacLeod, or China Miéville – offers a "poetic" rather than an instrumental exploration of the means of making radical change. Thus, in my focus on the political agency of the critical utopias (as enacted by individual characters, such as Le Guin's Shevek or Piercy's Connie, who both represent individual ethical choices as well as typify the collective political action of an entire movement), I identified the ways in which the utopias of those burgeoning, activist times called the 1960s zeroed in on precisely this imaginative operation, as they took the literary utopia's activist anticipation into a fuller consideration of directions and choices, and doing so in both pre- and post-revolutionary registers: thereby figuring not the *what* that is to be done but rather the *doing* that is, always, needed.[2]

---

2   In *Archaeologies*, Jameson recalls Perry Anderson's assertion that the utopias of the 1960s (Anderson focuses on Piercy) "were somehow the last traditional ones" (216). Thus, the break achieved by neo-liberalism and neo-conservatism and the crisis of socialism called forth a new creative moment, one in which we get not only the negativities of cyberpunk and the critical dystopia but also a

Working

> We left – onto the freeway shoulders –
> under the tough old stars –
> In the shadow of bluffs
> I came back to myself,
> To the real work, to
> "What is to be done."
> Gary Snyder, "I Went into the Maverick Bar"

As I continued my studies of utopian method as well as the, related, processes of political pedagogy and consciousness-raising/organizing, a period of living in Ireland in the mid-1980s turned my attention to a non-literary discourse: namely, liberation theology. As it developed out of both European contexts – such as the Catholic Action movement and progressive theologies (themselves influenced by philosophical anthropology, hermeneutics, existentialism, and the Marxisms of French communism and the Frankfurt School/Ernst Bloch) – and local sources – such as national liberation movements and writings by Bartolomé de las Casas, José Carlos Mariátegui, and Che Guevara – liberation theology took on a more politically engaged quality than its counterparts in Catholic "political theology" (see Johannes Metz) or Lutheran "theology of hope" (see Jürgen Moltmann). This situated and activist dynamic grew especially as the work of liberation theologians and philosophers such as Gustavo Gutiérrez, Leonardo Boff, Juan Luis Segundo, Enrique Dussell, and others was informed by, and in turn informed, the political alliances arising from the collaboration

---

"new formal tendency" that, as best seen in Robinson's work, does not represent Utopia as such but rather registers the "conflict of all possible utopias, and the arguments about the nature and desirability of Utopia as such" (216). While I agree with Jameson's recognition of this historical and formal development, for me, the critical utopias did not so much end the older tradition as begin this new set of tendencies, indeed informing the very utopian writing that Robinson has developed from the late 1980s to the present.

of indigenous and working peoples and left cadre in areas such as Brazil and Nicaragua.[3]

Speaking to the point of this essay, liberation theology articulated an overt utopian project in both its theological and pastoral dimensions. Unlike many Christian discourses since the Middle Ages, liberation theology does not attack Utopia as a heretical turn away from the narrative trajectory of redemption and salvation. More in keeping with the "Third Age" theology advanced by Joachim of Fiore in the twelfth century, the liberation theologians saw the collective political movement toward a just and emancipated future as a "graceful" sign of the larger promise of the Christian message – and further recognized humanity's participation as central to what they openly called a "revolutionary process" of transformation, thus positing an activist view of the redemptive process (Gutiérrez 213). Theologically, therefore, liberation theology drew on an eschatological understanding of a transformed humanity *in history*, as it figured the horizon of a salvation that was both spiritual and material, a horizon that grew out of a critique of contemporary capitalism and anticipated a better world in its engaged re-interpretation of the "signs of the times," as the Gospel of Matthew put it. Pastorally, it located the core of that process of transformation in the situated experiences and knowledges of the world's most oppressed, thereby expressing a preferential option for the poor that could inform the leading edge of spiritual and political work in the world. Indeed, it was the peda-

---

3   Living in Ireland in the mid-1980s, I saw a different version of the power of religious thought and practice in challenging a society, and I read of the deployment of liberation theology by progressive Irish political and social activists (many returned, and radicalized, missionaries). While by this time I had abandoned my beliefs, I still valued the linkages of spirituality and politics (indeed, Kovel's essay on materialist spirituality remains an important work on this matter); and I began to look at the role of the utopian persuasion in the progressive theologies that were so much a part of the left movements of Central and South America (as well as Ireland, black and Hispanic North America, South Korea, and in women's movements around the globe). In this essay, however, I focus on the utopian methodology and not the substance of liberation theology itself (one that by time of this writing has been systematically suppressed by the Vatican, under the leadership of both Pope John Paul II and Benedict XVI).

gogical and political work of the grassroots Christian base communities in Brazil, Nicaragua, and elsewhere that most directly created
what José Miguez-Bonino called the "new prophetic temper" of this
mode of religious and political praxis. Brought into action by the
emancipatory pedagogy of Paulo Freire (as it deployed the hermeneutic circle of experience, suspicious reflection, transformed experience, and new emancipatory knowledge), the empowering matrix
of worship, study, and action that shaped the *conscientization* process
in the lives of the base community members was the strongest force in
building what, in the spirit of Vatican II, was seen as a people's
church (quoted in "Denunciation" 46–7).

Thus, in several essays, I wrote about the *utopian* methodology
and pedagogy of liberation theology.[4] As a transformative method that
aims to change and not simply know the world, liberation theology
combines "a negative 'hermeneutics of suspicion' with a positive
'hermeneutics of recovery'" ("Denunciation" 44). Through this double
move, named by some as a process of "denunciation" and "annunci-
ation," liberation theologians provide a utopian "mediation between
faith and politics that challenges and transcends the limitations of the
present in the name of the dispossessed" ("Denunciation" 44). In this
context, I noted the resonance between liberation theology and its base
community work and that of Marxist theory and left activism (a
connection that was already evident in the politics of the religious
Left). I cited Jameson's argument that "a Marxist negative hermeneutic, a Marxist practice of ideological analysis proper, must in the
practical work of reading and interpretation be exercised *simultaneously* with a Marxist positive hermeneutic, or a decipherment of the
Utopian impulses of these same ideological texts"; and I linked that
process to liberation theology, as it is was "outraged and outrageous in
its demands for justice and freedom" (*Political Unconscious* 296;
"Denunciation" 59). Thus, following a similar hermeneutic trajectory,
in an equally utopian mode, liberation theology enacts its own "prob-
lem-posing" strategy that creates opportunities for the most oppressed

---

4   Besides "Denunciation/Annunciation" as discussed, see also "Anticipatory Fic-
     tion" and "Mission Impossible."

of people to interpret their situation and to change it within the world-ly perspective offered by a utopian horizon ("Denunciation" 45).

As seen in the base communities, this transformative method operates in a pedagogical/political as well as an analytical/theological mode. As they carried out their adaptation of Freire's "pedagogy of the oppressed," the base communities enabled their members to speak a "truth" appropriate to their needs and aspirations ("Denunciation" 46). Here, what Phillip Wegner calls Utopia's "pedagogical and transformative dialectic" arrives as a radicalizing knowledge that allows its engaged practioners to generate cognitive maps of reality that critique the existing society and prefigure new possibilities – again, realizing that such possibilities can only, like the Kingdom of Heaven or the Realm of Freedom, be pointed toward and not lived or known, until the "real work" of historical change occurs (58). Thus, the pedagogy of the base communities and the hermeneutics of liberation theology inform a praxis that accords with the utopian process, in that both provide the machinery of knowledge and action that the transformation of the present world system requires.

Finally, as I shifted my emphasis to a literary register, I noted that this "dangerous discourse" evinces a strong "skeptical edge," as feminist theologian Sharon Welch put it, that suspiciously breaks open the sutured world of contemporary power but mobilizes a fantastic mode that is overtly utopian in its creation "of dangerous memories and subversive visions" based in the cultural matrices of local populations ("Denunciation" 59–60; Welch 14). I concluded by way of a reference to the anthropological work of Michael Taussig, as I argued that:

> there is in the spirituality of liberation – tempered by the materialist theology that reflects upon it and the social practices that give it concrete existence – a "wildness" that challenges the unity of the established order and gives voice to new possibilities. It is a wildness in the spirit of Benjamin's notion of messianic disruption – one that "creates slippage and a grinding articulation between signifier and signified." The questioning hermeneutic of liberation keeps this wildness alive so that it can "speak truth to power" in the utopian name of the integrity of nature and the human community (Taussig, quoted in "Denunciation" 61).

After working on the wild, disruptive, and creative utopian elements in liberation theology, I looked back to the influence of Bloch's utopian philosophy on the development of progressive theologies, and on liberation theology in particular. While this allowed me to say more about liberation theology and its relationship with Marxist thought and practice, it also led me to focus on Bloch's utopian method. I therefore came back to considering the ways in which the *critical method* of Utopia can often conflict with the *prescriptive substance* of Utopia – or, how Utopia as *process* works with and against Utopia as *ideology* (a formulation not all my colleagues in utopian studies would be comfortable using).

And so I revisited Bloch's extensive exploration of the trajectories of hope in the imaginative surplus of world history, as he discovered insistent strands of utopian anticipation in an amazing array of human expression and action. More pointedly, I examined the ways in which he deployed a critical utopian method within his own body of work. Here, I was prompted by Jameson's call for the "coordination of the ideological with the Utopian" at the end of *The Political Unconscious*, as he moved beyond the familiar Mannheimian binary of Ideology and Utopia to the recognition that "the effectively ideological is also, at the same time, necessarily Utopian" and thus articulated a more nuanced utopian project that could trace the ways in which not only the ideological could "be grasped as somehow at one with the utopian" but also the utopian could be regarded as "at one with the ideological" (286). To be sure, working from Jacques Lacan and Louis Althusser, we can fairly readily see how a utopian appeal can inform and drive a process of ideological interpellation – be it within fascism, nationalism, or indeed feminism or communism. However, we need to understand that Jameson is also recognizing the ways in which the utopian project itself can resolve into an ideological amber, locking its open promise into a fixed state that preserves and maintains (or at most, or worst, reforms) rather than critiques and breaks open to a more distant, and more radical, horizon of possibility.

In the spirit of this critical dialectic, I re-read *The Principle of Hope*, following Bloch's moves from meditations on the daydreams of everyday life to the ultimate transformation of the world and its history in the name of his most concrete utopia, the Soviet Union. Thus, in "Bloch Against Bloch: the Theological Reception of *Das Prinzip Hoffnung* and the Liberation of the Utopian Function," I rehearsed this Marxist's contribution to Christian theologies and commented on the ways in which the dialogue between Christianity and Marxism opened both progressive discourses to pressing historical needs; but I also went on to explore how Bloch's utopian method interacted with his own, compromising, preference for the positive utopian ideology of Karl Marx and Soviet communism at the end of *Principle*. My essay opened with Walter Benjamin's recommendation that historical materialism could become the victor in the battle against fascism if it enlisted the services of theology (see "Theses on the Philosophy of History"), and I brought this productive suggestion up to the moment of the 1960s, when Bloch's Marxist utopianism helped to bring progressive theology down to earth and enlisted it in the service of the revolutionary transformation of society. In return, I argued, the debilitating authority of a closed, orthodox and teleological, Marxism was itself challenged by this new religious discourse as it contributed to that period's revival of the radical process of utopian anticipation in that same transformative process (see "Bloch Against Bloch" 96).[5]

However, a consistent use of his critical method was not an easy move for Bloch; for while his intellectual and political commitment to a radical utopian hermeneutic carries through his entire body of work, his affiliation (understandable, to be sure, in the face of the twin evils of Nazi and American power, of fascism and capitalism) with the counter-hegemony of the Soviet Union, and indeed later the German Democratic Republic, threatened to deflate the effectiveness of that very method. Drawing on the observations of Jan Bloch, Oskar Negt, Zipes, and others, I noted that Bloch's political commitment to the U.S.S.R. not only trapped him in a historically static loyalty, it also revealed a twofold error in his method: on the one hand, his "strategic belief in the power of the utopian telos" led him to locate the U.S.S.R. at the leading edge of that trajectory and thus displaced all other radical possibilities; on the other hand, his "ideological hypostatization" led him to set aside the "critical and negative aspects of the

---

5   Geoghegan's recognition of the emergence of a "post-secular" political position
     is a further elaboration of this tendency; see his essay in this volume.

utopian function that could have challenged and subverted" his concrete utopia and consequently enlisted him in the forward movement
that was desperately needed by an internal communist critique and an
emerging New Left ("Bloch Against Bloch" 110). Thus, in a move not
unrelated to Jameson's suspicion of the place of practical politics
within the utopian, I wrote of the conflict between Bloch's utopian
politics and utopian method; and I developed my analysis in the spirit
of what I had earlier written regarding the literary utopias of the
1960s. My commentary was couched in a retrospective caution:

> although [Bloch's] long-range vision enables humanity to move beyond the
> darkness of the lived moment, unless that vision includes an immediate critique
> of the ideological appropriation of the "utopian" achievements along the way,
> that vision itself can betray the very processes which are meant to lead toward
> it. [...] In other words, unless both moments of the critical dialectic of the
> utopian function are maintained – unless the negative, denunciatory moment
> and the positive, annunciatory moment are both employed so that each chal-
> lenges the limitations of the other – the utopian method will fail through an
> acceptance of the provisional "success" valorized by short-sighted ideology
> ("Bloch Against Bloch" 110–11).

Or, to put it more succinctly: if "the utopian goal is valorized at the
expense of the utopian project, the method fails" ("Bloch Against
Bloch" 111).

I then explored this political and methodological crisis, and
lesson, through a reading of *Principle* wherein I identified a "dialogic
tension" between a historically frozen orthodox Marxism with its
commitment to a linear progression toward the communist telos and
an unorthodox understanding of the fragmentary, disruptive work of
utopia throughout history ("Bloch Against Bloch" 112). I focused on
textual evidence of this tension in the final two sections of Volume
Three: "The Last Wishful Content and the Highest Good" and "Karl
Marx and Humanity: Stuff of Hope." In the penultimate "Last Wishful
Content," Bloch properly warns against the trap of "false," ideologically fixed utopias that prevent the actual movement toward
concrete utopia. Thus, he argues, the primary utopian drive "rooted in
hunger, in need" can be discovered in the cultural heritage of humanity throughout history, even as its radical surplus is again and

again trapped in the idealizations of ideologies (*Principle* III 1321). To be sure, even in this strongly critical utopian section, Bloch is tempted by his own desire for a linear, privileged, teleology: a desire revealed in his metaphors of "maturity" and "perfection" (*Principle* III 1192). And yet, the deeper force of his hermeneutic consistently pulls him beyond any privileged moment in history; for in this section he manages to move beyond the Faustian "temptation to 'stay awhile'" which carries the danger of becoming encased in a given ideological matrix" and identifies those moments "when one is on the edge of a 'good' that goes beyond what is offered" ("Bloch Against Bloch" 114).

In some of his clearest utopian maneuvers, Bloch insists that Utopia is not matter of a finished content but rather a phenomenon of motion toward a not yet existent reality, albeit a movement that necessarily has to work through, against, and beyond the actual tendencies and latencies of the given moment. Thus, while he evokes a "final figure" or a "kingdom figure" that bespeaks a revolutionary telos, he is usually careful not to equate that figure with an achieved reality: for these are anticipatory not established evocations, and thus are "*frontier* concepts [...] that [move] *toward* the Absolute of human wanting" (*Principle* III 1345, 1353, emphasis added). To be sure, Bloch's privileging of a specific historical trajectory arises again in those senses of "highest" good and an "Absolute" of wanting, but these figures nevertheless remain on the horizon of the ongoing process. In this section, then, Bloch is at his critical best, as he insists that the utopian function must include "the power to define fulfillment as well as the power to resist *all* efforts to contain its potentially unbounded hope in any hypostatized definition" ("Bloch Against Bloch" 115).

However, in the closing section of *Principle*, Bloch represses his utopian method at the moment when it is most needed, as he "commits the very act of mythical hypostatization he rails against throughout the three volumes" ("Bloch Against Bloch" 115). In his teleological "Karl Marx and Humanity," the radical utopian takes refuge in his ideological enclave, locating the consummation of utopian longing in the figures of the already existing Marx, and by implication, the Soviet Union. Marx thus arrives at the end of this great work as the "true architect" who finally empowers humanity to actively comprehend itself (*Principle* III 1354). Indeed, Bloch goes even further, as he names *theory* rather than material conditions and human actions as history's agent: e.g., "in those countries where *Marxism* took power [...] quarters are arranged for the future" (*Principle* III 1367, emphasis added). At this point, when his utopian method should especially be searching for a post-Soviet not yet that even he cannot imagine, Bloch loses the run of his own method as he "settles for a teleological end point in a militant hypostatization of those times which inspired its movement in the first place – reducing them to the limits of Soviet Marxism and the Soviet State" ("Bloch Against Bloch" 116).

Yet, even here, at his most ideologically fixated, Bloch's stubborn utopian yearning outdistances even his most adamant affiliation, as the utopian Bloch yet again turns against the ideological Bloch. At the beginning of the section, he infers his method in an introductory quotation, as he cites Gotthold Lessing's words: "It is not true that the shortest line is always the straightest"; and he holds to his forward gaze when he warns that "no dreaming may stand still" and invokes the necessity of an "open history, [as] the field of objective-real decision" (*Principle* III 1354, 1365, 1372). Thus, Bloch's failure of nerve in this last section does not bring down his entire argument and method, as even in the closing pages he speaks of "the process-world, the real world of hope itself" and reminds his readers that the "best still remains patchwork" (*Principle* III 1374, 1375). I therefore concluded my essay by asserting that throughout *Principle* Bloch continually ruptures the ideological suturing of his own system, teaching us to read against the ideological grain of the most compelling beliefs and affiliations by way of a critical utopian hermeneutic. Even as he himself falls short of that very method, locking himself into his own Soviet solidarities, he offers us the opportunity to turn the utopian impulse against his own position and to continue to learn from him even in his compromises and failures. As with the critical utopias that discovered the utopian germ in the hypostatizations of actually existing "utopias" and sought for ways to move forward yet again, so too Bloch invites us to read beyond his last chapter in an open process of utopian anticipation.

This invitation to engage a utopian method of reading beyond compromise, closure, or desperate affiliations recurred a few years later in the face of the revival of dystopian writing during the period of neo-conservative/neo-liberal hegemony and left oppositional uncertainty and diffusion. In *Scraps of the Untainted Sky: Science Fiction, Utopia, Dystopia* and *Dark Horizons: Science Fiction and the Dystopian Imagination* (jointly edited with Raffaella Baccolini), I wrote on the generic innovation that several of us came to call the "critical dystopia." In this new current of sf narrative, we found yet another manifestation of utopian anticipation: one that, like the earlier critical utopias, foregrounded the question of political agency; for here too the renewed possibility of oppositional political movement rather than the formulation of a utopian system was of central concern. Thus, in literary and filmic works from the late 1980s to the late 1990s – by the likes of Piercy, Robinson, Margaret Atwood, Octavia E. Butler, Gary Ross, and the Wachowski Brothers – critics such as Baccolini, Lyman Tower Sargent, Bryan Alexander, Peter Fitting, Jenny Woolmark, Ildney Cavalcanti, and I examined the refunctioning of the dystopian mode in this period when the radical anticipations of Utopia were being denied, suppressed, and refused (when they were not simultaneously being co-opted into the global commodity culture).

The dystopian mode had certainly made its mark in the twentieth century. From Jack London's *Iron Heel* to the great dystopian "trilogy" of Yevgeny Zamyatin's *We*, Aldous Huxley's *Brave New World*, and George Orwell's *Nineteen Eighty-Four*, to works such as Katharine Burdekin's *Swastika Night*, Ray Bradbury's *Fahrenheit 451*, and John Brunner's *Stand on Zanzibar*, the genre provided an avowedly pessimistic form wherein the closure and terror of modern societies could nevertheless be registered and wherein, in some, warnings could be issued to readers to take heed, or else. As Baccolini and I noted, this dark side of the utopian genre had faded in the period of the critical utopias but had reappeared in the 1980s and 1990s. The new dystopias thus confront "the devaluation of Utopia by an official, neo-liberal discourse that proclaimed the end of history and celebrated simultaneously the end of radical social dreaming and the achievement of an instantaneous 'utopia' of the Market" (6–7). Yet, these texts manage not only to rekindle the observant pessimism of their predecessors; for – in works such as Atwood's *The Handmaid's Tale*, Robinson's *Gold Coast* and *Antarctica*, Butler's *Parable of the Sower*, Piercy's *He, She and It*, the Wachowskis's *Matrix*, and Ross's *Pleasantville* – they also explore, within their pages, new possibilities of political opposition "based in difference and multiplicity yet cannily reunited in an alliance politics that speaks back in a larger though diverse collective voice" (Baccolini and Moylan 8). Consequently, as Phil Wegner notes in this volume, they not only critique the present system but also posit new forms of oppositional politics that supersede both the left micro-politics and social-democratic reformism of the time and build toward a new revolutionary vision and direction.[6]

As with the critical utopias, the political thought experiments of this new sf direction are best seen as poetic meditations on transformative possibilities. With their formal strategy of producing open texts by way of what Baccolini calls "genre blurring" and with their iconic generation of dystopian worlds that nevertheless include utopian enclaves of resistance (e.g., Earthseed in *Parable*, Tikva in *He, She and It*) and broad political alliances (e.g., the workers, scientists, feral Antarcticans, and government leaders in *Antarctica*; or the multiracial, sexual, class Resistance in *The Matrix*), the critical dsytopias tap into the "necessary pessimism of the generic dystopia" but also express an "open, militant, utopian" political vision and trajectory that refuse "the anti-utopian temptation that lingers like a dormant virus in every dystopian account" and challenge the dominant system imaged in the text's alternative world (*Dark Horizons* 7; *Scraps* 195).[7]

---

6   See also *Archaeologies*, in which Jameson discusses dystopia (including the critical dystopia) and recognizes the difference between critical dystopian texts, with utopian hope, and dsytopias, such as Orwell's, that are anti-utopian ("Journey into Fear"). Rather than stressing this difference as indicative of an epistemological, formal, political break, it might be useful to read these distinct textual positions along the continuum proffered in *Scraps*: wherein the entire dystopian genre can be seen as working within a militant, utopian pessimism to those adopting a resigned, anti-utopian pessimism (see *Scraps*, ch. 5 and 6).

7   Jameson's use of the term "enclave" in *Archaeologies* works at a different register than our textual analyses of the enclave as a formal element in the critical dystopia; however, there is a direct relationship between the two. As Jameson puts it, utopian space "is an imaginary enclave within real social space," and its "possibility is dependent on the momentary formation of a kind

This political charge, then, is not to be dismissed as a descent into practical politics, but rather it is best seen as the outcome of imaginative work that maps, warns, and delivers an activist hope in times that were bereft of a strong political opposition. Thus, "generally, and stubbornly, utopian," the critical dsytopias exemplify another moment in which the utopian method engages with an enclosed present. While their scenarios point toward a utopian horizon, their militantly pessimistic narratives "do not go easily toward that better world"; instead, they "linger in the terrors of the present even as they exemplify what is needed to transform it" (*Scraps* 198–9). Again, the utopian maneuver is one of breaking radically with the present in the name of a movement toward a transformed future, but this time not even daring systematically to image that future, opting instead for speculating on the next steps of a viable collective opposition – one which, as it happened, anticipated the anti-globalization and social forum movements of the turn of the twentieth century.

Keeping On

> All people who have ever lived on Earth have acted together to make a global history. It is one story. Certain patterns are evident in it.
> Kim Stanley Robinson, *The Years of Rice and Salt*

Looking back on all this work, I see the common thread that has been there from the beginning: namely, that of seeking and tracing evidence of the utopian function in the political imagination of the (ongoing) contemporary moment. Never regarding Utopia as static or normative, I have always valued its quality as a critical, negative, and deeply

of eddy or self-contained backwater within the general differentiation process and its seemingly irreversible forward momentum" (15). This description of utopian space as a productive holding mechanism or counter-hegemonic zone within the apparently unstoppable drive of history can stand as a referent for the very textual signifier of the utopian enclave found in the critical dsytopias.

political phenomenon, one that invites humanity to reach to horizons of possibility – even, and perhaps especially, in the most apparently achieved "utopian" situations. While Utopia's alternative social realities are in and of themselves compelling figures of total social transformation (and doubly inspiring, as they both name actual possibilities as well as point to those we cannot yet know), no singular utopian solution can ever do the job of bringing humanity into that much needed better world. The utopian *problematic*, therefore, must always enable further openings, further movement, so that its mobilization of desires and needs for a better world will always exceed any utopian visions that arise from that very process, always look through any utopian answers, and always seek for more.[8] In doing this, the utopian vocation – pursued by activists, artists, and scholars, not to mention each of us in our everyday lives – must include an apprehension of its own internal and external limitations and challenges.

To be sure, in the long, and varied, trajectory of anti-utopian thought (from Aristophanes or Augustine, Edmund Burke or Karl Popper, Francis Fukuyama or Joseph Ratzinger), utopian aspiration has been rejected as, at its most benign, an undertaking that is boring and stifling or, at its most demonic, one that is authoritarian and destructive; and, while utopian practioners and theorists consistently oppose these judgments, they are often the first to recognize the dangers of closure and concentration of power that can develop in the progression from initial utopian impulses to an organized movement toward a better society or indeed the building of that society. Thus, the tendency of disciplined political practice or the systematic ordering of a better society to temper or repress the transformative energy that started it all has been soberly recognized in the utopian tradition, most especially in the self-reflexive critical utopian work coming out of the 1960s and 1970s.

And yet, no utopian worthy of the calling would embrace a transformative impulse alone. Winning the revolution, not simply making the revolution, is essential. The risk of closure and control is unavoidable if utopian change, rather than reformist or gestural poli-

---

8   As Jameson puts it, the utopian calling comes "to us as barely audible messages
     from a future that may never come into being" ("Politics of Utopia" 54).

tics, is to be seriously pursed. The threat of an effacement of "utopian energy" (see Sargent in this volume) – as the movement is organized, as subversive energy is tamed in favor of a post-revolutionary equilibrium, or as the power of leading the movement or administering the new society settles into habitual hands – cannot be denied, but rather must be admitted and addressed at each step in the revolutionary process. The sheer tendency toward compromise and suppression cannot justify the step backward from revolutionary change that is called for in anti-utopian resignation; nor does the apparent freedom of total negation justify the refusal of the hard work demanded by the process of building concrete utopias. Utopian transformation is a *dangerous* act, but it is no less worthy, or less necessary, for being so.

Thus, in these "bad new times" (as Bertolt Brecht might have called them), neither a politics based on maneuvers within the current system nor a politics of sheer refusal is acceptable if one is still interested in being part of the historical movement toward a socio-economically just, ecologically healthy, fully inclusive, and fully emancipatory world – if, that is, one is still to be with the diverse alliance that is the Party of Utopia. In these times – replete with their own "reality paralysis" – it is more necessary than ever to "choose Utopia," as Sargent puts it in his essay in this volume, and to value the legitimation of the transformative work required by that choice. I want therefore to suggest that it is time to re-embrace, or more so to re-function, a bolder position: namely, to think of the power of the *strong thought* of Utopia. By using this phrase, I am arguing against the characterization of the spirit of our era as it was symptomatically captured in postmodern philosopher Gianni Vattimo's concept of "weak thought": that is, the *pensiero debole*, the "positive nihilism," that he pitted against the earlier strong thought of foundational, enlightenment master narratives. I suggest that it is time to move beyond this valorization of melancholy, exhaustion, and accommodation. It is time not simply to "allow" or "listen to" stances of difference and processes of opposition, but rather to enable them, to empower them, or, at least, to create the utopian spaces within which they can flourish so that humanity's needs and desires might one day be met.

It is time, therefore, to increase the charge on critical and political thought, in this post-postmodern period. Here, then, I do not use *strong thought* as a return of the repressed, but rather as a way to re-assert the fundamental quality of Utopia: one that nevertheless needs to be taken, to be quaint, as "under erasure," as it envisions a total socio-political transformation while it adopts the negative herm-eneutic, for example, of the critical utopia of the 1970s or Bloch's critical utopianism. Within this framework, then, Utopia can be grasp-ed as a force that is equal to opposing the globalizing forces of global capital and American imperialism. Such strong, utopian thought can allow us to opt for the bigger view and for the bigger, global-scale alliance politics required to give it flesh (as does the comparable, related, *totalizing* analysis of ecology that must take everything into account to understand anything).

In this light, I want also to suggest another description by which we can understand the nature of the utopian method, in an expression that bespeaks the strength of Utopia as specifically rooted in an ever-insistent need to be critical, negative, and open. Thus, I think it could be helpful to borrow the terminology of nuclear physics and apply it to Utopia: that is, to accept that any given instance of utopian aspiration has a certain *half-life*. In physics, half-life is the time span required for the quantity of a radioactive material to be reduced to one-half its original value – that is, the amount of time it takes for half of the atoms in a sample to decay (see "Radioactive Half-Life" online). Hence, as a metaphor for utopian dynamics, *half-life* captures the explosive energy of Utopia yet recognizes that that energy will event-ually diminish. By understanding the tendency of the utopian process to crack open the present, provincial moment but then, always, to recede after its catalyzing work is done (by being deflected, defeated, or simply exhausted), we are perhaps better able to understand Uto-pia's potential and thus to work more knowingly with its recurring cycle of openness and ordering.[9] Given this sense of Utopia's effec-tive duration, it is perhaps even more important to appreciate the primacy of its disruptive qualities. As Susan McManus argues, to stay

---

9   Utopia's half-life resonates with Sargent's "utopian energy" and the ways it can
     be taken forward in utopian work or "displaced [...] into activities other than the
     creation of utopias." Even when compromised or defeated – in an echo of
     Bloch's sense of cultural surplus – it remains available to future possibilities.

its course an authentic utopianism must be firmly based in its disruptive impulse even as it goes on to inform the building of movements, institutions, or societies. While both the disruptive and the institutional moments are "epistemologically and politically necessary, and dialectically related," the "second moment, of institutionalization must itself always be subject to the disruptive and imaginative moment" (McManus 3).

If, then, utopian justice and fulfillment are to be lived by all, what is needed, in this new century as in other times, is a courageous embrace of the utopian project, not self-denying resignation but self-aware engagement. As this volume, and this essay, argues, however, the political work of utopian transformation requires the (theorized) knowledge of its dangers *and* its opportunities, its negative and positive tendencies. If, and when, a political movement is again carried forward or a better social order is successfully established, the subversive and creative-utopian energy of the project at each and every moment must be protected within the very problematic and practices that inform and drive it. To prevent closure and privilege – or at least to enable successful challenges to any such that develop – the conditions for a renewable utopian function must be made available. Thus – along with these senses of Utopia's strength and its temporary duration – another important element in the utopian method is *memory*, in particular that form of memory that is productive rather than consoling or disempowering. While the maintenance of an open method that discourages exclusive power (be it in the form of overt force, wealth, information, or hierarchy) is essential, the ability to reach back and learn from the lessons of past victories and defeats is also required in that process of rekindling utopian opportunity. As Vincent Geoghegan argues, what is needed is that form of memory named by Bloch as *anagnorisis* (recognition); for with recognition, "memory traces are reactivated in the present" as "a repository of experience and value in an inauthentic, capitalist world" ("Remembering the Future" 22). In regard to the utopian process, the recognition of, and reflection on, past struggles can inform the contemporary process so that it becomes imbued with an educated grasp of previous campaigns even as it proceeds with the work of negation,

re-vision, transformation.[10] Thus, forward-looking memory can catalyze the refunctioning of Utopia and feed into what I call the
"temporal solidarity" of the world's many utopian efforts.[11]

As this new century continues, the dangerous project of Utopia
will continue. Emerging within the actual tendencies and latencies of
the current conjuncture, new utopian manifestations (be they cultural,
as in sf by the likes of Robinson or Miéville, or political, as in the
hopeful forms of opposition germinating in the World Social Forum or
in the independent left-wing governments of states such as Venezuela
or Bolivia) are taking us beyond the dark moments of the 1990s into
yet another era of struggle and possible change. As each utopian effort
breaks new progressive ground, and as each falters, the histories of
previous utopian moments need to be remembered; and the stories,
lessons, and inspirations of these past utopian efforts need, ever again,
to feed the emerging one. Utopia's work is never done.

10   See also Baccolini's work on memory and Utopia, especially the essay in this
     volume, and Gibbons's comments on the subversive power of tradition.
11   The utopian function of forward-looking memory is brought to life in Robin-
     son's *Years of Rice and Salt*. In this counter-epic, three characters (I, K, and B)
     reappear in historical episodes from the eighth century up to present day,
     revolutionary China. As they live, die, and are resurrected (in Robinson's
     materialist version of this process), the three take control of history by finding a
     way to retain their memories (and hence their power to know and revolt) that
     are always erased by the gods after each lifetime. This process enters its critical
     stage when one of the three, Iagogeh, draws on a text she had written in an
     earlier life in her efforts to retain a political memory and articulates their
     revolutionary strategy of refusing to drink the "vial of forgetting" (333). Fol-
     lowing her plan, the three spit out the god's liquid of forgetting and reach the
     shore of their new lives with memories intact. Iagogeh then reminds them that
     in this new life they can remember, and "make something new" (335).

Works Cited

Baccolini, Raffaella. "'A useful knowledge of the present is rooted in the past': Memory and Historical Reconciliation in Ursula K. Le Guin's *The Telling.*" Baccolini and Moylan. 113–34.

—— "Journeying through the Dystopian Genre: Memory and Imagination in Burdekin, Orwell, Atwood, and Piercy." *Viaggi in utopia.* Ed. Raffaella Baccolini, Vita Fortunati, and Nadia Minerva. Ravenna: Longo, 1995. 343–57.

Baccolini, Raffaella, and Tom Moylan. "Introduction: Dystopia and Histories." Baccolini and Moylan. 1–13.

—— (eds.). *Dark Horizons: Science Fiction and the Dystopian Imagination.* New York and London: Routledge, 2003.

Benjamin, Walter. "Theses on the Philosophy of History." *Illuminations.* Trans. Harry Zohn. New York: Schocken, 1969.

Bloch, Ernst. *Heritage of Our Times.* Trans. Neville Plaice and Stephen Plaice. Berkeley: University of California Press, 1991.

—— *The Principle of Hope.* Trans. Neville Plaice, Stephen Plaice, and Paul Knight. 3 Vols. Cambridge, Massachusetts: MIT, 1986.

Butler, Octavia E. *Parable of the Sower.* New York: Four Walls Eight Windows, 1993.

Daniel, Jamie Owen, and Tom Moylan (eds.). *Not Yet: Reconsidering Ernst Bloch.* London and New York: Verso, 1997.

Freire, Paulo. *Pedagogy of the Oppressed.* New York: Herder and Herder, 1970.

Vincent Geoghegan. "Remembering the Future." Daniel and Moylan. 15–32.

Gibbons, Luke. *Transformations in Irish Culture.* South Bend: University of Notre Dame Press, 1996.

Gutiérrez, Gustavo. *A Theology of Liberation: History, Politics and Salvation.* Trans. and ed. Sister Caridad Inda and John Eagleson. Maryknoll: Orbis, 1973.

Hall, Stuart. "The Emergence of Cultural Studies and the Crisis of the Humanities." *October* 53 (1990): 11–23.

Jameson, Fredric. *Archaeologies of the Future: The Desire Called Utopia and Other Science Fictions.* London: Verso, 2005.

—— "Introduction/Prospectus: To Reconsider the Relationship of Marxism to Utopian Thought." *minnesota review.* Special Supplement on "Marxism and Utopia" 6 (1976): 53–9.

—— *Marxism and Form.* Princeton: Princeton University Press, 1971.

—— "Of Islands and Trenches: Neutralization and the Production of Utopian Discourse." *diacritics* 7.2 (1977): 2–21.

—— *The Political Unconscious: Narrative as a Socially Symbolic Act.* Ithaca: Cornell University Press, 1981.

—— "The Politics of Utopia." *New Left Review* 25 (2004): 35–56.

Kovel, Joel. "Cryptic Notes on Revolution and the Spirit." *Old Westbury Review* 2 (1986): 23–35.

Le Guin, Ursula K. *The Dispossessed*. New York: Harper, 1974.

Matrix, The. Dir. Andy Wachowski and Larry Wachowski. 1999.

McRobbie, Angela. "The Politics of Feminist Research: Between Talk, Text and Action." *Feminist Review* 12 (1982): 46–57.

McManus, Susan. "Fabricating the Future: Becoming Bloch's Utopians." *Utopian Studies* 14.2 (2003): 1–22.

"Marxism and Utopia." Special Supplement. *minnesota review* 6 (1976).

Miguez-Bonino, José. *Doing Theology in a Revolutionary Situation*. Philadelphia: Fortress, 1975.

Moylan, Tom. "Anticipatory Fiction: *Bread and Wine* and Liberation Theology." *Modern Fiction Studies* 35.1 (1989): 103–21.

——— "Bloch Against Bloch: The Theological Reception of *Das Prinzip Hoffnung* and the Liberation of the Utopian Function." Daniel and Moylan. 96–122.

——— *Demand the Impossible: Science Fiction and the Utopian Imagination*. London and New York: Methuen, 1986.

——— "Denunciation/Annunciation: The Radical Methodology of Liberation Theology." *Cultural Critique* 19 (1992): 33–65.

——— "Mission Impossible: Liberation Theology and Utopian Praxis." *Utopian Studies III*. Ed. Michael Cummings and Nicholas D. Smith. Lanham: University Press of America, 1991. 20–30.

——— *Scraps of the Untainted Sky: Science Fiction, Dystopia*. Boulder and Oxford: Westview, 2000.

Piercy, Marge. *He, She and It*. New York: Knopf, 1991.

——— *Woman on the Edge of Time*. New York: Knopf, 1976.

Pullman, Philip. *The Subtle Knife*. New York: Scholastic Point, 1998.

"Radioactive Half-Life." 12 February 2005 <http://hyperphysics.phy–astr.gsu.edu/hbase/nuclear/halfi.html>.

Rich, Adrienne. "Natural Resources." *Dream of a Common Language: Poems 1974–1977*. New York: Norton, 1980.

Robinson, Kim Stanley. *Antarctica*. New York: Harper Collins, 1997.

——— *The Years of Rice and Salt*. London: Harper Collins, 2002.

Snyder, Gary. "I Went into the Maverick Bar." *Turtle Island*. New York: New Directions, 1974.

Suvin, Darko. "On the Poetics of the Science Fiction Genre." *College English* 34.3 (1972): 372–83.

——— "'Utopian' and 'Scientific': Two Attributes for Socialism from Engels." *minnesota review*. Special Supplement on "Marxism and Utopia." 6 (1976): 59–76.

Taussig, Michael. *Shamanism, Colonialism, and the Wild Man: A Study in Terror and Healing*. Chicago: University of Chicago Press, 1987.

Vattimo, Gianni. *The End of Modernity*. Trans. John R. Snyder. Cambridge: Polity, 1992.

Wegner, Phillip E. "Horizons, Figures, and Machines: The Dialectic of Utopia in the Work of Fredric Jameson." *Utopian Studies* 9.2 (1998): 58–74.

Welch, Sharon D. *Communities of Resistance and Solidarity: A Feminist Theology of Liberation.* Maryknoll: Orbis, 1985.

Williams, Raymond. "Utopia and Science Fiction." *Science-Fiction Studies* 5.3 (1978): 203–14.

NAOMI JACOBS

Utopia and the Beloved Community

Once, when organizing a utopian studies conference, I received a letter postmarked Waco, Texas. The writer asked me to recommend intelligent, "nubile" female professors who could help him breed children for the utopian society he was planning to create. The arrangement would include a trip to Orlando, he noted. Having dealt before with hoaxers who found the concept of Utopia inherently laughable, I thought he was joking, and responded in kind. In his next, somewhat agitated, letter, he laid out in elaborately mathematical detail the rules and regulations for his proposed society, specifying ideal numbers of breeding adults, numbers of children per couple, male/female balance, curriculum for each year in school, carefully calibrated jail sentences for infringements of the numerous rules, ad infinitum. Nonplussed, I sent my regrets that I did not know of anyone likely to join his project, and suggested that he might try advertising in other venues. His final letter looked like the work of a schizophrenic. Random lists of words and numbers, obscure formulae, bizarre drawings – well, let's just say that the content, together with the postmark from a city associated with a certain distorted cult mentality, left me looking over my shoulder for some time afterwards. He seemed quite capable of making a trip up to Maine to persuade me to assist his project. He certainly was not interested in modifications to his plan or input from anyone else. Altogether, his behavior bore out the common stereotype of utopian thinkers as potentially dangerous crackpots.

Utopia as we once knew it has become obsolete, and scholars have less and less interest in new versions of the magnificently, even obsessively assured texts by Charles Fourier, Étienne Cabet or Edward Bellamy that inspired discipleship and imitation in the past. Let's face it: most readers, myself included, feel little but dread at the prospect of reading a new utopia in the traditional mode, or of encountering a real-life utopian reformer. What could be more tedious, and less likely to inspire useful political activity, than yet another round of enumeration, exposition, explanation, and persuasion? Given our age's general skepticism about reform, few readers – at least, few secular readers – are willing to swallow wholesale the proposals of any single-minded reformer, and few writers of literary utopias expect readers to put their ideas into practice in any direct way.[1] There are no Piercy Clubs mounting electoral campaigns to eliminate the gendered pronoun, no Delany Societies agitating to establish unlicensed districts in cities, no fans of Ursula K. Le Guin setting up eco-communes in the Napa Valley and no Kim Stanley Robinson followers lobbying to terraform Mars. These days, to believe that a better world should be built to the dimensions of any one thinker's vision seems naïve at best, delusional at worst.

And yet, appeals to Utopia are everywhere. In 2003 an important outlet for contemporary art, the Venice Biennale, featured an installation called "Utopia Station." Poet Claudia Keelan recently published an award-winning book titled *Utopic* (see Peppermint). On a more mundane level, the yellow pages of any city phone book in the United States list Utopia beauty salons, coffee shops, and cafes. Our beverage choices include a juice drink named Fruitopia and the Boston brewer Sam Adams's "Utopias" beer (twenty-four percent alcohol by content, priced at a hundred dollars for a twenty-four-ounce bottle). Such uses of the word, however degraded, give evidence of the rhizomatous persistence of Utopia, its dispersal into daily life, its viral infection of consciousness, even in a supposedly post-utopian culture. It is in this complex of anti-utopian cynicism and pervasive utopian longing that utopian studies as an academic field takes place.

In this essay I will first consider the informal web of relations and the collaborative, sociable approach to intellectual work that lured me into the field of utopian studies. To my mind, the eclecticism of the field, its incoherence and irreverence, its very apolitical status, its

---

1   I speak here, of course, of the secular and skeptical context of academia, setting aside for purposes of this project those many charismatic religious and political leaders who find plentiful disciples these days for their fundamentalist utopian visions.

sometime frivolity, and its open, even indiscriminate welcoming of all comers and incorporation of all texts, are qualities perfectly suited to this postmodern utopianism that no longer aspires to transform the world, although it may hope to improve it – to Utopia as intermittent, a tendency or process, as opposed to Utopia as a monolithic goal. I will then suggest the ways in which a similarly collaborative/dialogic method and "a certain abandonment of mastery" can revitalize the form of the literary utopia (Kinnahan 33). My exemplar will be an important though little-known experimental text: Bernadette Mayer's 1984 *Utopia.*

Method

In creating the "Utopia Method Vision" lecture series, Tom Moylan asked us to reflect upon what brought us to this field and how our work with Utopia has affected our methods and approaches within our disciplines. I am a literary scholar, trained with a specialty in the history and theory of the novel. During my doctoral studies, I read Samuel Butler's *Erewhon* in a course on Victorian fiction and Bellamy's *Looking Backward* in one on American intellectual history. I had read Aldous Huxley and George Orwell as a teenager, of course, and was familiar with enough titles to put together a syllabus on utopia and dystopia when the year 1984 rolled around. But in my dissertation on postmodern American fiction, only one utopian work was mentioned, and that briefly. Neither I nor any of my teachers would have expected utopian literature to become my primary research area.

The story of how this happened is a tale of two conferences. Both took place when I was a newly minted Ph.D. on her first professorial appointment. Struggling like most new faculty under the pressures of unfamiliar course preparations, murky departmental politics, and the "publish or perish" syndrome, I was also struggling with the very fact of being an academic. Always an addicted reader, and sometimes a fiction writer, I had found myself doing doctoral work almost by default. Trained in the mode of New Criticism that demanded aesthetic analysis free of any taint of politics or personality, I chafed against its constraints. The magisterial tone of omniscience and objectivity I had been taught to affect felt alien and alienating to me, as did the requisite review of literature in which one established one's own authority by demolishing other critics' work. I could mimic that voice, take on that mask, but not without feeling I was perpetrating a scam. So it was with some reluctance that I went off to play that role at the professional conferences I was expected to attend.

One meeting was a conference in narratology: prestigious, highly theoretical, and crowded. I wandered among hordes of strangers, loitered unnoticed at cash-bar receptions, and listened to hotshot keynoters drone on with little apparent enthusiasm for either their subjects or the venue. In windowless hotel meeting rooms, I saw established scholars eviscerate graduate students who had asked the wrong question and watched ambitious younger scholars engage in a Darwinian struggle for position. It was a relief when the audience for my paper on the Brontës' use of the frame-tale was polite and reasonably responsive. Lonesome, often bored, and sometimes appalled, I experienced the event as a bizarre ritual of the profession, an arbitrary test of endurance I must perform to prove my worthiness to teach.

The second meeting was the tenth annual conference of the Society for Utopian Studies. It was a small event on a university campus, made even smaller by a hurricane that disrupted travel. When I walked into the opening-night reception, I was immediately welcomed by several people who saw that I was new to the group. The sessions were held in pleasant, high-windowed old classrooms. Discussions were respectful and constructive; I witnessed no personal attacks and little rank pulling. A senior scholar took the time to talk seriously with me about my paper on Nathaniel Hawthorne's *Blithedale Romance*. There was a general sense of people knowing each other and relishing each other's company. On one of those sunny autumn afternoons, I took a long walk on the hills behind the campus with Peter Fitting and Ken Roemer – two other contributors to this volume, as it happens – and on Sunday morning enjoyed a group visit to a Sufi community in the New York countryside.

You can easily guess which was the conference to which I have returned over the years. The field of utopian studies has become my scholarly home, a realm of human warmth and ongoing connection that has nurtured my intellectual work by modeling how such work can be collaborative, noncompetitive, and convivial. It has become a part of my "Beloved Community" (a term I use advisedly, knowing that some readers might find it trivialized by this application). Coined by American philosopher Josiah Royce and taken up again by Martin Luther King during the civil rights movement, the term describes the community of those dedicated to justice and peace. This may seem rather too much to claim for any academic enterprise, and of course, utopian studies could never embody Royce's ideal. When visionaries who believe they have found the solutions to the world's problems attend utopian studies meetings, they quickly realize they will find no disciples there; one such projector ultimately dismissed the Society for Utopian Studies as "a gaggle of bourgeois intellectuals whose idea of utopia is a free buffet." One must certainly grant the ironies involved when a group of academics, their bills often being paid by their universities, meet in expensive hotels to discuss visions of a more just and equitable world. Similarly, I can understand why a newcomer observing the intimate web of relationships connecting the loyal long-time participants might feel, as one said, as if she had "crashed some-body else's family reunion." But much more than many, the enterprise of utopian studies seems shaped by the conviction that, as Royce put it, one's work, indeed one's life, "means nothing, either theoretically or practically, unless I am a member of a community" (Royce 357).

Utopian studies – with its relatively marginal status and small size, as well as its notoriously loose self-definition – has augmented the ethos sustained by the founders of the field, many of whom came out of Left politics of the 1960s and 1970s. Unlike many professional organizations, utopian studies has been from its inception an enter-prise of friends. It has been informed by a desire to connect the world of scholarship with the world of politics, and to do so in a way that embodies egalitarian ideals. In this volume, Hoda Zaki comments that the study of utopia allows us to "merge an ethical component into our research and life work" (see 269 below). In my experience this has been true not only in the content of that work, but in the manner in which it is conducted as a social – and sociable – enterprise. More than once in my nearly twenty years with the Society for Utopian Studies, new participants have told me they have "fallen in love" with the group. Said one, "finally I've found where I belong as a scholar."

Today, when reading scholarship in utopian studies, I often encounter the work of people I know personally, people with whom I have laughed, argued, commiserated, and speculated. I know their stories, their faces, the very cadence of their voices. I have seen pictures of their pets, their houses, their babies; I have written letters to support their promotions or job applications and they have done the same for me. These are the people who have shown me ways to be a scholar that did not involve one-upmanship, pretense, or scorched-earth tactics of self-promotion.

Working in this scholarly community has affected my work as a literary critic in a number of ways. I was trained in a formalist tradition that values craft, unity, and harmony in literary texts, and frowned upon texts that were openly political. Criticism was to be a process of reading a "great work" with scrupulous attention, of unpacking all the nuances of the text's meaning toward the aim of delineating its perfections. The ideal work of art was one in which no part could be changed without loss of beauty or wholeness; all was intentional, all controlled. Indeed, this concept of the text bears striking resemblances to some older concepts of Utopia as a world of perfect harmony, unity, and completeness. Reading Ernst Bloch, Fredric Jameson, Ruth Levitas, and Moylan on Utopia, I have come to value openness, movement and surprise over balance and control. I find myself less drawn to stylistic or formal polish, and more drawn to those texts that take risks, that convey a sense of life in the moment, of a daring attempt rather than an accomplished goal. I have also become more willing to follow eccentric paths of study. The omnivorous interdisciplinarity of utopian studies has made it possible for me to range far afield from the subjects and method of my training, knowing that generous audiences will help to strengthen my work and not simply attack its failings. Furthermore, the simple question, "do you have anything?", from a friend organizing a conference panel or a book has more than once helped me to develop a vague notion into a finished project.

The changes in my own work are in many ways a microcosm of larger changes in literary studies and in thinking about Utopia over recent decades. Indeed, the situated analysis of everyday life, Foucauldian re-mappings of power, and feminist explorations of the intersectional and relational nature of identity, all lead to new understandings of Utopia and a correspondingly new form for the literary utopia: one that is decentered, fragmentary, multi-vocal, contradictory, irreverent, and perhaps not incidentally, collaborative.

As my understanding of both intellectual and political efficacy has become more fluid and decentered, I am increasingly interested in the dispersed utopian textualities that grow out of discursive communities such as the feminist poets and experimental writers of the 1970s and 1980s. These communal or dialogic discourses embody a process of utopian exploration rather than delineate an alternative way of being. Always unsettled and unsettling, they illustrate nothing, conclude nothing. They provide no map from here to where we might want to be. But in their method and form, they re-affirm the vitality of utopian hope and embody the practice of living this hope within a community of others.

Vision: Bernadette Mayer, Writing in the "future public tense"

Only a few of the utopian texts we commonly study, however self-conscious, critical, or ambiguous, have broken away from conventional narrative techniques and from an aesthetic of authorial control, of unity and completeness. Joanna Russ's *The Female Man*, Samuel R. Delany's *Trouble on Triton*, the essays of Hakim Bey, and Le Guin's *Always Coming Home* do come to mind as exceptions that begin to push the boundaries of form and style. Yet each is still the unified product of a single mind. Of course, it could be argued that all texts are collaborative in origin, to the extent that no literary practice arises out of a vacuum. Every author, no matter how original, must create in some relation to existing traditions and bodies of thought for their departures to have a meaning. But my focus here will be on the actual process of collaboration between living writers in the production of a single text. When Bernadette Mayer did so in the creation of her *Utopia*, she introduced into the *form* of utopia some of the conceptual moves of the "critical utopias" Moylan has defined.

Most readers of this volume are probably not familiar with Mayer. Nor was I, until a new colleague who specializes in the twentieth-century avant-garde told me of Mayer's utopia and of her significance to postmodern American poetry and prose. Born in 1945, Mayer is considered by some to be one of the most important experimental writers of her generation (see Baker; Vickery). As teacher and later director at the Poetry Project at St. Mark's Church in the Bowery, she was at the epicenter of New York's poetry scene in the 1960s and 1970s. Her famous workshops in experimental writing (1971–1974) introduced many poets to linguistic and poststructuralist theory and to a more critically self-conscious approach to writing (Kane 188). Mayer's substantial and provocative work deploys techniques of automatic writing, collage and cut-up, games and jokes, collaboration and chance – all quite different from the rational, unified world-building that has characterized most literary utopias. Yet like her utopian predecessors, she writes with a confidence that language has power to change the world, and utopian references are to be found throughout her oeuvre.[2] Mayer's radical uses of language, her open form, and her collaborative process show the way, I believe, to the future of utopia as a literary mode. Hers is a utopia grounded, like the discipline of utopian studies, in *friendship*, expressing a free exchange of ideas among friends rather than the solitary, potentially obsessive delineation of a private vision.

---

2   For example, her delightful poem "The Garden," a kind of ode to a public garden, imagines plants as models for the remaking of the world: "If all our eyes had the clarity of apples / In a world as altered / As if by the wood betony / And all kinds of basil were the only rulers of the land / It would be good to be together / Both under and above the ground / To be sane as the madwort, / Ripe as corn, safe as sage, / Various as dusty miller and hens & chickens, / In politics as kindly fierce and dragonlike as tarragon, / Revolutionary as the lily" (*Mayer Reader* 85–6).

The initial provocation for Mayer's utopia came in the early 1980s with the casual question from her poet friend Bill Berkson, "What's your idea of a good time?" In response she wrote a short poem, "We All Sleep on Royal Blue Satin Sheets like Cucumbers in Boxes of Snow"; it playfully describes an urban version of the Land of Cockaigne where kids, food, and good conversation abound and every poetry book becomes a best seller. At the time, Mayer writes, she had found herself in a situation where she had no choice but to become involved with local politics:

> it was the politics of my family, the politics of schools, the politics of the Poetry Project, the politics of the Lower East Side of New York City, and the politics of the American government. I was no longer a person living alone or exempt who could control her own destiny in some way or on some days (*Utopia* 16).

As a result, she found herself impelled toward a more directly political form of writing than the art installations and experimental writings for which she had been acclaimed in the 1970s.[3] This move to the political was not without difficulties for a writer whose previous work had explored the intricacies of individual consciousness and percep-tion through detailed examinations of her own experience. Mayer, well steeped in the history of utopian thought, seems to have initially questioned her authority to write a utopia, saying, "I couldn't figure out how to write this book" (*Utopia* 14). How *does* one embark upon a utopia, if not from a position of certainty and clarity about what the world should be? Mayer's solution was to de-authorize herself, saying, "it doesn't matter who I am in the utopian tradition I am no one, no woman no man no person in nowhere like a mad child who answers she is nobody likes nothing & lives no place" (*Utopia* 13). Declining the role of controlling visionary, Mayer also made her utopia a joint enterprise, drawing upon her longstanding experience with and theoretical commitment to collaborative writing. Her 147 page *Utopia*, written in part by nine of her friends, was published

---

3   Mayer's 1975 *Memory* installation, for instance, included over a thousand wall-mounted snapshots, taken at the rate of one roll of film per day for one month, and seven hours of taped narration about the pictures.

(probably not coincidentally, in 1984) by Mayer's own cooperative press, United Artists.

> *Maybe in the Utopia you are born knowing how to fix things* (Anne Waldman).

In some ways the utopian future projected in Mayer's text represents a fairly standard anarchist-socialist vision, if funnier than most. Like most utopias, it contains information on the necessary "nine subjects: food, money, sex, cities, work, marriage, children, machines, and art and literature" (15). No one is hungry, no one is rich or poor; war and exploitation have been replaced by peace and equality; there is freedom for all and abundant pleasures both physical and convivial, good talk and good food with friends and family. The utopians drive emissions-free vehicles to weekend stays at country houses available for general use; "there is no useless work [...] the air is clear" (28). But Mayer's vision is no sober plan for a sustainable society, for there are also zoos for the greedy, poetry readings that attract audiences of 100,000, and endless innocent, carefree sex, some of which happens while floating in the air:

> let's just say while we are making love, since we are together, no storm no earthquake and especially no bomb is going to be dropped or deployed [...] we are now again as little as the truly skipping kids (70).

Laundry is washed in a sort of swimming pool where the swimmers' movements provide the agitation. We are told that the utopian world of the future is brought about by a group of people "pretending to be from outer space" because nobody would believe what they had to say if they were not from another planet. The provisions of the new world government – which, as it happens, is only "one of many possible world governments" – include "come anytime, stay as long as you want to" and "no leaders to listen to, plenty of visions to see" (44). Mayer has described her utopia as "this nursery school teacher's world where theoretically nobody is ever unkind to each other," and her fantasy sustains both a sense of its own impossibility and a longing to regain that primal innocence of childhood (Rower 9–10).

> *Utopia is something civilized it's as simple as that.*
> *Not simple but simply that* (Rochelle Kraut).

Despite the pleasures of Mayer's playful utopian content, her work is most significant for its rethinking of utopian *form* and *style*. It represents a major intervention in the genre for several reasons. First, the book is notable for a mix of genres far more promiscuous than the conflation of the travel account, the ideal commonwealth, and the "dialogue of counsel" in Thomas More or other early utopian writers. In her contribution to this volume, Raffaella Baccolini has suggested that "the very notion of an '*impure* genre, with permeable borders which allow contamination from other genres [...] represents resistance to a hegemonic ideology'" (see 164 above). Mayer's work incorporates poetry, essay, fantasy, a play, letters, a listing of the leaders of every country in the world, and historical documents. It is framed by all the apparatus of a scholarly text, with a table of contents, an introduction, a bibliography of primary and secondary sources, and an enormously funny index that is a good read in itself. But each of these elements is distorted, undermined, or parodic. In its heterogeneity and disorder the book exemplifies what Jerome McGann calls the "nonnarrative" mode of writing, wherein "collections of diverse materials, anthologized structures where the relations between the parts are not determined by narrativities [...] their interrelations [...] have to be consciously constructed" by the reader (204). Among utopian texts, only Le Guin's *Always Coming Home*, to my knowledge, approaches the generic hybridity of Mayer's book. But Le Guin's text is unified in tone, language, and content; it is not difficult to make sense of her book as a whole. Mayer's, by contrast, has a moving and scintillating energy; ideas are thrown off like sparks without any overt attempt on the author's part to unify the whole.

I also know of no other utopia that expressly positions itself outside the realm of commerce and within the realm of the gift. Today one might pay fifty dollars or more to buy a used copy of this cheaply produced paperback – if one could even be found. Only 1000 copies were printed. But because the book carries a "utopian copyright – all rights unreserved" (n.p.), it is possible legally to teach it and share it in

photocopied form. This copyright grants express permission to any
reader to use any or all parts of the book in any way they find "useful
or enjoyable." It even provides the author's address and phone number
(now outdated, of course) for direct contact with her; "call me or write
me if there's any problem," she urges. Her words, she says, should be
regarded as "an expression of affection to each person in this world,
assuming each hopes for peace." In so positioning her writing, Mayer
echoes a common trope of avant-garde communities, in which
writings, especially collaborative ones, have often been characterized
as "acts of generosity; that is, as exchanges of gifts" in a "cultural
space from which the market was absent" (Herd 38, 60). To offer a
utopia as a gift is also to enter it into a structure of non-commodified
exchange in which readers are welcome to participate. As Jean Miller
comments, "none of what's written in this book is about owning
certain words. Instead it's about how the words are all of ours and we
can make the meanings, too" (online).

> *Gazing at the stars as we go astray* (Lewis Warsh).

Few other utopias share this book's raucous humor. The irony of
More, the satire of Butler can make us smile. But Mayer's utopia is
laugh-out-loud, stand-up-comic funny. It is bawdy, outrageous, and
silly. I can recall no other utopia whose inhabitants laugh so hard they
fall down. Reading it, we cannot take utopia too seriously, and yet we
must wish for the kind of absolute freedom and enjoyment that it
embodies. But Mayer also suggests that laughter can serve a social
function beyond the expression of shared enjoyment. Describing the
political process of the future, she writes that "Laughter / then thought
is born" (40). In laughter is the ultimate expression of freedom, and
the frequency with which people in her book laugh uncontrollably is
of a piece with their general resistance to control, bureaucratic or
social – a resistance that carries over into the open structure of the
book. Mayer's laughter also affirms the importance to utopia of
sociable pleasure. Like Emma Goldman, who famously wanted no
part of a revolution in which she could not dance, Mayer values group
pleasures like dancing, dining, drinking, and merriment, and at a level
of excess that would probably not meet More's standard of "reason-

able" pleasures. In fact, she has gone so far as to say that the desire to please *is* "the impulse of utopia" (Gordon online).

> *This secret)(dream)(is future public tense not re-membered never learned* (Bernadette Mayer).

Mayer's utopia is also unusual for an intimacy that strongly evokes the community that gave rise to it. Many sections read like a personal letter or diary entry. She makes offhand references to her friends, partner, and children; she tells us of her struggles with the utopian form; in a poem called "Some of This Decade's Things," dedicated to Henri Lefebvre, we read a long list of the objects found in her New York apartment. Most readers will not know "Bill Berkson" or "Hannah" or "Lewis." It does not matter, for the book was written as much for Mayer's friends as by them. Juliana Spahr has argued that Mayer's radical sonnets rewrite the lyric form, recreating intimacy as collective; we might see Mayer's utopia as doing the converse with its genre, recreating utopia as intimate. By this I do not mean that old truism, "the personal is the political," although Mayer is certainly alert to the ways in which personal experience is inflected by power. Rather, Mayer's work emphasizes the personal nature of the political activities that bring about social change. Politics happens when people get together to work toward a common goal; and often it happens most effectively when those people are friends who take pleasure in each other's company. Perhaps this is why, when trying to "figure out how to write this book," Mayer came to the conclusion that "it seemed like a utopia's stamina must be addressed to or based on or written by or for someone you love" (14). Thus, she begins her "Something & Everything" section, which provides a good many details about her imagined world and how it came about, as if opening an affectionate conversation with a lover: "Darling sweetheart honey baby my love my sweet my darling sweet [...] there are no countries anymore with governments, there is no more of that" (51). She figures the creation of a utopia not as the birthing of a coherent vision from the mind of a single thinker, but as the pleasurable exchange of ideas between people who love and care for one another.

*I'm not sure what to do about people who need to be
on life/support systems. Bernadette, what do we do
about them?* (Anne Waldman).

A similar intimacy was typical of the so-called New York School of
poets that preceded Mayer's generation – most notably John Ashbery,
Frank O'Hara, and Kenneth Koch. Many of their poems include a
casual noting of daily events in which the names of friends and
acquaintances are dropped along with those of New York streets,
cafes, art works, and landmarks. O'Hara called this "personism," his
"attempts to make the poem part of the everyday systems of inter-
subjective communication [...] while also making it a permanent
ongoing record of his friends and their day to day existence" (Watkin
31). Although some of Mayer's projects involved a "resistance" to
"New York writing," her style does sometimes resemble it (Rifkin
online). Like O'Hara's "lunch poems" or Koch's list poems, Mayer's
work has an offhand, easy tone, a good deal of personal detail, and
artfulness skillfully concealed beneath an apparently haphazard
surface. Like theirs, hers is a poetry of willful minutiae that foregoes
transcendence and self-seriousness; it aims to erase the boundary
between art and life, high culture and low, and to demystify the
"genius" status of the artist under Romanticism. According to Harvey
Finkelstein, such poetry is utopian because it locates a "vision of or
desire for perfection" in the blissful present of an eternally renewed
poetic moment (49).

THE ONLY UTOPIA IS IN A NOW (Charles
Bernstein).

A quite different poetic tradition is to be felt in other aspects of
Mayer's use of language. The unstructured and sometimes ungram-
matical sentences, the many run-ons and fragments, will puzzle and
frustrate most readers of traditional utopias and indeed of traditional
fiction. There are stretches of stream-of-consciousness and of free
association, of parody, and of poetry. There are sentences without
recognizable syntax, and familiar words with new meanings. Here we
see Mayer's links with the Language poets who have dominated the
experimental poetry scene in United States since the 1970s. Influenced

to varying extents by post-structuralist accounts of language, the Language poets – many of whom attended Mayer's workshops in the early 1970s – seek to escape the constraints of syntax and form, to write new kinds of sentences in which the materiality and arbitrariness of words are foregrounded. Language poetry is a participatory poetry that requires readers to construct their own meanings from the distorted, "deranged" words on the page. Sentence fragments, nonsensical juxtapositions, groups of words that violate every Chomskian principle for the order of sentences, are all used in the service of a utopian dream: that by transforming language, breaking apart its totalitarian power, poets might transform consciousness and thus open the possibility of true revolution in culture and society. If rational, grammatical language simply replicates and reinforces the discursive status quo, reinscribing our participation in dominant structures of power, then to "derange" the language becomes an act of resistance, a demonstration of the endless capacity for freedom in the human mind, a tool for a utopian transformation. As Charles Bernstein sloganized, "Language control = Thought control = Reality control" (Izenberg 145).

Mayer turned away from experimental writing in late 1970s as she became "interested not so much in the possibilities of language as such but in its relation to a more pressing subject, the concerns of everyday life" (Vickery 157). Her relations with other Language poets have been sometimes "troubled" as a result (Baker 165). Nevertheless, she continues to hold the view that to destabilize language can help to "remake" the world. One of her much-reprinted "Experiments for Writing" advises writers to "systematically derange the language" (online). Significantly, both system and madness are advised; this is to be an intelligent and intentional disruption. And in a later poem, "A Woman I Mix Men Up," Mayer exhorts:

to remake
the world is something not enough people dream of
[...] cast off the book & find
No expectations [...]
Scatter the dictionaries. They don't
Tell the truth yet (*Mayer Reader* 82).

In its innovative form and style, her *Utopia* does indeed "cast off the book" and "scatter the dictionaries" that have defined the utopian genre.

Finally, Mayer's utopia is significant for its collaborative nature. Collaboration, a central practice in many twentieth-century avant-garde groups, introduces an element of unpredictability to the writing process; it courts incoherence, forcing the writer to encounter and respect otherness.[4] A collaborative text will have only fractured unities and is unlikely to be swayed by the pull of totality. Most crucially, collaboration involves relinquishing control over the final product. In fact, there can *be* no final product, since writing is seen as praxis, something that "must be done rather than as something that is to be interpreted" (McGann 208). There were strong traditions of collaboration among Mayer's predecessors and contemporaries on the New York poetry scene. Social life and the writing life were at times so intertwined as to be almost indistinguishable. A landmark 1961 issue of *Locus Solus*, the literary magazine edited by Koch, was devoted entirely to collaborative writing. Poets from this circle would often get together to write, sometimes playing Oulipo games such as "Exquisite Corpse." According to Koch, collaboration provided "a way of having a party and working at the same time" (Herd 51).

Mayer has long shared this interest in the potential of collaboration. *Unnatural Acts*, the magazine she co-edited while teaching her experimental workshops in the early 1970s, included several collaborative issues. One was produced when a group of writers spent a day together, rewriting passages each had provided, in a sort of high-aesthetic version of the game of telephone. According to one participant:

> we were interested in collaboration and process [...] we were intending to be
> less precious about the actual product or outcome of writing experiments, and
> therefore, leaving more room for writing to be a present-time document of the
> writer's mind while writing (Kane 199).

---

4   A considerable literature exists on collaborative practice in the arts. Farrell
     studies the social dynamics of collaborative groups; McCabe's is a fascinating
     collection of essays on avant-garde collaboration, especially in visual art. For a
     sampling of work on collaboration between women, see Doane and Hodges;
     Ede and Lunsford; Kaplan and Rose; Laird; London; Peck and Mink; and York.

The resulting work went entirely without attribution, in an explicit rejection of hierarchy and ownership, with one cover proclaiming, "Our poems aren't our appearances [...] when you take out the I's/ everybody is matched" (Rifkin online). These writing sessions and their utopian ethos ultimately came to an end when writers began to want recognition for their own work. But throughout her long career, Mayer has continued to collaborate with friends, including well-known Language writers Clark Coolidge and Alice Notley; her twenty-four-year correspondence with Coolidge includes a seventy-one-page work titled "The Cave," produced between 1972 and 1978 (Durand). Suggests Ann Vickery, collaboration "involves a rejection of ego boundaries"; it "encourages spontaneity and promises a release from the habitual and the typical," thus creating a kind of utopian space for writing itself (254, 262).

This openness to multiple voices, to sharing the process of creation and welcoming the resulting contradictions, represents perhaps the most significant of Mayer's many notable departures from the utopian genre as we have known it. Approximately one-fifth of Mayer's utopia is written by her writer-friends, and even the sections apparently written by Mayer include many statements attributed to friends or to other writers. Anne Waldman contributes a "Utopia for the sick & dying," Ann Rower a note on the military budget, Hannah Weiner a "Note" that is a slightly modified copy of the "Great Law of Peace of the Longhouse People," John Fisk a list of all the nations of the world and their leaders, Rosemary Mayer an essay on Utopian Chairs, Rochelle Kraut a general note on utopia, Lewis Warsh a poem "for Bernadette's Utopia," and Grace Murphy the instructions for that utopian washing machine. Some of these contributors are skeptical about the entire enterprise, and say so. Yet Mayer's commitment to multiplicity is so strong that she even gives Language poetry spokesman Bernstein several pages to rebut her merciless Gulliverian satire of that movement.

Mayer can be said to collaborate with writers from the past as well as with the living writers who appear as characters in her work. One of the book's funniest sections is a mock "Debate of the Utopians" in which several dozen utopian thinkers, writers, and politicians, as well as poets living and dead, come knocking on Mayer's door and participate in a free-for-all of name-calling, non sequiturs, didactic pronouncements, and bawdy jokes. Elsewhere Mayer quotes extensively (and without attribution) from other texts such as the Constitution of the Six Nations of the Iroquois and *Gulliver's Travels*. These practices are of a piece with a number of her writing experiments that are directed toward breaking up the concept of the writer as solitary genius; "rewrite someone else's work," she suggests:

> experiment with theft and plagiarism.
> [...]
> Create a journal that is meant to be shared and commented on by another writer – leave half of each page blank for the comments of the other.
> [...]
> Trade poems with others and do not consider them your own (online).

Mayer's willingness to collaborate extends even to her relationship with readers. Several passages toward the end of the book ask readers to continue the project, urging a collaboration that exceeds the bounds of this particular publishing event. Inviting readers to add to what she and her friends have made, she writes:

> I hope the future was fine and you enjoyed being in it with us, we tried to make you comfortable and clear. *Not everything's been attended to yet though*, but when you know more, and I do, then tell me more about the naïve and serious and perfect and telltale and generous and satiric things, and we will have together an adjectival future which already lives in our kitchens (116, emphasis mine).

These requests make Mayer's work more radically open-ended than critical utopias like Marge Piercy's or Le Guin's in which the outcome of the fictional events remains undetermined. Her book *itself*, the actual text, is not finished. Claiming no primacy, no last word, Mayer could not be more different from those magisterial utopian dreamers who have been, sometimes rightly, accused of a totalitarian hubris.

Phil Wegner cautions that we need to "distinguish between utopia as an hermeneutic [...] and utopia as a particular literary genre" (see 111 above). While I take his point, I have attempted to suggest here that genres and forms are also hermeneutics, with evolving histories of their own. What we can learn from Utopia varies with the kind of utopia we are reading, and the kind of utopia we write grows out of what we need to know. As Jennifer Burwell writes, "the political effect of a particular literary form is tied to the subject positions that the social discourses circulating within the work express" (45). The social discourses circulating within Mayer's work – and underpinning its very composition – express subject positions that make all readers welcome participants in the creation of a utopia. We are not being asked to work toward a specific future imagined by someone else. Rather, we are being asked to add to, and by implication modify, the book itself, to become part of the creative process, for as long as it takes to bring about a world we might want to live in. In Mayer's hands, Utopia thus is thoroughly postmodernized: disorderly and disunified, wacky and eloquent, fanciful and serious, sarcastic and hopeful, it leaves open the questions of where the world should go, and of the roads we ought to take to get there. These very qualities, of course, also indicate the political limitations of the postmodern utopia. The book presents no coherent social critique, no workable political program; it is not *instructive* in any practical way. And yet, Mayer has written, "the only write I like is change the world ridden" (*Mayer Reader* 129). For her, to write and to share one's writing are acts of freedom which can, to the extent that language creates the world, also change the world.

Am I then advocating frivolity, a playfulness without product? I fear that I am arriving at just such a position, although the high seriousness of many of the essays in this volume makes me hesitant to admit it. Still I believe that Mayer's *Utopia* demonstrates that the utopian enterprise can benefit from at least intermittent bouts of fun and foolishness – from finding ways to "have a party and work at the same time." Political scientists might find little of interest in a text like this, but common readers who need an occasional break from making sense and being productive will relish the humor, inventiveness, downright silliness, and affectionate affirmations of Mayer and her friends, who together have created an exhilaratingly utopian reading experience.

As befits a book that Mayer has described as "all introduction," this utopia ends with an Epilogue that comes to no conclusions:

here's a utopia 1984
which is more a clue
than a place or book
at which you'll look
you haven't given up
on a world have you?
you know traditional
utopias are no place
as ours will ever be
we were all the same
& remain in any name
here is some utopian
some – and everything
add all you would to
what is already here
together we will put
things on paper that
've never been there (123).

This statement, it seems to me, is not a bad description of the ethos of the discipline of utopian studies. We have not given up on a world, have we? In this scholarly "no place," we each add our "utopian some – and everything," *together* putting things on paper that have never been. Laughing, wining, dining, and dancing, we gather as friends to think, talk and write about the "good place," and then, perhaps, to act accordingly. As Mayer says, why would anybody write if they did not want to change the world?

Works Cited

Baker, Peter. "Bernadette Mayer." *Dictionary of Literary Biography. American Poets Since World War II.* Fourth Series. 165. Ed. Joseph Conte. Detroit: Gale, 1996. 165–72.

Burwell, Jennifer. *Notes on Nowhere: Feminism, Utopian Logic, and Social Transformation.* Minneapolis: University of Minnesota Press, 1997.

Doane, Janice, and Devon Hodges. "Writing from the Trenches: Women's Work and Collaborative Writing." *Tulsa Studies in Women's Literature* 14.1 (Spring 1995): 51–7.

Durand, Marcella. "Bernadette Mayer & Clark Coolidge: Correspondence & Collaboration." 18 June 2004 <http://epc.buffalo.edu/authors/coolidge/durand.html>.

Ede, Lisa, and Andrea Lunsford. *Singular Texts/Plural Authors: Perspectives on Collaborative Writing*. Carbondale: Southern Illinois University Press, 1990.

Farrell, Michael. *Collaborative Circles: Friendship Dynamics and Creative Work*. Chicago and London: University of Chicago Press, 2001.

Finkelstein, Norman. *The Utopian Moment in Contemporary American Poetry*. Lewisburg: Bucknell University Press; London and Toronto: Associated University Press, 1993.

Gordon, Nada. "Utopia." *Form's Life: An Exploration of the Works of Bernadette Mayer*. 25 May 2004 <http://home.jps.net/~nada/mayer11.htm>.

Herd, David. "Collaboration and the Avant-Garde." *The Critical Review* 35 (1995): 36–63.

Izenberg, Oren. "Language Poetry and Collective Life." *Critical Inquiry* 30 (Autumn 2003): 132–59.

Kane, Daniel. "Bernadette Mayer and 'Language' in the Poetry Project." *All Poets Welcome: The Lower East Side Poetry Scene in the 1960s*. Berkeley: University of California Press, 2003. 187–201.

Kaplan, Carey, and Ellen Cronan Rose. "Strange Bedfellows: Feminist Collaborations," *Signs* 18.3 (1993): 547–61.

Keelan, Claudia. *Utopic*. Farmington: Alice James Books, 2000.

Kinnahan, Linda A. *Lyric Interventions: Feminism, Experimental Poetry, and Contemporary Discourse*. Iowa City: University of Iowa Press, 2004.

Laird, Holly A. *Women Coauthors*. Urbana and Chicago: University of Illinois Press, 2000.

Le Guin, Ursula K. *Always Coming Home*. New York: Harper and Row, 1985.

London, Bette Lynn. *Writing Double: Women's Literary Partnerships*. Ithaca and London: Cornell University Press, 1999.

Mayer, Bernadette. *A Bernadette Mayer Reader*. New York: New Directions, 1992.

—— *Utopia*. New York: United Artists, 1984.

—— "Writing Experiments." 12 June 2004 <http://poetryproject.com/features/mayer.html#exper>.

McCabe, Cynthia Jaffee (ed.). *Artistic Collaboration in the Twentieth Century*. Washington: Smithsonian Institute Press, 1984.

McGann, Jerome J. "Contemporary Poetry, Alternate Routes." *Social Values and Poetic Acts: A Historical Judgment of Literary Work*. Cambridge: Harvard University Press, 1988. 197–220.

Miller, Jean. "Notes on Bernadette Mayer's *Utopia*." *HOW(ever)* 4.1 (April 1987). 8 November 2004 <http://www.scc.rutgers.edu/however/print_archive/0487post.html#jmpost>.

Moylan, Tom. *Demand the Impossible: Science Fiction and the Utopian Imagination*. London: Methuen, 1986.

Peck, Elizabeth G., and JoAnna Stephens Mink (eds.). *Common Ground: Feminist Collaboration in the Academy.* Albany: SUNY Press, 1998.

Peppermint, Heidi. "Review of *Utopic.*" 12 December 2004 <http://www.poetry.org/ issues/issue3/text/prose/peppermint1.html>.

Rifkin, Libbie. "'My Little World Goes On St. Mark's Place': Anne Waldman, Bernadette Mayer and the Gender of an Avant-Garde Institution." *Jacket* #7. 18 December 2004 <http://jacketmagazine.com/07/rifkin07/html>.

Rower, Ann. "Interview with Bernadette Mayer, 18 December 1984." *Bench Press Series on Art: Interviews with Contemporary Writers and Artists.* Ed. Madeleine Keller. New York: Bench, 1985.

Royce, Josiah. *Josiah Royce's Late Writings: A Collection of Unpublished and Scattered Works.* Ed. F. Oppenheim. Bristol: Thoemmes, 2001. 16 December 2004 <http://www.thoemmes.com/american/>.

Spahr, Juliana. "'Love Scattered, Not Concentrated Love': Bernadette Mayer's Sonnets." *differences: A Journal of Feminist Cultural Studies* 12.2 (2001): 98–120.

Vickery, Ann. *Leaving Lines of Gender: A Feminist Genealogy of Language Writing.* Hanover: University Press of New England, 2000.

Watkin, William. *In the Process of Poetry: The New York School and the Avant-Garde.* Lewisburg: Bucknell University Press; London: Associated University Press, 2001.

York, Lorraine. *Rethinking Women's Collaborative Writing: Power, Difference, Property.* Toronto: University of Toronto Press, 2002.

PETER FITTING

Beyond This Horizon:
Utopian Visions and Utopian Practice

In the following essay, I want to explain how I came to the study of Utopia as well as to outline the theoretical and methodological framework of my work. Simply put, my interest in Utopia (the literary utopia as well as utopianism) grows out of some crucial friendships and out of the merging of my interest in science fiction (sf) with my own political evolution – developments which have shaped my academic career even as they have led me to the study of utopianism. My utopian method and approach have evolved, following from my discovery of utopian fiction, in terms of what I understand it to be and the role I see it playing in the world. To describe this method, I will outline three overlapping moments in my study of Utopia, before concluding with some thoughts about the place of the utopian today.

To begin at the beginning, I do not come from a politically active background, but from a solid middle-class family. Until graduate school, I attended private Catholic schools in California, first with the Carmelite nuns, and then with the Jesuits in high school, and with the Christian Brothers in college. While I retain little of the religious part of that Catholic education, and while there was little in the way of explicit politics in the California schools of the 1950s, or at home, for that matter, I somehow became aware of the social message contained in a certain Catholic tradition – certainly against the grain of Catholic orthodoxy of the time.[1] But in terms of politics, or utopianism, there

---

1   Although Vatican II and the espousal of socially progressive ideas did not take place until 1962–1965, Moylan has pointed out to me how much was already happening in the time leading up to Pope John XXIII's momentous redirection of the Church, "including existentialist work; and what became the theology influenced by Bloch and the Marxist-Christian dialogue begun in France" (personal communication).

was certainly none of that until I reached graduate school – the University of Minnesota, first of all (and it is serendipity that Lyman Tower Sargent and I were there at the same time at the beginning of the 1960s, although we did not meet until almost twenty years later!). Of course, the early 1960s were marked by the civil rights movement and then by the increasing opposition to the U.S. intervention in Vietnam, and by feminism. This context was undoubtedly the background to my growing social awareness. And I use the word "social" deliberately, since this awareness was not yet political – my response to the war and to existing social inequities were determined by ethical considerations rather than by an analysis or understanding of how they had come about. That would come later, during the 1970s.

I began my teaching career at the University of Toronto in 1966, as a professor of French language and literature, where I soon became involved in anti-war actions. But still, I had not made any real connections between the war and my academic work. I was, however, an avid reader of sf; and it was a meeting with the sf writer and critic Judith Merril that led me to start thinking about what I was doing.[2] Judy had just moved to Toronto (in 1968) to express her opposition to

---

2   Merril (1923–1997) was the author of a number of sf stories and novels, including her first sf story, "That Only a Mother," in 1948, which is seen as an important pre-feminist story that brought a woman's perspective to the genre. Other important works include *Daughters of Earth* and two collections of her stories, *Survival Ship and Other Stories* and *The Best of Judith Merril*. Her biggest impact on the genre, however, was as a critic and especially as an editor. She edited numerous sf anthologies beginning in 1950, notably Dell's series of *Year's Best SF* from 1956–1967; and she was the "Books" columnist for *The Magazine of Fantasy and Science Fiction* from 1965–1969. She became interested in and a proponent of the "New Wave" in sf during her trips to London in the mid-1960s, leading to the anthology *England Swings SF*. When she moved to Rochdale College in Toronto (a housing co-operative which was at the same time a free university and the center of Toronto's counter-culture), she established its library, based largely on her own private collection. When Rochdale closed, she donated the collection to the Toronto Public Library, creating the Spaced Out Library, now called The Merril Collection. During the 1980s she did much to encourage Canadian sf, founding Hydra North in 1984 (Canada's first association of sf professionals) and, in 1985, editing *Tesseracts*, an anthology of Canadian sf that has now become a series.

the Vietnam War, and we would meet to talk about sf and politics. We started a "speculative fiction" reading group, and then, in 1970, I was able to offer an sf course at the university – in what was then called "interdisciplinary studies," since the English department was not yet interested in sf. Through our conversations, she made me realize that it might be possible to take the critical tools and methodological approach I had been given for the study of French literature and apply them to sf; and she helped me to realize that there was a connection between contemporary sf and what was happening in the world.

As a French professor, I was aware of the French tradition of Left cultural theory and practice, particularly under the impetus of the French Communist Party and the upsurge in left political activity during the late 1950s in opposition to France's continuing colonialist rule in Indochina and (after the fall of Dien Bien Phu in 1954) in Algeria. In the early 1960s, under the influence of Russian Formalism, some literary critics had begun to consider the question of the politics of form itself; turning the debates about politics and literature from questions of the artist's political commitment (Sartrean *engagement*, etc.) and about the *contents* of art (as in "socialist realism") to questions about the role that the very forms of literature – as well as its teaching and consumption – played in maintaining the status quo. (All of this is epitomized in the work of Louis Althusser and his rethinking of the concept of ideology.)[3]

---

3   For a brief synopsis of these issues as they appeared at the time, see Eagleton's *Marxism and Literary Criticism*. Althusser's "Ideology and Ideological State Apparatuses" was published in 1970. While I can hardly do justice to Althusser and the ideology debates here, let me briefly sum up the issues that concerned me. Before Althusser, the Marxist concept of ideology was usually considered as a form of false consciousness, an illusory view of reality that could be dispelled through education and the disclosure of the true reality of class struggle and capitalist exploitation. Under the influence of Jacques Lacan and psychoanalysis (and in reaction to the growing popularity of the recently published "humanist" texts of the early Marx), Althusser made some substantial revisions and additions to this concept, beginning with the emphasis that "ideology has a material existence"; ideology is not just false ideas or misunderstandings, but the ways that we live and experience the world we live in, through our daily activities, rituals, and the like. Moreover, Althusser insists, there will always be ideology; reality will always be mediated (and constructed)

With this background in mind, I would like to call this first political moment *pre-utopian*: the moment of sf and of Marxism, but without any real understanding or awareness of Utopia and its possibilities. There were three components to my reading and political work at this time that then led me towards the study of Utopia.

First of all, my interest in sf as political was influenced by a particular French variant of Marxism: the *Tel quel* group – which, in the United Kingdom, was a tendency that manifested itself in film studies around the journal *Screen* and the work of Colin McCabe and Stephen Heath – while in terms of literary studies, this position was summed up by Rosalind Coward and John Ellis in their book *Language and Materialism* (1977).[4] In short, this was the attack on representation and realism and an argument for a subversive potential to be found in certain kinds of non-representational and avant-garde writing, a literary direction exemplified for the *Tel quel* group by James Joyce's *Finnegans Wake*. (I tried to apply this method to sf, as can be seen in my article on Philip K. Dick's *Ubik*; while *Tel quel*'s own turn to the right in the 1980s suggests the obvious political limits in such a position.)[5]

through the various "positions" which constitute our subjectivity – our race, class, gender, nationality, religion, and so on. In his *Ideology: An Introduction*, Eagleton defines the Althusserian moment as the passage "from a *cognitive* to an *affective* theory of ideology": "For Althusser one can speak of descriptions or representations of the world as being either true or false; but ideology is not for him at root a matter of such descriptions at all, and criteria of truth and falsehood are thus largely irrelevant to it. Ideology for Althusser does indeed represent – but what it represents is the way I 'live' my relations to society as a whole, which cannot be said to be a question of truth or falsehood. Ideology for Althusser is a particular organization of signifying practices which goes to constitute human beings as social subjects, and which produces the lived relations by which such subjects are connected to the dominant relations of production is a society" (18).

4   There have been some recent accounts of *Tel quel* in English: see, ffrench; Marx-Scouras; and ffrench and Lack. For a less sympathetic view that uses the analytical approach of Pierre Bourdieu to demystify *Tel quel*, see Kauppi.

5   For a presentation and critical analysis of the structuralist moment, see Jameson, *Prison House*, as well as "The Ideology of the Text."

At the same time, in North America, the mid-1970s saw the founding of the Marxist Literary Group (MLG). Many college and university teachers were trying to integrate Marxism into their teaching, particularly Marxist aesthetic theory, as a way of doing political work. Leaving aside for a moment the question of how political this was anyway, it is important to point out that such an approach was primarily analytical, and consisted of the (ideological) analysis of the works of the past and of the present, and of the canon and the profession; but also that there was often little sense of what political writing should be – apart from the subversive option I have just mentioned.

Third, I was dissatisfied with what could be done at the university, and I tried to do politics by going "outside," to a "socialist school" (the Toronto Marxist Institute) where we gave courses open to the public on a range of topics; and where I taught a series of courses on Marxism and culture as a way of trying to understand what I was reading.

Meanwhile, on the sf front, in the aftermath of the World War II, U.S. sf was ostensibly no more political than U.S. society in general. But as Merril and others have pointed out, during the McCarthy era "science fiction became, for a time, virtually the only vehicle of political dissent" (Merril 74); this developed as a form of critique epitomized by Frederick Pohl and C.M. Kornbluth's novel, *The Space Merchants* (1953). Of course, as the 1960s unfolded, sf reflected both the larger fractures in U.S. society and the sense that another world was possible. In her reviews of sf, in the *Magazine of Fantasy and Science Fiction*, Merril wrote about the work of some younger sf writers in terms of the search for a "new mythology," a term which might best be understood as her own word for ideology. Shaken by the civil rights and later the women's movements, and especially by the mounting opposition to the U.S. intervention in Viet Nam, the tranquility and harmony, and the apparently shared values of U.S. society in the 1950s collapsed, a narrative which is summarized in the events of the film *Pleasantville*. In writing about a new mythology, Merril was calling for sf to play a role in imagining and developing new values for a society in transition.

Here it is important to acknowledge sf's special ability to deal with reality – a position which would soon become codified in Darko Suvin's definition of the genre as "cognitive estrangement":

> sf is, then, a literary genre whose necessary and sufficient conditions are the presence and interaction of estrangement and cognition, and whose main formal device is an imaginative framework alternative to the author's empirical environment (7–8).

Thus, in the 1960s and 1970s, sf offered writers a means of thinking critically about the present and the possibility of alternatives in a way that mainstream "realist" fiction could not. The classic illustration of this can be found in Ursula K. Le Guin's novel, *The Left Hand of Darkness* in 1969, in which she takes an issue very much on the feminist agenda of the day and uses sf to pose it in a way which was (and remains) impossible for realist fiction to do: could sex and gender be separated?[6] The utopian moment of the early 1970s was the moment in which writers began to go beyond Le Guin's speculative separation of sex and gender to imagine utopian worlds in which the whole panoply of feminist demands have been realized, as in Le Guin's own extraordinary *The Dispossessed*.

As we can see from this example, if an estranged critique of the present could be seen as a first element of political awareness, this critique soon led to attempts to imagine *alternatives* to the present. Already, in the late 1950s and early 1960s we can see the genre's interest in alternatives, from alternatives to the technological world-view of earlier sf, as in Arthur C. Clarke's *Childhood's End*, the telepathic collectivity of Theodore Sturgeon's *More than Human*, Robert Heinlein's Michael Valentine Smith in *Stranger in a Strange Land*, or, a few years later, Samuel R. Delany's questing hero in *The Einstein Intersection*. This was followed, in the 1970s, then, with a series of feminist influenced utopias which include (all from the period 1974–

---

6   On the world of Gethen, in Le Guin's novel, people have no sexual characteristics nor sexual drives most of the time. But then, for a few days a month, like animals in heat, their lives are given over entirely to the sexual drives. They take on female or male sexual characteristics in a more or less arbitrary fashion. See *The Left Hand of Darkness*, chapter 7.

1980): Le Guin's *The Dispossessed*, Delany's *Triton*, Marge Piercy's *Woman on the Edge of Time*, and Joanna Russ's *The Female Man*. Along with these, one should mention a more traditional utopia, Ernest Callenbach's *Ecotopia*, as well as Suzy McKee Charnas's "science fantasy" *Motherlines*, and one important instance of a feminist utopian fantasy, Sally M. Gearhart's *The Wanderground*.[7]

One of the features of second-wave feminism was a renewed interest in what a world without sexual exploitation and domination would actually look and feel like and how men and women might live together according to new social and sexual relationships. While many feminists concentrated on the analysis of the forms and nature of capitalist patriarchy, and many more women (and men) were involved in struggling against the institutions and practices of patriarchy, some writers set out to imagine non-patriarchal societies. In the 1970s, then, there was a revival in the literary depiction of alternate societies based on new social and sexual relationships, as writers attempted to portray non-hierarchical and non-oppressive social and sexual relationships and patterns of behavior, to imagine the society which would be created by these new patterns and structures of behavior as much as it would enable them.

For me, this newer sf seemed to present the ideal fusion of art and politics: sf was not only a genre which was outside the mainstream (and thus perhaps less corrupted by it, with a credibility that the works of the canon did not have); but it was also a type of fiction which many people read for pleasure, and which seemed to be dealing with the very political questions which concerned me – questions which seemed further and further from the aesthetic preoccupations of university critical practice. This was the moment when I began to realize that what was important about this new kind of sf was its ability to go beyond some estranged representation of the present, to actually imagine a different future.

This then was the Utopian Moment. In this way, our awareness and interest in utopian writing grew out of developments in sf in the early 1970s, especially under the impact of feminism. In terms of a

---

7   I tried to tell this story in my "The Modern Anglo-American SF Novel." See also my "Ideological Foreclosure and Utopian Discourse."

utopian method, I was increasingly convinced that what these works were doing – why they were needed, why they were important – had to do with their ability to give us a glimpse of what an alternative might actually look and feel like; and in that sense the "critical utopia," under the influence of feminism, focused not so much on alternative structures, constitutions, and governing bodies, but on daily life in a different world, with new values and structures of feeling, gender relations, and so on. Such visions seemed essential to the struggle for human emancipation because they helped us to articulate what we understood by a qualitatively *different* society, something we often lost sight of in the midst of our day-to-day lives. These alternate visions were important because they reached beyond the restricted public of the already politicized and spoke to a wider audience which often seemed to no longer believe in the possibility of desirable or feasible alternatives to the fundamental insufficiency of the present.[8]

Here, I would like quickly to point to a few historical circumstances which might help to understand the specificity of this particular utopian development. For however predominant U.S. sf has been since the 1930s, there are other significant sf traditions: in Britain, France, Germany, Russia, and Japan. But this is not the case for the utopian revival of the 1970s which is almost exclusively a U.S. phenomenon.[9] Why is this so? The first part of an answer may lie in what is often called "American exceptionalism," a concept which refers to the fact, often noted by social scientists and historians, that unlike Canada, where I live, or most European countries, there is virtually no Left tradition in the U.S., no socialist or communist or even social-democratic parties, at least not in the sense that they play any significant electoral or extra-parliamentary role.[10] While I do not

---

8   This certainly influenced my teaching and critical writing in the 1980s, as summed up in my article "So We All Became Mothers."

9   The best-known exception – Monique Wittig's *Les Guérillères* – was written in France by an author who was soon to move to the U.S. While this experimental utopian fiction was little-known in the sf community, it was widely embraced by U.S. feminists – and much less so by feminists in France. See Anderson.

10   "American exceptionalism refers to the curious situation in which the United States is the only major industrial country of the twentieth century without the

think that this is the only or even the principle reason for the upsurge in utopian writing in the U.S. in the 1970s, I think that it is a factor that should be looked at in trying to understand why utopian writing emerged so strongly at this moment in American sf. In this way, it might be argued that it is the absence of a Left tradition which has made that utopian revival possible. Although Marxism can certainly be seen as a utopian philosophy of hope, it is important to remember that classical Marxist thought has often juxtaposed utopian thinking and writing to "true" political practice, as if the utopian was the impractical and unrealistic, a juxtaposition explicit in the title of Friedrich Engels's *Socialism Utopian and Scientific*. In these terms, Utopia is seen as a distraction from the urgent task of organizing the working class and of making a revolution. The absence, then, of a Left tradition, along with the vitality of sf and its ability to refract the present through the lens of the future may have contributed to the ability to think of alternatives without focusing very much on the transition, and on such practical questions as how we are to actually get to this new society.[11]

In today's bleak times, it is also important to remember that in the late 1960s and early 1970s there was a strong sense that things were changing for the better, hopes that were summed up in the title of Tom Moylan's book, *Demand the Impossible*, a title which was the second half of a slogan, "Be realistic, demand the impossible," taken from May 1968 in Paris, the most intense manifestation (in the developed countries at least) of that belief that the world was changing.[12]

---

presence of a significant socialist/social democratic and/or communist party in its polity" (Markovits and Hellerman 7).

11   In a complete study of this issue, one would also have to discuss the specificity of this utopian moment in terms of the particular nature of U.S. feminism. One should also mention in this context, the absence of historical thinking or awareness more generally, made worse or seemingly sanctioned by structuralism and postmodernism.

12   For an overview of this moment, see Jameson, "Periodizing the 1960s." There he reminds us of a number of other utopian developments in the "third" world beginning with the Bandung Conference, the Cuban and Algerian revolutions, and so on.

These unleashed utopian energies and hopes obviously had a lot to do with the upsurge in utopian writing at the time.

My discovery of the literary utopia and its importance and potential role in political action was hardly an isolated event: across North America, other students and scholars were making the same connection, and this led to some academics, with Sargent playing a leading role, to organize a scholarly association devoted to the study of Utopia, one that would investigate all of the various and many strands of the utopian tradition: not just the literary, but the political and historical, as well as the revival of utopian experiments in various communes and small communities in the 1960s.[13] The founding of the Society for Utopian Studies, in 1975, was followed by Sargent's launching of the journal *Utopian Studies*, which he edited from its inception in 1988 to 2004. I started attending the meetings of the Society in the early 1980s, and under Lyman's sometimes not-so-gentle prodding, I started to learn that there was already a significant utopian tradition, and that these recent literary utopias were not a completely new development.[14]

So what was my utopian method in all this? As I started to explain, it was posited on the conviction that these utopian novels had a role to play in political work, precisely as visions of an alternative – and "alternative" was for many of us a code word for socialism. That is to say, these novels provided us with a way of showing people that there *were* alternatives, as well as what those alternatives would look

13   For an explanation and description of the many strands of utopianism, see Sargent, "Three Faces."
14   The Society for Utopian Studies has always been an interdisciplinary organization – following Sargent's three interests – as well as a place where there seemed to be less competition than in the academy generally, and where there has always been support and encouragement. Like the women's movement that gave it a kick start in the 1970s, the Society tries to live out its utopian ideals in its practice as a scholarly group. This is also the place to mention the importance of the role of Moylan in the development and promotion of utopian ideas. I first met Moylan through sf and then shortly afterwards at the MLG's summer institute (in St. Cloud Minnesota); and *Demand The Impossible* stands as the most important articulation of these positions – of what I saw as the union of a Marxist politics and of an involvement in sf, along with the realization that feminism had introduced a new, utopian dimension into sf.

and feel like – as opposed to the perceived abstractions and tired slogans of much traditional Left discourse. In fact, they could even serve as a place for outlining and debating the forms and structures of the new society we were interested in building. Thus, despite my own supposed theoretical sophistication, I and many others looked at these novels "literally," at least in the sense of how they analyzed and dealt with the contemporary situation, how they imagined the new society would emerge, and what that society would look like. The literal-mindedness of some critics – myself included – often went further than that of the authors themselves; and in this context, one could perhaps map the principal authors of the utopian revival on a spectrum, from "literalists," like Callenbach, to the more "critical" utopians – those writers who, in their awareness of the utopian trad-ition, distanced themselves from it as a way of trying to moderate and qualify this tendency towards reading the work as a literal repre-sentation of an alternative – and I am thinking especially of Le Guin's *The Dispossessed* and Delany's *Triton*.

The literal approach involved not only the discussion of the structure and forms of the new society, but the question of the "transition" as well: of how we go from here to there. The classic example of the question of the transition in the literary utopia can be seen in William Morris's *News from Nowhere*, which constitutes a critique of the peaceful transition to socialism portrayed in Edward Bellamy's *Looking Backward*, a changeover which is unrealistic and naïve since it implies that those in power would voluntarily give up their privileges. This is an important component of the Marxist critique of utopianism which often dismisses utopian visions as the "imaginary resolution" of real problems, a wish-fulfillment that di-verts our energies from working for change to dreaming about it. In sf terms, this critique could also be seen as referring to the familiar trope of the "frontier" of so much U.S. cultural production – visions of an empty and "untamed" American West, or of an uninhabited planet, just waiting to be discovered and developed.[15] At the other end of the spectrum of critiques of the transition, the fervor of the 1960s also produced those who argued that such a transformation could come

15   On this subject, see Mogen.

from within, through a change in consciousness, as summed up in Charles Reich's best seller, *The Greening of America*.[16]

To sum up this utopian moment, then, if we see writing, or any artistic production, more generally as what Fredric Jameson has called – in his Sartrean mode – a "verbal thrust," a response and reaction to historical events as much as to the writing of others, we can appreciate more fully the remarkable exchange of utopian ideas and visions throughout the 1970s among a number of writers and readers. Obviously (and in hindsight, predictably) this writing did not and could not in itself produce those new societies we so longed for; but they did stir up reactions and responses, as did the calls for equity and the larger advances of feminist and movement politics more generally throughout the decade. Positive responses as well as negative ones, the latter in the form of a backlash – one that is still with us today. This is without doubt the case in the larger, historical sphere: as marked by the elections of Margaret Thatcher and Ronald Reagan, the rise of neo-liberalism, and the attacks on the many gains in the areas of equity and equal opportunity (all of which are chronicled, for example, by Susan Faludi in her book *Backlash*). Within sf, there was as well a reaction against some of this writing, and a decline in the writing of utopias.[17]

Thus, we come to a third *moment*, that of a retreat or, at least of a rethinking of the utopian optimism I have been describing. This has produced several different reactions or ways of negotiating this shift, (one that is the focus of Moylan's *Scraps of the Untainted Sky*). I will attempt to address these differing, but not contradictory, positions on Utopia and utopian methodology by introducing the work of my next interlocutor, one who has been there since the beginning but whose ideas about Utopia it has taken me longer to understand and in-corporate into my own practice. (As you may have gathered, these

---

16 This is also relevant to the critique of *Tel quel* which believed (at least for a while) that changing our perceptions would change the world. The best sf novel on this theme is Ian Watson's *The Embedding*. I tend to side with Marx's reply to these positions, in the Preface to *The Critique of Political Economy*: "It is not the consciousness of men that determines their being, but, on the contrary, their social being that determines their consciousness" (Marx and Engels 182).

17 For the impact of this backlash on sf, see Fitting, "The Turn From Utopia."

interlocutors have all been or become friends, and this particular friendship is the oldest of them all, going back forty years.) Jameson and I have been talking about Marxism, sf, and Utopia for some time; and while our positions and focus may seem somewhat different, his work has been essential to my own approach and development.[18]

While there have been other, more sophisticated applications and descriptions of Jameson's theory of Utopia, I will only mention briefly three ideas I have taken from his work and which definitely do not exhaust his writing on Utopia.[19] Jameson's most fruitful and troubling intervention lies in his proposal that the literary utopia should not be seen as the representation of an ideal society, but as a reflection on "our own incapacity to conceive [utopia] in the first place" ("World Reduction in Le Guin" 230); or, as he wrote a few years later, our "constitutional inability to imagine Utopia itself, [is not due] to any individual failure of imagination but is the result of the systemic, cultural, and ideological closure of which we are all in one way or another prisoners" ("Progress versus Utopia" 153). I take this point in what I consider its classical Marxist sense, as a gentle reminder of the illusion or trap of Utopia:

> the utopian text [...] hold[s] out for us the vivid lesson of what we cannot imagine [...] our own incapacity to see beyond [our] epoch and its ideological closures. This is the correlative, the obverse and the negative side, of Marx's great dictum [...] namely that the world has long since dreamed of something of which it needs only to become conscious for it to possess it in reality (*Seeds of Time* 75).

One way to attempt to summarize Jameson's argument is to say that the imagined utopia in the literary work is limited to a kind of reformism since we can only conceive of what is already there, making the utopia what Phil Wegner (following Ernst Bloch) has called a *repairing* of the present rather than its transformation. In this same

---

18   I am not sure I can claim to have introduced him to sf and utopia, since he had a student in the early 1970s who went on to become one of the most important contemporary sf/utopian writers – Kim Stanley Robinson. Jameson's influence on Robinson is also crucial since Robinson began his Ph.D. thesis on Dick with Jameson before he moved to Yale. See Fitting, "The Concept of Utopia."

19   See Fitting and Moylan, "Special Section on the Work of Fredric Jameson."

vein, I should mention that, in other places, Jameson has stressed that rather than seeing them as representations of a future society, one should read these literary utopias as calling attention to and identifying what in our society needs to be changed.

The second point I take from Jameson comes from his interest in popular culture and the observation that there is always a utopian dimension or core in the most degraded popular works as well as in even the most oppressive and hateful forms of consciousness. In *The Political Unconscious*, like Bloch before him, Jameson extended the concept of Utopia, explaining that the deepest appeal of even the most reprehensible forms of class consciousness lay in a buried utopian vision of "a specific historical and class form of collective unity" (291):

> all class consciousness – or in other words, all ideology in the strongest sense, including the most exclusive forms of ruling-class consciousness just as much as that of oppositional or oppressed classes – is in its very nature Utopian (289).

Here I think that he is reminding us that while these anticipatory utopian instances are to be found in some unlikely places, these utopian yearnings are not necessarily positive or (even) transformative; and it is up to critics to explain and draw these distinctions, as well as to detect and describe the utopian mechanisms to be found in the cultural productions which surround us. It is up to us to recognize and foster utopian desire, and to develop and encourage its critical edge. This dialectic of "ideology and utopia" at work in cultural texts has long influenced my own readings of sf. At the same time, the concern for tracking the utopian has led me beyond the literary utopias of the 1970s in a variety of directions, to the utopian tradition of the eighteenth and nineteenth centuries, to the generic possibility of right-wing utopias, to the question of the reading pleasure of utopia, and especially to film – in the question of what a utopian film would be as well as to asking how this dialectic works in popular film.

The third suggestion that I have taken from the work of Jameson is his presentation of "dialectical thinking" in *Marxism and Form*, where he argued (as Althusser did for ideology) that Utopia has a history and that its function changes and evolves. This stress on the historicity of concepts and strategies informs all of his subsequent work and is essential for understanding and tracking the dialectic of "ideology and utopia" I mentioned above:

> for where in the older society (as in Marx's classic analysis) Utopian thought represented a diversion of revolutionary energy into idle wish-fulfilments and imaginary satisfactions, in our own time the very nature of the utopian concept has undergone a dialectical reversal. Now it is practical thinking which everywhere represents a capitulation to the system itself, and stands as a testimony to the power of that system to transform even its adversaries into its own mirror image. The Utopian idea, on the contrary, keeps alive the possibility of a world qualitatively distinct from this one and takes the form of a stubborn negation of all that is (*Marxism and Form* 110–11).

Those words were written in 1971, even before the utopian revival which was only just beginning; and I shall return to the question of the timeliness of Utopia in a moment.

Each of the points I have taken from Jameson and described brings us back, I think, to a paradoxical reaffirmation of the need for utopian imagining, even as these visions and descriptions are not meant to be taken literally, but – to put it crudely – to remind us of all that we lack and are denied by the crushing mechanisms of capital. Where does this leave us? What place is there for utopian studies or Utopia itself in these increasingly dark times? I think that my own evolution – from a more *positive* view of Utopia (as models or visions) to a more (Jameson influenced) dialectical and *negative* view (Utopia as a reminder of what we do not have) – is but one way of reacting to the present situation. To conclude, then, I want to review what I see as some of the different ways of negotiating the present.

First of all, it is important to emphasize that utopian writing did not end with the elections of Thatcher and Reagan, that however powerful the backlash, inside the sf community and in the outside world, some writers continued, and continue today, to use the utopian form. There are, however, differences in post-1980 utopian fiction that acknowledge these changed times. This change is demonstrated for me by two novels by Piercy. In the first, *Woman on the Edge of Time*, we can see a classic 1970s utopia, one in which there is still a struggle going on to ensure and defend the utopian future, but one in which, nonetheless, most of our planet constitutes a utopian society, while the corporate forces which are attacking the utopia are mostly confined to a satellite from which they launch their attacks. This situation is reversed in her 1991 novel, *He, She and It* (U.K. title, *Body of Glass*), in which the earth is a bleak, corporate dystopia, a wasted and plundered planet, and where the events of the novel are centered around a small utopian enclave which is threatened on all sides.[20]

Another form of utopian writing can be seen in the *Mars* trilogy of Kim Stanley Robinson (*Red Mars*, *Green Mars*, and *Blue Mars*). If Piercy's later utopia was characterized by a change from the depiction of a utopian world under attack (and struggling to come into being) to a utopian enclave in the midst of a larger dystopian world, Robinson's Martian novels focus on the transition itself – hundreds of pages of meetings, debate, and discussions about what the new world of Mars should be: discussions involving the various stakeholders, investors, corporations, states, as well as those who are attempting to transfer an ideology or a world-view, or to build a better world, or to guarantee a profit, or to bring about the triumph of or more simply the survival of their way of life, or to protect some "original" Mars, or to avoid the mistakes made on Earth, and so on. In this way, we are given some two-hundred years of Martian history – as expressed in the progression of the three titles: beginning with the adventures of the first men and women to arrive, through the gradual transformation of the red desert planet into a world closer to our own, with green fields and forests and then dotted with blue lakes and seas. In the beginning Mars is not yet a utopia, and humans can only live there with great

---

20   In chapter 15 of *Woman on the Edge of Time*, Piercy describes an alternative to the utopia of Mattapoisett: a terrible, bleak future in which sexism and capitalism have flourished. In *Woman*, that brief nightmarish chapter was limited to Gildina's windowless 126th floor apartment. A surgically "built-up contracty [...] [Gildina was born] with brain deficiencies from protein scarcity in foetus and early childhood" (*Woman* 299). It is from this sex-slave that we learn of life in a toxic, polluted future, where the rich live segregated from the diseased and undernourished masses who to survive were often forced to sell their bodies, or their organs. This dystopian vision is the basis for the future of 2059 in *He, She and It*.

difficulty. It is only in the third novel, *Blue Mars*, that this flash of recognition must vary for different readers, when one realizes, in the midst of the description of one activity or another, someone hang-gliding or a shared meal, that this is in fact a utopia and that Utopia is a process rather than a realized goal.[21]

When coming to terms with this apparent retreat from the utopian optimism of the 1960s and 1970s, it is also important to remember that, however inhospitable the present moment is to Utopia, it is essential to defend and maintain what we have accomplished in the past few decades, and to continue that scholarly and critical work. This is exemplified in Sargent's ongoing scholarly projects: his bibliography, his studies of national character and Utopia, as well as his questions about the existence of non-western utopias, his work for the Society for Utopian Studies, the journal, and so on: all this in preparation for better times.[22]

Another way of negotiating the present can be found in the work of Raffaella Baccolini and Moylan on the "critical dystopia" – research which, in these terms, can be seen as a means of recovering the utopian dimension from what has perhaps too quickly been seen as the abandonment of Utopia. This involves distinguishing those works which simply assume and use a dystopian background as a setting for their adventures (most famously this is a critique often made of cyberpunk) from the militant pessimism of other works which reject resignation even as they attempt to confront the present. However dystopian the worlds they portray, these latter dystopias display some critical awareness of the present, as they attempt to explain how this dystopia came about rather than simply taking it for granted; and these

---

21 In fact, this pause on the threshold of utopia, as it were, is typical of a number of 1980s utopias, or at least of their titles, and they might be summed up as "liminal" utopias, societies on the verge of becoming utopia, with titles like: Pamela Sargent's *The Shore of Women*; Joan Slonczewski's *A Door into Ocean*; and Sherri Tepper's *The Gate to Women's Country*. See also Wegner, as well as Jameson's reading of the *Mars* trilogy, "'If I find one good city I will spare the man.'"

22 This basic scholarly position is essential, for without it we are doomed to begin over, like the people of the planet Lagash in Isaac Asimov's story "Nightfall," or Walter Miller Jr.'s *A Canticle for Leibowitz*.

works, too, also hold out some utopian hope. The model of the critical dystopia in this sense is Margaret Atwood's 1985 *The Handmaid's Tale*, for it holds out the prospect of hope (Offred's escape, and the novel's Epilogue, in a distant future in which Gilead is nothing more than the subject of historical research).[23]

These attempts to track the utopian in dystopian times point more generally to the question of refocusing the discussion of Utopia, beginning with questions about Utopia and national identity and whether utopianism is limited to the western tradition. But I think, too, that it may be that new utopian struggles and the seeds of change are emerging from outside the developed countries of the west. This concern has taken me most recently to the World Social Forum (WSF) in Porto Alegre (whose slogan is "Another World Is Possible"). With all its flaws and limitations, the WSF is an alternative utopian vision, one which not only gives voice and hope to the voiceless, to groups like that of landless workers (MST) or the Via Campesina network of peasant organizations from around the world; indeed, the WSF has developed into a global association working alongside existing state forms, but without seeking to reproduce or replace them. I do not have time here to describe the range and activities of this convening of extra-governmental groups opposed to neo-liberalism and committed to an alternative globalization, but it too constitutes a significant utopian vision which has taken an extra-literary form.

At the same time, this looking outside the developed countries in the context of the formulation of an alternative globalization is a promising new way of considering world events, one which is summed up for me in Michael Hardt and Tony Negri's political treatise *Empire* from which I draw, perhaps too simplistically, some important lines of reasoning. Rather than simply denouncing or attacking globalization – in the name of a threatened nation-state, for instance – Hardt and Negri's book develops some very relevant

---

23   For a discussion of *The Handmaid's Tale*, see Fitting, "The Turn from Utopia."
     In recent work, I have tried to find such positive dimensions in contemporary
     dystopian film, by juxtaposing the "false" escapes of the heroes of *Dark City*
     and *The Truman Show* to the more complex situations in *The Matrix* and
     especially *Pleasantville*. See Fitting, "Unmasking The Real?"

themes, beginning with the vision of a global utopia. Summarizing quickly, I take their concept of the *multitude*, as reminding us that social transformation may come from actors from outside the developed world and/or from outside the proletariat as traditionally defined.[24] Significantly, in these utopian terms their book concludes with three demands which not only reiterate many of the visions of the utopias of the 1970s, but which – in true utopian fashion – are impossible under a market economy: the demand for the realization of these all too reasonable and necessary goals would spell the end of capitalism. These three demands are: global citizenship, a social wage, and the "the right of reappropriation," a broadening of the familiar call for the seizing of the means of production, which now includes a full range of human activities and potential.

In the above, I have tried to outline some avenues of research and of struggle for utopian scholars and for those committed to those new visions in what may seem like especially discouraging times. In this context, Jameson – more than thirty years ago – gave some very good reasons for the continuing relevance of Utopia:

> [There is] not a crisis in Marxist science [but] in Marxist ideology. If ideology [...] is a vision of the future that grips the masses, we have to admit that, save in a few ongoing collective experiments [...] no Marxist or Socialist party or movement anywhere has the slightest conception of what socialism or communism as a social system ought to be and can be expected to look like. That vision will not be purely economic. [...] It is, as well, supremely social and cultural, involving the task of trying to imagine how a society without hierarchy, a society of free people, a society that has at once repudiated the economic mechanisms of the market, can possibly cohere ("Cognitive Mapping" 355).

Whereas, in the earlier quotation (from *Marxism and Form*) it was the appeal to "practical thinking" that represented the closing down of thinking about a better world, today the rejection of alternatives is even more insidious and dangerous, as it masquerades under the very banner of socialism, under which, we are told, we must be prepared to accommodate and accept capitalism. With the fall of the Soviet Union and the apparent triumph of a single mighty world power, progres-

---

24   This concept was expanded in their subsequent book, *Multitude*.

sives are told that there is only one alternative, the so-called "third way," in which the market economy can somehow be disconnected from the social sphere. Utopia stands, in Jameson's terms, as a fierce rejection of this bogus option along with the reminder that there still are alternatives.

Works Cited

Althusser, Louis. "Ideology and Ideological State Apparatuses." *Lenin and Philosophy, and Other Essays*. London: New Left Books, 1971. 136–70.

Anderson, Kristine. "Encyclopedic Dictionary as Utopian Genre: Two Feminist Ventures." *Utopian Studies* 2.1–2 (1991): 124–30.

Atwood, Margaret. *The Handmaid's Tale*. Toronto: McClelland, 1985.

Bloch, Ernst. *The Principle of Hope*. Trans. Neville Plaice, Stephen Plaice, and Paul Knight. 3 Vols. Oxford: Blackwell, 1986.

Eagleton, Terry. *Marxism and Literary Criticism*. London: Methuen, 1983.

—— *Ideology: An Introduction*. London: Verso, 1991.

Faludi, Susan. *Backlash: The Undeclared War Against American Women*. New York: Anchor, 1992.

Fitting, Peter. "The Concept of Utopia in the Work of Fredric Jameson." *Utopian Studies* 9.2 (Fall 1998): 8–17.

—— "Ideological Foreclosure and Utopian Discourse." *Sociocriticism* 7 (1988): 11–25.

—— "The Modern Anglo-American SF Novel: Utopian Longing and Capitalist Cooptation." *Science-Fiction Studies* 6.1 (1979): 59–76.

—— "Reality as Ideological Construct: A Reading of Five Novels by P.K. Dick." *Science-Fiction Studies* 10 (1983): 219–36.

—— "'So We All Became Mothers': New Roles for Men in Recent Utopian Fiction." *Science-Fiction Studies* 12 (1985): 156–83.

—— "The Turn from Utopia in Recent Feminist Fiction." *Feminism, Utopia, and Narrative*. Ed. Libby Falk Jones and Sarah Webster Goodwin. Knoxville: Tennessee University Press, 1990. 141–58.

—— "*Ubik*: The Deconstruction of Bourgeois SF." *Science-Fiction Studies* 2 (1975): 47–54.

—— "Unmasking The Real? Critique and Utopia in Recent SF Films." *Dark Horizons: Science Fiction and the Dystopian Imagination*. Ed. Raffaella Baccolini and Tom Moylan. New York: Routledge, 2003. 155–66.

Fitting, Peter, and Tom Moylan (eds.). "Special Section on The Work of Fredric Jameson." *Utopian Studies* 9.2 (1998): 1–78.

ffrench, Patrick. *The Time of Theory: A History of Tel quel.* Oxford: Clarendon, 1995.

ffrench, Patrick, and Roland-Francois Lack (eds.). *The Tel quel Reader.* London and New York: Routledge, 1998.

Hardt, Michael, and Antonio Negri. *Empire.* Cambridge, Massachusetts: Harvard University Press, 2000.

—— *Multitude: War and Democracy in the Age of Empire.* New York: Penguin, 2004.

Jameson, Fredric. "Cognitive Mapping." *Marxism and the Interpretation of Culture.* Ed. Cary Nelson and Lawrence Grossberg. Urbana: University of Illinois Press, 1988, 347–60.

—— "The Ideology of the Text." *The Ideologies of Theory.* Minneapolis: Minnesota University Press, 1988. vol.1. 17–71.

—— "'If I find one good city I will spare the man': Realism and Utopia in Kim Stanley Robinson's *Mars Trilogy.*" *Learning from Other Worlds: Estrangement, Cognition and the Politics of Science Fiction and Utopia.* Ed. Patrick Parrinder. Liverpool: Liverpool University Press, 2000: 208–32.

—— *Marxism and Form.* Princeton: Princeton University Press, 1971.

—— "Periodizing the 60s." *The Ideologies of Theory.* Minneapolis: Minnesota University Press, 1988. vol.2: 178–210.

—— *The Political Unconscious.* Ithaca: Cornell University Press, 1981.

—— "Progress Versus Utopia: or, Can We Imagine the Future?" *Science-Fiction Studies* 27 (1982): 13–92.

—— *Postmodernism: Or, the Cultural Logic of Late Capitalism.* London: Verso, 1991.

—— "Reification and Utopia in Mass Culture." *Social Text* 1 (1979): 130–48.

—— *The Seeds of Time.* New York: Columbia University Press, 1994.

—— "World Reduction in Le Guin: The Emergence of Utopian Narrative." *Science-Fiction Studies* 7 (1975): 221–30.

Kauppi, Niilo. *The Making of an Avant-guard: Tel quel.* New York: Mouton De Gruyter, 1994.

Le Guin, Ursula K. *The Left Hand of Darkness.* New York: Ace, 1969.

Markovits, Andrei S., and Steven L. Hellerman. *Offside: Soccer and American Exceptionalism.* Princeton: Princeton University Press, 2001.

Marx, Karl, and Frederick Engels. *Selected Works.* Moscow: Progress, 1968.

Marx-Scouras, Danielle. *The Cultural Politics of Tel quel: Literature and the Left in the Wake of Engagement.* University Park: Pennsylvania State University Press, 1996.

Merril, Judith. "What Do You Mean: Science? Fiction?" *SF: The Other Side of Realism.* Ed. Thomas Clareson. Bowling Green: Bowling Green University Press, 1971.

Mogen, David. *Wilderness Visions: The Western Theme in Science Fiction Literature*. San Bernardino: Borgo, 1994.

Moylan, Tom. *Demand the Impossible: Science Fiction and the Utopian Imagination*. London: Methuen, 1986.

—— *Scraps of the Untainted Sky: Science Fiction, Utopia, Dystopia*. Boulder: Westview, 2000.

Piercy, Marge. *He, She and It*. New York: Knopf, 1991.

—— *Woman on the Edge of Time*. New York: Knopf, 1976.

Robinson, Kim Stanley. *Blue Mars*. New York: Harper Collins, 1996.

—— *Green Mars*. New York: Harper Collins, 1993.

—— *Red Mars*. New York: Harper Collins, 1992.

Sargent, Lyman Tower. "The Three Faces of Utopianism Revisited." *Utopian Studies* 5.1 (1994): 1–37.

—— "Utopianism and the Creation of New Zealand National Identity." *Utopian Studies* 12.1 (2001): 1–18.

Suvin, Darko. *Metamorphoses of Science Fiction*. New Haven: Yale University Press, 1979.

Wegner, Phillip E. *Imaginary Communities: Utopia, the Nation and The Spatial Histories of Modernity*. Berkeley: University of California Press, 2002.

HODA M. ZAKI

New Spaces for Utopian Politics: Theorizing About Identity, Community, and the World Conference Against Racism

It's terrific, there is a great deal of momentum with what's happening in Latin America being shared with Asia, being shared with Africa and Europe. Economists, environmentalists, human rights activists, development people, are for the first time sharing across regions and I think that this is the beginning of an alternative power system which will increasingly oblige governments to implement in this century the legal commitments drafted and refined in the last half of the 20th century.
Mary Robinson, "Making 'global'"

The more revolutionary the social transformation contemplated, the more Daniel could make sense of the radically unrecognizable in his own life. [...] As she spoke of cross-border organizing, the borders Daniel himself had crossed became part of a common atlas. He was part of the same process which involved all the other people in the hall, none of whom were where they'd started life either.
Robert Newman, *The Fountain at the Center of the World*

All writing is autobiographical, although the connections between lived experience, action, and the printed page are complicated and at times difficult to discern. In this essay, I will weave the personal and the political with the theoretical and the global, ending with an analysis of the 2001 World Conference Against Racism (WCAR).[1]

I wish I could say that I have loved utopian literature since I was a child, and that its imagined worlds provided relief in this heartless world. The truth is that I backed into utopian theory and then into its literature as a way to understand an early fascination with science fiction (sf). I was born in 1950 to Egyptian diplomats. Although I was an Egyptian citizen, and a subject of an Egyptian king, I was also a subject of the British Empire. Even after 1952, when Egypt underwent an almost bloodless revolution and gained its sovereignty, the cultural connections that bound the former colony to its British mother-country remained firmly in place for many years for those of us who were westernized and middle class. So it was that in growing up in North Africa and the Middle East, on the cultural margins of the west, we of the middle classes in the former colonies continued to read the works of Enid Blyton, Agatha Christie, and magazines such as *Argosy*. And it was in the pages of *Argosy* that I first encountered, and fell in love with, sf. Many years later, in the mid-1970s, when I was enrolled in a Ph.D. program in political science, and it was time to decide on what to focus on, I decided to focus on sf.

Growing up for part of my childhood in post-1952 Egypt also meant that I had a long experience of living in a country that had established its constitution and the ideology of its ruling party along certain utopian lines, that of Nasserism, Arab Socialism, and Pan-Arab and Pan-African unity. This political and economic system tried, how-ever imperfectly, to abolish the legacy of colonialism and its attendant inequalities. I was used to living under a one-party system, to using ration cards, to supporting African freedom fighters and students from colonized African countries, to living in subsidized housing and with policies of rent control, to having free education from primary school to post-graduate university levels, and the like. These features felt normal and were justified ideologically, and the rights of national

1   I want to acknowledge the support of Alex Willingham, Birgit Van Hout, Carol Kolmerten, and Lyman Tower Sargent who read versions of this essay, and Ruth Levitas, for her feedback and suggestions. A Hood College Board of Associates grant in 2002 supported some of this research.

entities to experiment with their social institutions was confirmed even more upon my living in Yugoslavia for two years in the mid-1950s. Thus, when I encountered some of these socialist features later in Utopia, I did not deem them as problematic.

My area is political thought, which of all the areas in political science is the most expansive in terms of its terrain, and most closely aligned to the study of literature. Within it, utopian thought is a time-honored though marginalized tradition, and using it allowed me to legitimize my project in popular culture. I selected characteristics of traditional utopian thought that, for me, represented its essential qualities and applied them to the genre of sf to determine whether utopianism was alive and well in popular culture. Utopian thought, I determined, fulfilled four functions: descriptive, critical, exhortative, and anticipatory. The theorists I used to construct my argument included Karl Marx and Friedrich Engels, Karl Mannheim, Herbert Marcuse, and Ernst Bloch. From that project, I moved on to examine black- and lesbian-authored sf. Did these authors represent politics in ways that were more radical than mainstream sf, I wondered? How did their politics differ, if at all, from the writings of other authors of sf? I was able to answer these questions by examining the contents of their utopias and the ways they imagined social change would take place. In terms of Ruth Levitas's classification of how utopias are defined and used, I would fit squarely in her "content" box since the formal attributes of utopias were of little concern to me.[2]

In the 1980s, like many others, I was looking for radical politics in unexpected places, and utopian thought (Bloch was especially useful in this regard) was a tool that allowed me to do that. After spending almost a decade on sf, I became a little impatient and disenchanted with it, and I moved on to study protest movements and other sources of dissent and social justice and their ideals. I focused on the political thought of individuals active in the civil rights movement in the United States. The leadership provided by black communities in their struggle for equality proved to be compelling, especially

2   Levitas has distinguished between three definitions of utopia: those that highlight its contents; those that examine its formal characteristics; and those that examine its social function.

the kinds of leadership that emerged from places other than the church, such as educational institutions. I was interested in the intersection of this form of activism with the institutional bases that provided the space for such action and thought. This intersection defined temporary, alternative political arenas for black Americans, who at that time were denied entry into mainstream spaces, such as the voting booth. I thought that I had put Utopia aside.

But as I examined the speeches and writings of the civil rights leader Alonzo G. Moron, the utopian elements of his writing, and the context within which he functioned, begged for further analysis. I resisted at first, but then relented. I allowed that educational institutions established after the Civil War in the U.S. South were utopian experiments both in terms of their mission – the education of freed people, who as the formerly enslaved were forbidden education, and their integration into society as full and equal citizens – and in terms of the communities that flourished within them. Perhaps, I thought, such educational institutions could be construed as utopian spaces and as forms of intentional communities.

So I stepped back into the utopian river, but a slightly different one. This time, I was interested in the community aspect of utopian thought. Utopian literature is both a direct and meta-commentary on community; critical of the author's own society, utopias describe ideals and promote solutions in fictive, and better, communities. They describe, model, rehearse, promote, and anticipate alternative communities. In the broadest sense of the word, utopian thought can be interpreted as an expression of longing for community. Finally, utopian literature can create communities in its various readers, who are bound by their experiences of reading the texts and, if converted, to its ideals.

My interest in community was shaped also by the politics of the times. In the U.S., in the civil rights litigation in the late twentieth century, the term "community of interest" had begun to be used by civil rights lawyers and their plaintiffs to argue for the construction of voting districts that would favor the election of minority candidates in an electoral system that was biased toward whites. Lawyers were arguing against a more conservative approach to the construction of these districts, which purported to draw their lines to encompass populations in spaces that were compact and contiguous, deemed to be more "natural," and not political. A small group of black social scientists and lawyers from the civil rights community began to meet on a regular basis to exchange ideas. From this exchange, it became apparent that a historical understanding of how community had been defined in recent social and political thought would be of help to the legal activists interested in promoting egalitarian voting rights. In response to this need, I wrote an article about the evolution of the definition of community (see Zaki).

Searching for unexpected sources of utopian thought in sf had been a search for sources of resistance to the status quo. My research on private educational institutions, which are non-profit organizations in the U.S., led me to examine the role of non-governmental organizations (NGOs) as possible sites for democratic action. This project prompted me to attend the 2001 Non-Governmental Organizational Forum of the World Conference Against Racism, and I returned from it feeling that something new and important was developing. It felt like I had visited Utopia for a week and, from the testimony I have read from the other attendees, others felt the same way. It then took over a year for me to forge the connection between the WCAR, Utopia, and community.

Since all writing is to some extent autobiographical, my attraction to fictive community can be partly explained by the nomadic existence that I led for all of my youth in a family that followed my father's career transfers to four continents. Yet I am not defining community in the fashion of communitarians, who include a moral content and a conservative slant to their ideas, since that definition has been used to promote conservative, pro-family policies in the U.S. and U.K. (see Burnett). I also think that my research interests mirror those of others of my generation and political leanings. For the study of Utopia has allowed us to merge an ethical component into our research and life work.

Immanuel Wallerstein says something along these lines when he links three usages of utopianism to three varieties of Marxism and three stages of development in the social sciences. He summarizes how social scientists have searched for methods of analysis after World War II. In this era of "a thousand Marxisms," there is no orthodoxy. It is a time when social scientists look for ways to engage with the world while rejecting scientism and visions of inexorable progress: "The Marxist utopia of the era of a thousand Marxisms is a utopia in search of itself," he states ("Marxism" 179). He tasks Utopia with the function of "illuminating historical choices rather than to presume to make them" (184). He also invents the word "utopistics" to substitute for utopian thinking, which he maintains has brought about disillusionment. Wallerstein defines utopistics as: "the sober, rational, and realistic evaluation of human social systems, the constraints on what they can be, and the zones open to human creativity" (*Utopistics* 1–2). As we search for method, resistance, and Utopia, I propose yet another place and another text in what I call "anti-globalization literature" where Utopia today is being created. To do so, I have to describe the evolution of community in the theoretical literature to demonstrate where Utopia and community are being used as ways to challenge and change the world today.

Theorizing About Community

Within academic circles the topic of community has long interested scholars from many disciplines, especially sociology, history, and political science. I approach community from my work with utopian thought in the context of political theory, but I am impressed with the immense cross-disciplinary implications involved in any inquiry into issues of community.

Theorizing about community follows the general rule that all theorizing is a reflection of, and a response to, material events occurring in the author's society and beyond. The efforts to establish alternative social groupings in the 1960s gave rise to scholarly interest in types of communities and to examining the origin, evolution, and character of the experimental communities established during this period. There was little agreement among scholars as to the salient characteristics of intentional communities, including what to call them. All the definitions before the 1980s are similar in that they included the geographical grounding of a group in a particular location and a shared way of life which usually countered values deemed significant in mainstream society. A second shared assumption was that membership in these communities was voluntary. Both of these axioms were to be challenged a few decades later.

The best-known work of the 1970s on intentional communities was sociologist Rosabeth Moss Kanter's *Commitment and Community: Communes and Utopias in Sociological Perspective*. Her definition of community is worth quoting:

> [They are] voluntary, value-based, communal social orders. Because members choose to join and choose to remain, conformity within the community is based on commitment [...] rather than on force or coercion. [...] A commune seeks self-determination, often making its own laws and refusing to obey some of those set by the larger society. It is identifiable as an entity, having both physical and social boundaries, for it has a physical location and a way of distinguishing between members and nonmembers. It intentionally implements a set of values. [...] Its primary end is an existence that matches the ideals. All other goals are secondary. [...] These ideals give rise to the key communal arrangement, the sharing of resources and finances.
>
> The utopian community may also be a centralized, coordinating organization, often combining all of life's functions under one roof. [...] The community may be at the same time a domestic unit (large, extended family), a production unit (farm or business), a political order (village or town), and a religious institution (2–3).

Utopian experiments, Kanter argued, were formed because individuals and groups made three types of critiques of mainstream society: religious, political-economic, and psychological.[3] Kanter focused on the mechanisms by which communities created commitments to the group on the part of their members, and she illustrated her points through case studies of utopian communities. Kanter's definition al-

---

3   These were roughly chronological with the major reasons for the formation of the thousands of U.S. social experiments. Thus, the earliest of such community-building experiments were religious; the second wave emerged with U.S. industrialization, roughly in the mid-1800s; and the third, largest, and greatest number of communities were being created at the very moment of her writing, the late 1960s and early 1970s (Kanter 3–7).

lowed her to include within the universe of utopian communities a variety of associations that had explicit missions of service toward a particular population. Often urban in nature, these communes were usually characterized by a strong leader and a sense of superiority on the part of their members. They also had a well-defined ideology and focused on education. Kanter and other analysts of alternative communities of the late 1960s and 1970s argued that these experiments were relevant to understanding dissent, desire, and change (see Case and Taylor).

More than twenty years later, political theorist Lyman Tower Sargent made another contribution to the definition of community. He took issue with Kanter for equating the success of utopian communities with their longevity. Sargent preferred to highlight the intentions of the founders and members of such communities when evaluating them. He sought to establish a link between intentional communities and communitarian thought. Although as many as nineteen terms have been used interchangeably to refer to utopian communities, such as "intentional communities" and "communitarian thought," and after noting that the sheer variety of intentional communities made it difficult to offer any definition that could encompass this universe, Sargent provided his own definition:

> I shall define intentional community as a group of five or more adults and their children, if any, who come from more than one nuclear family and who have chosen to live together to enhance their shared values or for some other mutually agreed upon purpose ("Three Faces" 13–15).

In defining community, Sargent foregrounded the element of intent. If a clearly discernible intent can be evidenced in the establishment of a group, then for Sargent such a group could be included within the realm of intentional communities: "the group must share some project, values, goal, vision, or what have you. The definition does not specify any of the content of what is shared" ("Three Faces" 10).

Sargent agreed with Kanter in that communities were finite and discrete entities, having "beginnings, a point of establishment (usually fairly easy to determine), a life, and, for most, a period of disintegration and an end point" ("Three Faces" 16). He offered a taxonomy of intentional societies of eight main categories, some of them re-ferring to geographical place, others defined in terms of intent, and some by their ideological origin. For Sargent, the taxonomy provided evidence of the link between utopian thought and its practice: the establishment of intentional communities. Sargent can be seen as a transitional figure in the evolution of the definition of community, for although he accepted the need for communities to be grounded in some locality, his stress on intentionality allowed him to include groups whose members did not live in the same place, "but [who] continued to think of themselves as a community" ("Three Faces" 15).

In the mid 1980s, a sharp turn took place in the study of community. What was once the province of sociologists and political scientists became a highly interdisciplinary enterprise. I date the new beginning to 1983, with the publication of two works. The first was *The Invention of Tradition*, edited by Eric Hobsbawm and Terence Ranger. Hobsbawm defined "invented tradition" to:

> mean a set of practices, normally governed by overtly or tacitly accepted rules and of a ritual or symbolic nature, which seek to inculcate certain values and norms of behavior by repetition, which automatically implies continuity with the past (1).

Hobsbawm demystified "traditions," many of which, although they appeared to be old, were often new and sometimes invented. Of particular interest is the application of Hobsbawm's ideas to the devel-opment of nationalism and the nation. Sometimes, Hobsbawm noted, the development of nationalism was so new, that "existing customary traditional practices – folksong, physical contests, marksmanship – were modified, ritualized and industrialized for the new national pur-poses" (6). Under other conditions, even the historical antecedent was invented. Hobsbawm identified three, not necessarily distinct, types of invented traditions that emerged since the Industrial Revolution:

> a) those establishing or symbolizing social cohesion or the membership of groups, real or artificial communities, b) those establishing or legitimizing in-stitutions, status or relations of authority, and c) those whose main purpose was socialization, the inculcation of beliefs, value systems and conventions of be-havior (9).

Thus, he pointed to the ways in which "traditions" have been put to use as mechanisms to create community and power, and legitimate it with the patina of age; and he characterized the nation state, its symbols, and the emotions it generated as "exercises in social engineering" (13).

Hobsbawm's invitation to examine the invented nature of the nation-state community was taken up by Benedict Anderson in *Imagined Communities*, published in the same year. Anderson examined the rise of nationalism in the eighteenth century in the New World and its subsequent spread to Europe. Of particular importance were the interconnections between print-capitalism, language, and élite behavior in the Americas. For Anderson, nationalism first emerged when nationalist leaders used "textual communities" created from print journalism and increasing rates of literacy to build new groups linked by language. A common language alone could not create community, said Anderson, but "textual communities" allowed nationalist élites to create a sense of national unity where none had existed before. The first to do so were "Creole" élites in South America, frustrated at their denial of social mobility by Spain's rulers. Anderson's work discussed nationalism as an ideology designed and created by élites who wanted to create positions of power for themselves and their class. This view of nationalism runs counter to its self-understanding, which maintains that nationalism evolved naturally from the decline of the Roman Empire and feudalism. Thus, Anderson's work denaturalized nationalism and separated it from the pillars of shared culture, language, history, geography. Anderson's work extended Hobsbawm's ideas of invented tradition to posit that a national community is an imagined and created community whose members function as though they know, and are related, to each other.

This interrogation of the notion of a national community raises difficult issues. If true, then it can be said that the creation of the nation-state was also not a voluntary act for those who lived within its borders. The nation-state has served to impose and, in some instances, obliterate sub-national loyalties and identities. This imposition is being enacted again on many fronts in the western world and the European Union, as we shall see later.

Philip Abbott's *Seeking Many Inventions: The Idea of Community in America* is provocative on the topic of community in the U.S. Abbott, a political scientist, states that Americans have not rejected but have experimented and created new forms of community. He calls these new forms "social inventions" and looks at five such fluid communities in popular culture: the telephone, which created electronic neighborhoods; the penitentiary, which spawned a number of social welfare groups dedicated to making penitentiaries institutionalize their differing and contentious philosophies; the automobile, which engendered the creation of motels and "leisure communities"; revival camps; and the quilting bee. Abbott believes that humans are ingenious in their ability to create new forms of community. What is new about these "instant communities" is that they "not only disregard geographic organization but in some cases defy any conception of natural space" (164). They engender new bonds between people other than familial, and use social space in new ways (165–6). Furthermore, they share a number of characteristics, including fragility and specificity of purpose: "most new invented communities in America do not attempt to create whole new societies. They are [...] makeshift inventions designed to provide temporary support for people" (175). Abbott's work makes it possible to define community in ways that go beyond looking at a common terrain as necessary and to define community in terms that are fragile, fleeting, imaginary, and bounded by common interests.

More recently, cultural studies and American studies have been two sites where work on community, nationalism, race, and identity similar to Abbott's have appeared. In 1998, the president of the American Studies Association, Janice Radway, discussed recent developments in the study of identity, culture, and geography. What was important is not only the content of her talk, but the fact that she was urging the members to pursue these new lines of inquiry, suggesting that these formulations of community had begun to make considerable headway. Radway characterized the more traditional approach to identity as essentializing. Sub-national identities were usually seen as based upon some immutable aspect, such as race, and were seen as secondary, and even antagonistic to, the national community (9). She welcomed recent approaches taken by some scholars, which she saw as sharply different. These approaches interpreted U.S. nationalism as historically contingent and dependent upon élites who defined this imagined community in relational terms, i.e., in ways that excluded certain groups and privileged others (9–10). Radway also highlighted newer work on culture and geography. This work did not take geography or culture as organic, homogeneous, or fixed, but rather as tied to politics and its exercise. The contributions of Border and Chicano/ Chicana studies was especially noted.[4] Just as race, identity, and culture are changing and inherently unstable notions, so the study of geography and space follows the same logic.

It is possible to speculate about the origin of these views on community. Certainly, technological developments such as the internet have given rise to new ways for individuals to connect with one another. Scholars are divided on the issue of whether these new ways can replace the functions of the older forms of association (see Wu Song). However, it also could be hypothesized that globalization has reordered space in ways that have challenged traditional accounts of it. Academics have responded by using space as an analytical category in order to understand this reorganization at a global level (see Cacho). Along with these changes, the very definition of community has become even more destabilized. The politics of community-building have therefore been exposed in new ways and applied to venerable institutions. This leaves us with a clearer understanding of the critical role played by imagination and politics in the formation of global, national, and sub-national communities.

---

4   For instance, Radway pointed to the notion developed by some on how living in border zones generates a point of view that is called by some "inbetweenness" (13). Usually this has been designated as a perspective that results from living "between" two or more cultures. The newer work, however, sees this condition as one generated by the dissonance individuals sense from the competition among, and the differences in power between, the various communities in which they live. These differences in power relationships are prior, and primary, and give rise to a sense of alterity, of difference. Put another way, it is the unequal distribution of power between communities that creates a difference in perspective amongst groups of people, and not a clash of cultures. Radway offers extensive documentation of the advances made in these areas.

The groundwork has thus been laid to consider many sorts of associations as forms of community. I now want to describe one global, anti-racist community that existed for ten days in Durban, South Africa.

The World Conference Against Racism

Racial discrimination has been a topic of deep concern to the international community for decades, and it has been the focus of three United Nations-sponsored conferences and many declarations.[5] The third UN-sponsored World Conference Against Racism was held over a two-week span in late August 2001, in Durban, South Africa. Choosing to hold the conference there was a significant and celebratory decision. Long a symbol of extreme racial oppression, South Africa had become, with the establishment of majority rule, a progressive democracy.

This UN-sponsored conference was actually composed of three parallel conferences: the first was an international Youth Summit; the second was the NGO Forum of the World Conference Against Racism, Racial Discrimination, Xenophobia, and Related Intolerance; and the third was composed of the world's governmental leadership, which met as the Third World Conference Against Racism, Racial

---

5   The first two world conferences on racism were held in 1973 and 1983 in Geneva, Switzerland, and focused primarily upon the ways to eradicate racial discrimination in South Africa, where the ideology of apartheid, a comprehensive national policy of racial separation, was the doctrine of the ruling minority party. In 1963 the UN adopted the "Declaration on the Elimination of All Forms of Racial Discrimination," in which it declared that racial discrimination violated the principles of the UN Charter. Almost ten years later, the UN General Assembly designated 1971 as the International Year to Combat Racism and Racial Discrimination, and specified that the next three decades, from 1973 to 2001, should be focused on the elimination of racism. The final year of the third decade, 2001, was named by the UN as the International Year of Mobilization Against Racism.

Discrimination, Xenophobia and Related Intolerance. At each of the meetings, the conferees deliberated and crafted two documents: a Declaration of Principles and a more action-oriented Programme of Action. My focus is the NGO Forum, which I attended as a delegate of the Arab American Institute, a civil rights organization for Arab Americans. I first describe some aspects of the conference, highlight one of its accomplishments, and then theorize its utopian elements, drawing upon the ideas discussed above.

The Forum was organized by an international steering committee of the NGOs led by a South African NGO. The UN facilitated the conference. NGOs, representing civil society, have played an increasingly important role in global affairs over the past decade, and it was felt that the global NGO community had a perspective and agenda different from those of governments.[6] The NGOs spent fifteen months planning for this conference. A number of pre-conference regional planning meetings (called "PrepCom") were held in Strasbourg,

---

6   At the first PrepCom, the motto was adopted ("United to Combat Racism: Equality, Justice, Dignity") and five objectives were chosen: to understand the history and sources of current manifestations of racism, discrimination, and intolerance; to ascertain who were and are its victims; to suggest ways to protect victims while working to eradicate racism; to provide remedies to racism at all levels; and to suggest strategies to achieve equality. Additional work was accomplished at the PrepComs, including selecting issues. Twenty-five were chosen, from trafficking of women and religious intolerance, to migrant rights, reparations, and hate crimes. Twenty-five commissions were set up to deliberate and formulate ideas and language for the final documents. NGOs worked together in caucuses, of which there were forty (International Human Rights Law Group, "Combating Racism" 5). The twenty-nine topics discussed and voted upon in the NGO Forum were as follows: African/African Descendants; Slave Trade and Slavery; Reparations; Anti-Semitism; Arab and Middle East [Islamophobia]; Asians and Asian Descendants; Caste and Discrimination Based on Work and Descent; Criminal Justice and Judicial Systems; Colonialism and Foreign Occupation; Persons With Disabilities; Education; Ethnic and National Minorities and Groups; Environmental Racism; Gender; Globalization; Hate Crimes; Health and HIV/AIDS; Indigenous Peoples; Labor; Media and Communication; Migrants and Migrant Workers; Palestinians and Palestine; Refugees, Asylum Seekers, Stateless and Internally Displaced Persons; Religious Intolerance; Roma Nation; Sexual Orientation; Young People and Children; The Girl Child; and Trafficking.

Santiago, Dakar, and Tehran. The PrepComs were venues of intense lobbying by the NGOs. It was in response to the lobbying done by some groups that the decision was made that the conference would have a broader focus than racial discrimination. This time, it would include other forms of discrimination perpetrated on the basis of disability, gender, religion, sexual orientation, xenophobia, and all other excuses for intolerance. At the PrepComs, U.S. black delegates put the discrimination against Latin American blacks and the issue of reparations on the table (see Crossette). The PrepComs were sites where decisions were made about the agenda and drafts of the final two Durban documents.

Many NGOs did a great deal of preparatory work for the Durban meeting, gathering information and writing reports.[7] The UN came under criticism for its lack of funding and support staff to organize the conference (see Themba-Nixon, and Narasaki). Notwithstanding these shortcomings, because the UN funded NGOs that lacked the resources to pay for travel expenses, and because interpreters translated the proceedings in a number of languages, the Forum was successful in bringing together a global group of human rights activists and in overcoming barriers of distance and communication. This is important when examining final documents of the conference, which, I argue, represent a global utopian perspective on human rights.

The NGO Forum of the WCAR

At the Forum, the vanguard of the world's NGO leadership committed to eradicating all forms of intolerance met to talk, strategize, and craft the two final documents. These documents were to be shared with the

---

7   Examples of such reports to come out of the U.S. included: American Friends Service Committee; Transnational Racial Justice Initiative; "Report of the US Leadership Meetings"; International Human Rights Law Group "Bellagio"; International Possibilities Unlimited; Lawyers' Committee for Civil Rights Under Law; Leadership Conference on Civil Rights; and TransAfrica Forum.

UN Commissioner for Human Rights, Mary Robinson, who was then to share it with the world leaders.

Six thousand delegates representing 2,000 NGOs came to Durban (see American Friends), many of them taking dangerous journeys to promote their issues. Some groups braved hostility and displeasure from their own governments (see Polakow-Suransky). At Durban, religious orders, international and domestic labor unions, international student unions, professional associations, women's groups, children's rights groups, and organizations designed to protect and further migrant workers' rights and those of indigenous populations in North and South America sent delegates if not delegations.

International human rights activists spoke and participated, such as the President of South Africa, Thabo Mbeki; Rigoberta Menchú; and Angela Davis. President Fidel Castro, who had come to attend the governments' WCAR, was the key speaker at the Forum's final session. Those who could not be there in person sent greetings, such as Mumia Abu-Jamal, a former member of the Black Panther Party convicted of allegedly killing a police officer in Philadelphia, Pennsylvania, and placed on death row since 1981 (see Abu-Jamal). Many of the delegates attending the Forum also attended the World Conference and were able to address world leaders in panels and plenary sessions (see "Call to Eradicate").

The venue where much of the action took place was Kingsmead Cricket Stadium, which lies in the center of the city. In the stadium's central arena, half a dozen large tents were set up to accommodate panels of speakers. Smaller tents were placed around the perimeter of the stadium to allow caucuses a place to meet and discuss lobbying and voting activities. Nearby, two large exhibition halls were filled with tables to allow organizations to display their materials, much of it educational in nature. Every day, hundreds of attendees wandered through the aisles to browse through the materials and to talk with representatives of organizations from every continent.

The NGOs pursued a number of ways to communicate their agendas: some focused on working within the thematic commissions, while others held workshops, gave briefings, and organized panels. Workshops were held all over the city: in museums, schools, hotels, art centers, the aquarium, and in technical colleges. Durban's City Hall was completely given over to the conferees.

One of the most effective means NGOs used was to hold open meetings in which the victims of racism and intolerance were encouraged to testify. For example, the U.S.-based Center for Women's Global Leadership, active for over a decade in the field of women's human rights, organized a six-hour hearing in which the audience listened to testimonies from women who were, and are, subjected to many forms of gendered discrimination, from Roma bride-selling in Serbia, to the treatment accorded to black women in prisons in the U.S., to Haitian women migrant workers in the Dominican Republic who often are not allowed to give birth in public hospitals and who, if admitted, are segregated in hospital wards. Migrant women workers in Malaysia testified to working conditions in which wages were withheld and physical abuse was common. As painful as the testimonies were, what struck many in the audience were the commonalities of women's experiences; the intersection of xenophobia, racism, and gender discrimination; and the ability of these women to transform their pain into organizing for change.[8]

A great deal of cultural activity took place throughout the ten days. A Film Festival Against Racism was free and open to the public. Films and documentaries from around the world were screened and a number of directors, including Ousmane Sambene and Haile Gerima, discussed their work. Musical and theatrical productions by anti-racist artists took place in different locations by artists such as Hugh Masekela, Miriam Makeba, and Johnny Clegg. Dance and musical performances punctuated the day's events and were held on stages near the stadium and around the city. If the events became too overpowering, delegates could retreat to a small hut in the stadium called a meditation room, where candles were lit and solitude could be obtained. Delegates set up impromptu displays on the grounds of the stadium, and some delegates played their musical instruments.

---

8   A videocassette of this panel was produced in 2003 by the Center for Women's Global Leadership. Other videocassettes include *Journey to Durban*, and *Bringing Durban Home*.

What the Forum Accomplished

While significant events took place at the Forum, I focus on the discourse of the delegates. The Forum was an organizing space for liminal, marginalized, groups to articulate and promote perspectives on globalization and its inequalities. An example is the adoption by the Forum of the resolution that the Trans-Atlantic Slave Trade was a crime against humanity.[9] Although this declaration was seen by supporters as long overdue and but a first step toward remedying past injustices, it was significantly added to the Forum's final documents, and it gave voice and standing to groups which have long struggled for acknowledgement of this historical injustice. At the governmental WCAR, former colonial European governments resisted a similar resolution in fear that would have legal and economic repercussions.[10] This led governments to approve a weaker statement on slavery that stopped short of declaring it as a crime against humanity. The dia-

9   Resolution Number 64 stated: "We affirm that the Trans-Atlantic Slave Trade and the enslavement of Africans and African Descendants was a crime against humanity and a unique tragedy in the history of humanity, and that its roots and bases were economic, institutional, systemic and transnational in dimension" ("WCAR NGO Forum Declaration" 10).

10   The resolution can be partly credited to the UN's creation of space for black activists. In April 2002, the 58th Session of the UN Commission of Human Rights established a Working Group for African Descendants in the Diaspora. African, U.S. blacks, and West Indians (African and African Descendants Caucus) collaborated to define slavery as a crime against humanity included in the final declaration. The milder Resolution Number 13 states: "We acknowledge that slavery and the slave trade, including the transatlantic slave trade, were appalling tragedies in the history of humanity not only because of their abhorrent barbarism but also in terms of their magnitude, organized nature and especially their negation of the essence of the victims, and further acknowledge that slavery and the slave trade are a crime against humanity and should always have been so, especially the transatlantic slave trade and are among the major sources and manifestations of racism, racial discrimination, xenophobia and related intolerance, and that Africans and people of African descent, Asians and people of Asian descent and indigenous peoples were victims of these acts and continue to be victims of their consequences" ("Declaration of the World Conference" 6). It was seen as weak without an analysis of the economics of slavery.

logue and interaction that took place between delegates as they shared information allowed for new information to be brought to the world's public opinion, for theorizing about race and intolerance, and for links to be forged by and between the global activists.

First, all three Durban meetings presented groups with opportunities to inform and gain the sympathy of the world's public opinion, and many groups seized that opportunity and used it well. Three groups were particularly effective in presenting their cases: the Dalits, the Roma people, and the Palestinians. Much of this information was new to many. Some of these items have been important components in post-Durban meetings.

Second, the dialogue between delegates included a theorizing dimension, where the roots of intolerance, its consequences, and the methods best used to eradicate it, were debated, leading one of the conveners to describe this dialogue as "a historic discourse" that broke new ground in describing discrimination in the third millennium (see McDougall). For example, in a panel dedicated to the discussion of hate crimes committed against Asians globally, organizers of Asian communities in Great Britain discussed how they had to deal with anti-Muslim skinhead groups and the police. The summer of 2001 was the time when a great deal of racist violence took place against Asians in the U.K. At the same panel, a representative of an Asian American civil rights group discussed hate crimes perpetrated against Asians in the U.S., and how Asian Americans are viewed as perpetual foreigners. The treatment of Asians in Canada was the subject of another presentation at the panel; there, Asians are on the receiving end of harsh treatment especially with regard to immigration and detention laws. Such discriminatory treatment was seen as arising from a deep-rooted fear that Canadians have about an Asian influx into their country. At this panel, the links between xenophobia and racism were explored, and racism as an analytical category was applied to populations other than African or African-descended.

Many groups defined racism and intolerance as a contagious disease that could be contained, rooted out, and conquered. A bright red headband distributed by a Guyanese group dedicated to children's rights summarized this utopian, can-do attitude: "I am a race-free zone," it proclaimed in large black letters, and many conferees wore these headbands in solidarity during the debates. Many groups accepted the notion of the intersectionality of race, class, and gender. And the solutions to discrimination advanced by different groups included reparations and the truth and reconciliation commissions, adopted in South Africa and in some Latin American countries, that stand in sharp contrast to a Nuremberg-style of court-room justice. For many, racial discrimination was seen as the hardest discrimination to endure and eradicate, and groups wishing to promote their cause would often present their experiences with oppression as that of racial discrimination. Ideas about the sources and reasons for racism have been shared across continents throughout the twentieth century. Theoretical advances made by U.S. groups in their national struggle for human rights have been found useful by groups in other continents, who used them to define their particular situations. The Dalits, for example, described casteism as a form of racial discrimination.[11] Yet sixty years ago, U.S. social scientists imported from India the concept of caste and used it to explain Jim Crow in the U.S. South.[12]

Third, as a result of this intense dialogue, many delegates left with the knowledge that there were a number of crosscutting issues that connected them to other global activists. This was particularly revealing to U.S. delegations. As Clarissa Rojas, a U.S. delegates for INCITE Women of Color Against Violence, an organization in San Francisco, stated a few months after the conference:

> going to Durban has impacted my work here in a number of ways. [...] We are really beginning to see that if we are working for social justice issues and if we are committed to a post-Durban strategy, there is no way to consider issues without a transnational focus. It's kind of a double consciousness. [...] The U.S. is almost in everybody's back yard. We have this incredible presence in the world. Yet here we are blinded by that reality. We need to not just learn about the world, but about the connections between us and the world and what we are doing in [the] world (online).

11 See Dalit Caucus; and Tupaj Amaru.
12 See Dollard. It is pertinent to remember that Durban was the place where Gandhi first used the principles of *satyagraha* which were to influence Martin Luther King, Jr.

The Forum gave its participants a sense of belonging to a global movement dedicated to the eradication of discrimination. A community had been created at the Forum.

This community allowed the delegates to see connections and compare solutions, and the opportunity to learn from each other. In his essay in this volume, Lyman Tower Sargent coins the term "utopian energy," which is a useful and an appropriate way to describe the feelings of belonging, strength, and possibility that infused the Forum and its delegates (see "Choosing Utopia" below). Reports of similar feelings have been discussed at other gatherings, such as the World Social Forum.[13]

If the Forum was utopian, it and the WCAR also had its anti-utopian enemies. The decision of the U.S. government to boycott the WCAR was received by the NGO delegates with dismay, although not with surprise. To many observers, the U.S. government's decision was a confirmation of its reluctance to engage in a fruitful discussion with the rest of the world on these issues. Some governmental delegates, however, were relieved when the U.S. group walked away; for in the brief time it had been there, U.S. delegates had mounted numerous challenges to the documents under discussion (see Tanzer).

The U.S. government after September 11th continued its offensive against the resolutions passed in Durban and the individuals who endorsed them. One example is its action against Mary Robinson, the former president of Ireland and then UN Commissioner. Robinson had supported compensation for slavery and had taken positions on the Middle East that were unpopular with the U.S. The U.S. government lobbied very hard, and successfully, to drive her out of her position. Her contract was not renewed.[14] Most recently, Congressman Tom Lantos (D-CA) has labeled Durban a "circus" and its documents "hateful," and the U.S. continues to not participate in any of the post-

---

13   See the special issue of *ColorLines* 7.1 (Spring 2004,) devoted to the World Social Forum; Fitting; and Poldervaart.

14   See Williams, "Bush's Hit List" and "Interview." For a detailed narrative about the pressures the U.S. government levied on Robinson by an insider unsympathetic to her and the Palestinians, see Lantos.

Durban meetings organized by the Office of High Commissioner for Human Rights (Lantos 46–7).

A Utopian Text, Community, and the NGO Forum

> I think we've gone as far as we can in saying this system is just nature, Louis-Rend had begun. You know, you can only tell people God put the king in Versailles for so long. So: I think we have to spend less time saying globalization is a force of nature, like rain, and spend more time in making the case for this philosophy as a philosophy.
> Why? Evan had asked.
> Because, he'd replied after a little pause, at the moment of greatest success you are exposed to greatest risk.
> Robert Newman, *The Fountain at the Center of the World*

At the Forum, a fleeting community of ten days was created out of shared commitments. But was it utopian? I believe so, given its mission, attendees, and location. Furthermore, the utopian energy left textual footprints. The delegates crafted and voted the "WCAR NGO Forum Declaration" and the "NGO Forum Programme of Action." The process of writing the NGO Document began before the Durban meeting and continued throughout it. It contains 473 resolutions and statements. Its seventy-two pages express a global community's analysis of global problems pertaining to race as well as recommendations on how to resolve them. They also include voices of groups that ordinarily are excluded because of their location and poverty. I propose that this document is both an intervention and a significant utopian text, and I connect it to Raffaella Baccolini and Tom Moylan's model of "critical dystopia," although I include it here as one form of anti-globalization literature.[15]

The Forum Document provides a snapshot of the contemporary world, focusing on the many forms of discrimination in existence. The document is not an easy read and bears the mark of the urgency of the delegates and their strong feelings. In some parts, the focus is on specific groups, such as women and the girl-child, while in other parts, the focus is on more general remedies and processes. The NGO Document includes both analysis and theorizing. Discrimination is described as having an intersectional quality that makes its victims experience intolerance differently. It describes the consequences of racism and its related intolerances. Some of the most interesting theorizing takes place in the way that the Document exposes the relationships between racism, xenophobia, and intolerance. In all of its descriptions and recommendations, the Document includes a gendered dimension for women and girl-children. Discrimination itself is theorized: some forms of racism are based in the historical fact of slavery, while others are not. Some groups and individuals are identified as discriminated against because of ethnicity, religion, language, sexual orientation, age, work, caste, national origin, and disease. Finally, race is recognized as an ideological construct used to exploit persons.

The Document also lists and describes the ways in which various discriminations are expressed, such as trafficking and environmental racism. Specific groups of victims are named and their experience of discrimination is described. The Document sees that the legacy of history continues to live in contemporary times: it maintains that there is an unbroken line of events beginning with the trans-Atlantic slave trade, then moving to slavery, and later to colonialism and the activities of multinational corporations, eventually exposing the uneven

---

15   Enloe urges feminist audiences to read similar reports for the most comprehensive and feminist analysis of women's issues. Literary anti-globalization texts include Octavia E. Butler's *Parable of the Sower* and Margaret Atwood's *Oryx and Crake*. Robert Newman's *The Fountain at the Center of the World* is the first to take as its subject matter anti-globalization demonstrations.

development of globalization for different populations and nation-states.

It argues that globalization is not a natural or unstoppable phenomenon. In Resolutions 123 and 124, the Document defines "globalization" as:

> the continuation of colonial and imperial control. It is inherently racist and anti-democratic, and creates a network of laws and policies that unevenly integrate the world. [...] The wealth and the power of globalisation is concentrated in the global capitalist class and is inherently linked to racism and casteism, environmental racism, [...] leading to many different forms of violence, militarisation and nuclearisation of countries and cities (20).

In Resolution 121, globalization was also determined to be a set of:

> processes [...] that concentrate power in the hands of powerful Western nations and multinational corporations. [...] It widens economic inequalities within and between countries [and] [...] leads to economic and social disintegration, unemployment and marginalisation. It particularly implies both feminisation and racialisation of poverty (20).

Categories of institutions are mentioned as perpetrating this global inequality, such as the multinational corporations and governments. The "tools" of globalization include "structural adjustment policies, privatization, trade liberalization and unequal terms of trade" (Resolutions 121 and 120 20).

In its critique, the Document demystified and denaturalized globalization, and called for a variety of interventions. It affirmed specific rights as human rights, including self-determination, freedom of expression, freedom of the press, individual dignity, equality and justice, humane working conditions, freedom of association, participation in decision-making processes, and compensation against racist acts (victims of all discriminatory acts are eligible). The Document also affirmed the previous international conventions crafted by the international community in the past.

The Document included recommendations for remedies, and it is with these that the reader can ascertain the utopian world envisaged by the delegates. These recommendations seek a more just and equitable world, free of racism and intolerance. In doing so, they place responsibility on key institutions: the UN, the nation-states, multi-national corporations, and civil society. All need to ensure that this future will come about. The UN should, for example, establish new Covenants to control multinational corporations and restructure its Security Council so that it does not give preference to, and perpetuate, an imbalance of global power (33). Nation-states should respect and protect human rights, seek to promote tolerance, and fulfill the human rights of their citizens. They should protect their citizens from corporate power and allow them to express dissent and build "a democratic and anti-racist globality" (54). Third World countries' debts should be cancelled and nation-states should develop action plans and institutions for human rights (Res. 301.4, 48). Finally, there was recognition that crimes had, and are, being committed against groups, and that institutional processes had to be put in place to address these. Reparations were offered as one solution (Res. 237.46, 3–39), but others were mentioned as well, beginning with the acknowledgement of the crime itself. Overall then, the NGO recommendations provide glimpses of an egalitarian world, as well as strategies to struggle against the status quo. A self-understanding about the role of the NGOs is also made clear. As part of civil society, NGOs should work in tandem with governments to provide data, advocate for human rights policies, support victims with legal advice, develop ways to increase participation in society, identify the human rights issues, publicize human rights violations, and educate the larger society. Finally, they should be funded by nation-states and the UN to do these tasks. Instruments to ensure that nation-states and multinational corporations are made accountable should be devised (Res. 222; Res. 227, 37; Res. 303, 48; Res. 313, 50).

A number of nation-states, such as China and the U.S., came in for especially strong criticism. Israel was also criticized for its treatment of the Palestinians and was described as an apartheid state (Res. 160.5, 26–7). This characterization of Israel led Mary Robinson, who officially received the document, to decide not to pass it on to the governmental WCAR. Consequently, the governmental WCAR crafted and voted on its own set of documents, the *Declaration and Programme of Action*. Today, this is the better-known text and is the one that the UN, governments, and NGOs are trying to keep alive and to use to set up post-Durban national action plans and other mechanisms to study, control, and work toward eliminating racism.

Having discussed the document, I would like to describe how the Forum itself was utopian from the standpoint of community. Marx said that it would take an international solidarity of the working class to end capitalism. However, until the working classes can do that, I propose that the global NGO community is one of the primary movements challenging globalization. Joining together in Durban solidified this community. A central conviction binding the delegates was the belief that politics, as a process, was the preferred agent of change and that non-governmental groups had an important role to play in that process. While delegates did not agree on all issues and struggles occurred over language and items to be placed in the final documents, most concurred that discrimination could be conquered by human agency.[16] This utopianism was reinforced by the very venue of the conference, the new South Africa.

The Forum therefore gave delegates a sense that winning the fight against intolerance was possible. It engendered a sense of empowerment and an optimism grounded in the experience of shared work and commitments and in the strength of numbers. Many took away from the Forum a sense of hope because they felt they were part of a larger, global, imagined movement committed to working against intolerance and for human rights. Their dialogue, sharing of ideas, tactics, and strategies were important steps in the consolidation of a global progressive force that can develop goals and strategies.

This new, imagined, utopian community has, however, a history. Several global conferences on colonialism and racism were held in the twentieth century, called by the colonized to discuss ways to eradicate racism and colonialism. Before World War II, Africans and blacks in the New World held Pan-African Congresses to discuss these mutual

16 The Palestinian-Israeli issue was only one of the difficult topics dealt with. Three others were the question of which groups should be named as victims of racism, xenophobia, and related intolerances; the historical debate surrounding slavery and its aftermath; and the definitions of colonialism, slavery, and reparations. See Constable, "Slavery's Legacy"; Swarns; American Friends Service Committee.

problems, and these meetings helped to foster African national liberation movements. In 1927, the Congress of Oppressed Nationalities met in Brussels; while in 1955, in Bandung the heads of twenty-nine newly sovereign nations of Africa and Asia met to discuss world peace, racialism, and colonialism. From Bandung emerged the Non-Aligned Movement that responded to problems of development, world peace, and the Cold War.[17] Richard Wright, an observer at Bandung noted in his report how the atmosphere at the conference developed:

> before Bandung, most of these men had been strangers, [...] bristling with charge and countercharge against America and/or Russia. But, as the days passed, [...] another and different mood set in. [...] As they came to know one another better, [...] their ideological defenses dropped. Negative unity, bred by a feeling that they had to stand together against a rapacious West, turned into something that hinted of the positive. They began to sense their combined strength (175).

In this passage, one of the most powerful in the book, Wright describes the community engendered by history, politics, and the conference itself. The similarity here to the mood at the Forum is striking.

In constructing a history for our imagined, anti-racist, global community, I am suggesting that the Forum signaled a re-birth. What is new about this utopian frontier is that its basic organizing unit is not the nation-state; for the NGOs, which cut across nation-states, have provided an organizing space for the multiple identities individuals and groups create for themselves, and for liminal groups that have fallen between the cracks of the nation-state's "totalizing grid" (see Anderson). NGOs, therefore, address not only inequalities between nations, but within and across nations, and this global reach is distinctly different from the earlier internationalisms of the twentieth century.[18]

In a personal conversation in 2003, Levitas raised the question about the sustainability of such forms of community, and whether the

17   On Pan-Africanism, see Esedebe; and Raheeem.
18   See Malkki for a provocative treatment of internationalism and nationalism. Although it is tempting to posit that NGOs themselves constitute utopian spaces, I refer readers to the debate about the politics of civil society between Rieff and Clough.

utopian community I describe represents a Mannheimian chialistic type of brotherhood. In this form of utopian mentality, said Mannheim, the dominant feeling is a presentism, a feeling that everything is possible, that the past and the future did not exist. For the moment, my answer is no: the delegates at the Forum were well aware of the obstacles ahead and understood that Durban was but a temporary relief. I partially base my response on my observations of one of the post-Durban meetings, hosted by the UN, that took place in Belgium in December 2003, at which the European NGO delegates were trying to work with governments, but also posing harder questions to the UN, governmental representatives, and expert witnesses about "Fortress Europe," detention centers, and attempts by European governments to diversify an aging workforce with immigrant labor while shelving issues of equality.[19]

In conclusion, the Forum was a significant moment where those whose lives have been distorted by various systems of oppression had a rendezvous with each other. Durban should be remembered and celebrated as the site and catalyst for the rebirth of a long-dormant, global, anti-racist civic community.[20] In so doing, we will be participating in community, inventing and fashioning a more democratic version of it to better prepare for the struggles ahead. Marx was right: the aim of knowledge is to change the world and not only to understand it. Ultimately, time will prove whether my method and vision are correct.

19   The Regional Seminar of Experts for Western States was organized by the Office of the High Commissioner for Human Rights and hosted by the Government of Belgium and took place 10–12 December 2003.

20   New and urgent battles are being waged in the U.S. for civil rights and new populations, most notably the young, the Muslims, and the Arab Americans have been galvanized into action. In May 2003, a conference (Movement Beyond Borders: After Durban: U.S. Communities Building a Multiracial Justice and Human Rights Vision) was convened at George Washington University. Thirty-seven U.S. NGOs sent delegates and it was opened by a youth conference. The group worked to develop an agenda, demonstrated at a Justice for Janitors rally, and discussed future strategies. Doudou Diene, the UN Special Rapporteur on Racism, attended the conference.

Works Cited

Abbott, Philip. *Seeking Many Inventions: The Idea of Community in America.* Knoxville: University of Tennessee Press, 1987.

Abu-Jamal, Mumia. "Greetings from Mumia Abu-Jamal to All Participants at the 3rd UN World Conference Against Racism, Racial Discrimination, Xenophobia and Related Intolerance." 31 August–7 September 2001.

All for Reparations and Emancipation. "Progress For Reparations and Emancipation." Press Release, 6 May 2002. 1–3. 13 May 2002 <http://www.ncobps-575W @ncat.edu>.

American Friends Service Committee. "Durban and Beyond: A Report on the American Friends Service Committee's Involvement in the 3rd World Conference Against Racism, Racial Discrimination, Xenophobia and Related Intolerance." Board Supporting Paper 14.

Anderson, Benedict. *Imagined Communities: Reflections on the Origin and Spread of Nationalism.* New York: Verso, 1983.

Baccolini, Raffaella, and Tom Moylan (eds.). *Dark Horizons: Science Fiction and the Dystopian Imagination.* New York: Routledge, 2003.

Bringing Durban Home: Combating Racism Together. Breakthrough. Videocassette. 2002.

Burnett, Jonathan. "Community, Cohesion and the State." *Race & Class* 45.3 (2004): 1–18.

Cacho, Lisa Marie. "Situating Space in 'Local' and 'Global' Struggles." *American Quarterly* 53.2 (2001): 377–85.

"Call to Eradicate Discrimination and Intolerance Marks Conclusion of World Conference Against Racism." 8 September 2001. New York: Department of Public Information, News and Media Services Division. 11 September 2001 <http://www.un.org/WCAR/pressreleases/rd-d45.html>.

Case, John, and Rosemary C.R. Taylor (eds.). *Co-ops, Communes & Collectives: Experiments in Social Change in the 1960s and 1970s.* New York: Pantheon Books, 1979.

Clough, Michael. "Reflections on Civil Society." *The Nation* (22 February 1999): 16–18.

ColorLines: Race Culture Action 7.1 (Spring 2004).

Constable, Pamela. "Mideast Dominates Racism Meeting." *The Washington Post* 1 September 2001: A1, A22.

—— "Slavery's Legacy: Divisions on How to Make Amends: Debate at World Racism Conference Focuses on Apologies vs. Reparations." *The Washington Post* 2 September 2001: A16.

—— "Israel, U.S. Quit Forum on Racism." *The Washington Post* 4 September 2001: A1, A16.

Crossette, Barbara. "Global Look at Racism Hits Many Sore Points." *The New York Times* 4 March 2001: A12.
—— "Rights Leaders Urge Powell to Attend U.N. Racism Conference." *The New York Times* 11 July 2001: A9.
Cushman, John H. Jr. "U.S. Delegates in Durban Practiced Minimalism." *The New York Times* 4 September 2001: A8.
Dalit Caucus. "Handout No.1: Caste Discrimination Against Dalits Is Racial Discrimination: Work and Descent based Caste Discrimination Against Dalits Is Racial Discrimination." n.d.
"Declaration of the World Conference Against Racism, Racial Discrimination, Xenophobia and Related Intolerance." 21 March 2002 <http://www.icare.to/31decwebversion.html>.
Dollard, John. *Caste and Class in a Southern Town.* New York: Doubleday, 1957.
Dudziak, Mary L. "Desegregation as a Cold War Imperative." *Stanford Law Review* 41 (November 1988): 61–120.
Enloe, Cynthia. "Crucial Reporting: Human Rights Reports and Why We Should All Be Reading Them." *The Women's Review of Books* 21.5 (2004): 21–3.
Esedebe, P.O. *Pan-Africanism: The Idea and the Movement, 1776–1963.* Washington: Howard University Press, 1982.
Fears, Darryl. "Threat to Boycott U.N. Race Talks Praised, Attacked." *The Washington Post* 1 August 2001: A3.
"Forecast: High Winds, Hot Air." Editorial. *The Washington Post* 28 August 2001: A14.
Herbert, Bob. "Doomed to Irrelevance." *New York Times* 6 September 2001: A27.
Hoagland, Jim. "Speak Out Against Mugabe's Racism." *The Washington Post* 26 August 2001: B7.
Hobsbawm, Eric, and Terence Ranger (eds.). *The Invention of Tradition.* Cambridge: Cambridge University Press, 1983.
International Human Rights Law Group. "Bellagio Consultation on the UN World Conference Against Racism." Washington: International Human Rights Law Group, 2000.
—— "Combating Racism Together: A Guide to Participating in the UN World Conference Against Racism." Washington: International Human Rights Law Group, 2001.
—— "Report of the US Leadership Meetings on the World Conference Against Racism." Washington: International Human Rights Law Group, 2001.
International Possibilities Unlimited. *Journey to Durban.* Silver Spring: International Possibilities Unlimited, n.d.
Journey to Durban: Migrant Rights at the UN World Conference Against Racism. National Network for Immigrant and Refugee Rights. Videocassette. 2003.
Kanter, Rosabeth Moss. *Commitment and Community: Communes and Utopias in Sociological Perspective.* Cambridge, Massachusetts: Harvard University Press, 1972.

King, Albert I. "What Durban Could Learn From Jim Nabrit." *The Washington Post* 1 September 2001: A29.

Lantos, Tom. "The New World Disorder: The Durban Debacle: An Insider's View of the UN World Conference Against Racism." *The Fletcher Forum of World Affairs* 26 (2002): 31–52.

Lawyers' Committee for Civil Rights Under Law. "Global Injustice: An Overview of Racism, Racial Discrimination, Xenophobia, and Related Intolerance: Produced in Preparation for the United Nations World Conference Against Racism, Racial Discrimination, Xenophobia, and Related Intolerance in Durban, South Africa." Washington: Lawyers' Committee for Civil Rights Under Law, 2001.

Leadership Conference on Civil Rights. "'American Dream? America Reality!' A Report on Race, Ethnicity and the Law in the United States In Preparation for the Initial Country Review of the United States by the United Nations Committee on the Elimination of Racial Discrimination." Washington: Leadership Conference on Civil Rights and Lawyers' Committee for Civil Rights Under Law, 2001.

Levitas, Ruth. *The Concept of Utopia*. London: Philip Allan, 1990.

"Making 'Global' and 'Ethical' Rhyme: An Interview with Mary Robinson." 17 February 2004 <http://www.opendemocracy.net/debates/article-6-27-1627.jsp>.

Malkki, Liisa. "Citizens of Humanity: Internationalism and the Imagined Community of Nations." *Diaspora* 3.1 (1994): 41–68.

McDougall, Gay. "The Durban Racism Conference Revisited: The World Conference Against Racism: Through a Wider Lens." *Fletcher Forum on World Affairs* 26 (2002): 135–51.

"A Mean-Spirited Conference." Editorial. *The New York Times* 17 August 2001: A18.

"Missing the Boat at Durban." Editorial. *The Berkshire Eagle* 31 August 2001: A6.

Morin, Richard. "World Image of U.S. Declines." *The Washington Post* 5 December 2002: A26.

Narasaki, Karen. "Personal Experiences at the WCAR." 21 March 2002 <http://www.ngoworldconference.org/ach010701.html>.

Newman, Robert. *The Fountain at the Center of the World*. Brooklyn: Soft Skull Press, 2004.

Perlez, Jane. "Powell Will Not Attend Racism Conference in South Africa." *The New York Times* 28 August 2001: A7.

Polakow-Suransky, Sasha. "A Politics of Denial." *The American Prospect* 13.1 (2002): 1–14.

Poldervaart, Saskia. "Free Places: Utopian Aspects of the Globalization-from-below Movement." 4th International Utopian Studies Conference, Madrid. 25–29 June 2003.

Radway, Janice. "What's in a Name? Presidential Address to the American Studies Association, 20 November 1998." *American Quarterly* 51.1 (1999): 1–32.

Raheem, T. Abdul. *Pan Africanism: Politics, Economy, and Social Change in the Twenty First Century*. New York: New York University Press, 1996.

Rieff, David. "The False Dawn of Civil Society." *The Nation* (22 February 1999): 11–16.

Rojas, Clarissa. "Personal Reactions to the WCAR, 28 February 2002." 21 March 2002 <http://www.ngoworldconference.org/arch022802.html>.

Sargent, Lyman Tower. "The Three Faces of Utopianism Revisited." *Utopian Studies* 5.1 (1994): 1–37.

Sipress, Alan. "Powell to Avoid Racism Forum." *The Washington Post* 27 August 2001: A1, A12.

Slevin, Peter. "Decision to Skip U.N. Meeting Lamented." *The Washington Post* 28 August 2001: A4.

Steele, Shelby. "War of the Worlds." *The Wall Street Journal* 17 September 2001.

Swarns, Rachel L. "Walkout Staged by U.S. and Israel at Racism Talks." *The New York Times* 4 September 2001: A1, A8.

—— "At Race Talks, Delegates Cite Early Mistrust." *The New York Times* 5 September 2001: A1, A8.

—— "Overshadowed, Slavery Debate Boils in Durban." *The New York Times* 6 September 2001: A1, A12.

—— "Rancor and Powell's Absence Cloud Racism Parley." *The New York Times* 31 August 2001: A3.

Tanzer, Charles. "Dispatch From Durban." *The Nation* (4 September 2001): posted 5 September 2001 (web only) at <http://www.thenation.com/doc.mhtml?i=20010903&s=tanzer>.

Themba-Nixon, Makani. "Durban Diary: Up Close and Black at the World Conference Against Racism." 13 March 2002 <http://www.seeingblack.com>.

TransAfrica Forum. "United Nations World Conference Against Racism, Racial Discrimination, Xenophobia and Related Intolerance." Washington: Trans-Africa Forum, 2001.

Transnational Racial Justice Initiative. "The Persistence of White Privilege and Institutional Racism in U.S. Policy: A Report of the U.S. Government Compliance with the International Convention on the Elimination of All Forms of Racial Discrimination." Oakland: Transnational Racial Justice Initiative, 2001.

Tupaj Amaru. "Causes and Origin of Racial Discrimination." World Conference Against Race, Racial Discrimination, Xenophobia and Related Intolerance. 31 May 2001.

Wallerstein, Immanuel. "Marxisms as Utopias: Evolving Ideologies." *Unthinking Social Science: The Limits of Nineteenth-Century Paradigms*. 2nd edn. Philadelphia: Temple University Press, 2001: 170–84.

—— *Utopistics: Or, Historical Choices of the Twenty-first Century*. New York: New, 1998.

"WCAR: Next Steps in a Painful Journey?" The Network of Alliances Bridging Race & Ethnicity. 15 December 2001 <http://www.jointcenter.org/nabre/whatsnew/wcar>.

World Conference Against Racism, Racial Discrimination, Xenophobia and Related Intolerance. *Declaration and Programme of Action*. New York: UN Department of Public Information, 2002.

"WCAR NGO Forum Declaration." 3 September 2001 <http://www.icare.to/31dec webversion.html>.

Williams, Ian. "Bush's Hit List at the United Nations." *Foreign Policy in Focus* (2001). 13 May 2002 <http://www.alternet.org>.

—— "Interview with Mary Robinson." 17 February 2004 <http://www.salon.com/people/interview/2002/07/26/mary_robinson/>.

Women at the Intersection of Racism and Other Oppressions. Center for Women's Global Leadership. Videocassette. 2003.

Wright, Richard. *The Color Curtain: A Report on the Bandung Conference*. New York: World, 1956.

Wu Song, Felicia. "Virtual Communities in a Therapeutic Age." *Society* 39.2 (2002): 39–45.

Zaki, Hoda M. "The Politics of Space and Spaces for Politics: Theorizing About Community Then and Now." *Beyond the Color Line: Race, Representation and Community in the New Century*. Ed. Alex Willingham. New York: Brennan Center for Justice, 2002. 174–90.

LYMAN TOWER SARGENT

Choosing Utopia: Utopianism as an Essential Element in Political Thought and Action

Why would anyone take Utopia and utopianism seriously? After all, according to Thomas Molnar in *Utopia: The Perennial Heresy*, utopianism is heretical and, according to Karl R. Popper in *The Open Society and its Enemies* and J.L. Talmon in *Utopianism and Politics*, leads to totalitarianism and violence. Also, utopias are alleged to be generally badly written and to attract the seriously nutty. It is hard to disagree. Ernst Bloch makes the latter point also, saying:

> the paranoiac is often a project-maker, and there is occasionally also a mutual connection between the two. So that a utopian talent slips off the rails in a paranoid way, indeed almost voluntarily succumbs to a delusion (473).

Alternatively, as F.L. Polak argues in *The Image of the Future*, utopianism is essential for the continuation of civilization, and Harvey Cox similarly notes that "the rebirth of fantasy as well as of festivity is essential to the survival of our civilization, including its political institutions" (82). Both Barbara Goodwin and I ("Authority and Utopia") have argued that utopianism is one of the main opponents of totalitarianism and violence. Far from being heretical, it permeates Christianity (Eden, the Millennium, and Heaven/Hell) and, as such, is a central motif for many Christian theologians such as Paul Tillich and Gustavo Gutiérrez. And, one could say with Bloch:

> So far does utopia extend, so vigorously does this raw material spread to all human activities, so essentially must every anthropology and science of the world contain it. *There is no realism worthy of the name if it abstracts from this strongest element in reality, as an unfinished reality* (624).

Utopia expresses much of the best and some of the worst of us. I have argued that what I called "body utopias," or utopias of sensual gratification, express the most fundamental needs and desires of the human being, such as food, shelter, and safety. Typical examples of such utopias are the earthly paradises found in most cultures and other fantasies of the good life with little human effort, like the "Land of Cockaigne" and "Big Rock Candy Mountain." But human beings do not like relying on nature or the gods, and they turn to what I have called "city utopias" or utopias of human contrivance ("Three Faces"). Typical examples of such utopias are Thomas More's *Utopia* and Edward Bellamy's *Looking Backward: 2000–1887*. How, utopias ask, can we ensure food, shelter, safety, and fulfillment for all human beings? And what could be more important, more fundamental?

The opponents of Utopia are fearful types who are unwilling to risk their comfortable positions so that others could leave their uncomfortable ones. In its simplest form, this is the dynamic that Karl Mannheim captures in his characterization of the work of ideology, which he opposes to Utopia. The proponents of Utopia are hopeful types who are sometimes willing to take great risks to make life better for all. They are, perhaps, too optimistic for their, and, sometimes, our, own good.[1]

Those who see heresy are happy to keep people brainwashed so that religion can be used to enrich themselves on the backs of the poor. Joe Hill's song "The Preacher and the Slave," with the chorus, "You will eat, bye and bye, / in that glorious land above the sky; / work and pray, live on hay, / You'll get pie in the sky when you die," is an excellent popular critique of the position some religions take vis-à-vis human betterment (*Songs of the Workers* 9). Karl Marx argued in the "Introduction" to his "Contribution to the Critique of Hegel's Philosophy of Law" that religion contained the best of human aspirations while also arguing that religion placed such aspirations outside human experience rather than within it, where such aspirations belong.

---

1   Anyone who joins a secular commune is staking a great deal on a vision of a possible better life. The turnover in such communities is very large and few people find such communities more than a stage in their lives. These people are risking their own well-being, not ours, but there have always been "true believers" who have been willing to impose their vision on us. See, for example, Dohrman; Hoffer; and Festinger, Riecken, and Schachter.

The opponents of Utopia seem to have rarely read an actual utopia and misread those they do read. For example, few of the classic anti-utopian writers like Popper, Talmon, and Molnar refer to actual utopias beyond Plato and More, and their readings of these works are open to question. The proponents of Utopia are often naïve about the problems of the transition from today to the utopian future and some few of them behave as the opponents suggest all utopians behave, being willing to impose their utopian dreams on others. The Taliban were only the most recent example of a utopia that was imposed on believers and non-believers alike.

My argument is that while Utopia can be dangerous, it is absolutely essential. As Carl Sandburg put it in "Washington Monument by Night," "The Republic is a dream. / Nothing happens unless first a dream" (282). The King James Version of the Bible also has a statement of what I am saying: "Where there is no vision, the people perish" (Prov. 29:18, KJV).[2]

Studying Utopia

I initially came to Utopia in the late 1950s as an undergraduate because in my very first readings of utopias I recognized that they corrected a fault I found in most political science literature, which was only marginally better in political thought. Utopias are concerned with all of human behavior rather than the narrowly political. At the time, political science was narrowly focused, and I recall, as a minister's son, being dumbfounded at being told (by that time in a doctoral seminar) that there were no politics in churches. While political science eventually changed, my interest in the broader outlook provided by utopias grew.

My own position became centered on the simple statement that it is easier to get somewhere if you know where you want to go. Indeed,

---

2   I have compared the King James version to a dozen other translations on this passage, and they all suggest that the passage is mistranslated.

many political theorists agree that utopianism is important or even essential. Nancy Hartsock wrote:

> there is a real need for a vision of utopia, a vision that seems particularly difficult to develop and retain in the final years of the twentieth century, with its unrelieved celebration of the market as the solution to all social problems (80).

Quentin Skinner wrote:

> I have never understood why the charge of utopianism is necessarily thought to be an objection to a theory of politics. One legitimate aspiration of moral and political theory is surely to show us what lines of action we are committed to undertaking by the values we profess to accept (78–9).

In a number of articles, I have written about the nature of utopianism and its role in political thought, but there are two reasons for re-thinking that work.[3] First, as Tom Moylan has shown in *Demand the Impossible* and *Scraps of the Untainted Sky*, both eutopia and dystopia have changed and are now more complex than they used to be. Second, I have never sufficiently elaborated my position; therefore, here I update this argument, add to it recent work on personal and national identity and explore two areas that I have previously referred to in passing but not developed: the relationship of Utopia to the past and what I have begun to call *utopian energy*.[4] The result seriously complicates my understanding of Utopia and utopianism but is, I hope, a better reflection of the roles they play in political thought and action.

Our understanding of utopianism in political thought and action has been marred by misleading statements made about the literature. As I began my research, the more I read of and about utopias, the more I began to wonder about the scholarship on the subject. The utopias I read did not seem to me to be saying what the people writing about them said they were saying. In addition, I became aware of

---

3   See, for example, Sargent, "A Note on the Other Side of Human Nature"; "Human Nature and the Radical Vision"; "Authority and Utopia"; "Three Faces"; and "Necessity of Utopian Thinking."

4   See Sargent, "Utopianism and National Identity"; "Utopianism and the Creation of New Zealand National Identity"; and "Utopische Literatur."

biases in the utopias themselves. As a now well-known example of such bias, in what I think was my second article on the subject, I pointed to a strong male bias in the utopias that had been ignored by scholarship (Sargent, "Women in Utopia"). In addition, utopias do not, with a few exceptions, present "perfect" societies inhabited by "perfect" people; they represent better or good societies inhabited by people who are better *because* they live in a better society. This became a constant theme of my work because the misrepresentation of the literature has been used as a basis for dismissing it and dismissing the implied argument that it is possible to radically improve human society. This misrepresentation continues, and scholars who should know better use the word "perfect" constantly. But, at the same time, there can be a problem with utopians who, convinced that they have the right answers to the world's problems, are not averse to forcing or manipulating others into following their lead, even if that lead turns out to end in a cul-de-sac. In fact, one of the first utopias I read, B.F. Skinner's *Walden Two*, was, to me, a dystopia even though I recognized that Skinner saw it as presenting a good place. Thus, from the very beginning of my career in utopian studies, I recognized that the concept of Utopia was complex, and I came to view it as involving contradictory, even tragic, elements.

Utopias have significant differences from most attempts to discuss social improvement. First, utopias depict whole, or almost whole, societies with the various institutions interacting rather than focusing on politics, the economy, the family, child-rearing, education, or some other sub-set of social institutions. They, for example, show how child-rearing and education are transformed together with the political and economic systems to bring forth a significantly better life for all. Utopias are concerned with all human behavior.

Second, utopias generally contend that *radical* change is needed, not just piecemeal reform. As a result, utopias opposed most of the major tendencies within social science and public policy research, which, recognizing the need for change, has generally been reformist. Reform is good and necessary, much better than no reform; but unless informed by Utopia, reform is at best insipid and, at worst, pointless. It is easier to get somewhere, even if that somewhere is reform, if you have a clear idea of where you want to go (see Sargent, "Revolution,

Evolution, and Reform"). Reform is only useful if we know where we want to go, as steps toward a larger transformation that will radically improve the human condition.

If we look at utopias historically and their connections with both reform and revolution, it can be argued that such improvement has taken place. Lewis Mumford quotes Anatole France, without attribution, as saying:

> without the Utopians of other times, men would still live in caves, miserable and naked. It was Utopians who traced the lines of the first city. [...] Out of generous dreams come beneficial realities. Utopia is the principle of all progress, and the essay into a better future (22).

Choosing Utopia

Thus, we must choose Utopia. We must choose the belief that the world can be radically improved; we must dream socially; and we must allow our social dreams to affect our lives. The choice for Utopia is a choice that the world can be radically improved.

But there are many different utopias to choose from – including ones that are racist, sexist, and nationalist – all creating "others" outside the charmed circle of the utopia. We cannot dismiss the utopias that do not meet our approval; we must admit that they exist and were thought of as positive alternatives by their authors. Some of these utopias reflect the time periods in which they could reasonably be thought of as positive. For example, More's *Utopia* is patriarchal and hierarchical and imposes slavery for seemingly minor infractions of the law, but it would have been a truly vast improvement for the poor of the time. Others, that are harder to see as positive, may reflect personal or cultural pathologies that have come to be recognized as such and have begun to be eliminated, or at least reduced. For example, the racist utopias that flourished in the early twentieth century are much rarer than they used to be; and there are fewer sexist utopias than there used to be, although they cannot yet be called rare.

Thus, in my version, the choice for Utopia also includes a clear choice that the selection that I prefer *not* be imposed on others and that choices made by others *not* be imposed on me. Choice must be based on educational and persuasive discussion, not coercion. Obviously, these comments reflect a utopian vision where such "others" are no longer created.

Utopians believe that improvement in human life is the appropriate goal of any change: that we can know what improvement means; and that we can, therefore, be quite clear about where we want to go. Moral judgment is one of the strengths of utopianism, but sometimes that strength hides a weakness because while each utopia is based on a moral principle or set of moral principles, each also excludes other utopias and, thus, other moral principles or sets thereof.

Utopians will, of course, disagree both about where to go and how to get there. As I noted earlier, some utopians will ignore or only suggest or imply the "how to get there" part, and this could be a problem. There are at least two answers to this concern. First, there is only so much that can be done in one book.[5] Second, and much more important, is the fact that many utopians are quite aware of the problem and address it. One may not think that Bellamy's evolution will work or that Morris's bloody revolution will succeed, but they certainly address the issue. So does Everett Edward Hale in both *Ten Times One Is Ten* and *How They Lived in Hampton*, and so do hundreds of other writers of utopias. Most fall into a limited number of fairly obvious categories like evolution or revolution, systematic reform in a chosen direction brought about by enlightened people or ones, like Hale and so many others, aware of what being a good Christian entails. Education is another frequently used tool, for the assumption is that once a number of people are aware of the problems of the present the possibility of a better future will follow – which is, after all, one of the reasons for writing a utopia in the first place. Even dystopias often give a message about how to avoid getting to the undesirable future. Many dystopias are jeremiads warning us about what will happen if we continue as we are: as Aldous Huxley put it in

---

5   On the question of "how to get there," see the related genre of literature, once called the economic novel; and in particular, see Rose; and Taylor.

describing his *Brave New World*, they are extrapolations into the future of trends the authors see at the time of writing. And Huxley clearly meant *Brave New World* as a warning. Thus, while many utopians do not explicitly light the way between now and the future, many do and many more do so by suggestion and implication. As readers, we probably miss the transition because we focus on the utopian future, which is, of course the center of most utopias.

Getting there includes overturning rules followed by new rules created by and for whole human beings, whole for the first time. Utopians believe they can suggest a better future, but they disagree on what that future will look like. In choosing Utopia, the details of the proposed society are best evaluated from the perspective of those portrayed in other utopian texts. More broadly, does the utopia fill the needs that we posit as essential; does it correct the problems identified in the present? These are core questions in studying any political theory, and the fact that the theory is presented fictionally is irrelevant.

Also irrelevant is whether or not the utopia is deemed to be possible or impossible, realistic or unrealistic. It simply does not matter. When we choose Utopia, we are choosing the possibility of a better life in the future, not necessarily choosing a particular set of institutions. Utopianism in political thought is not primarily about specifics; it is about an attitude to change. Utopias hold up a fun fair mirror to society that corrects the distortions in the present by showing a better alternative. Once seen, it becomes the responsibility of the viewer to work to achieve that or some other better world. The past shows us that better worlds can be achieved; utopias suggest that still better can yet come.

Utopia and Identity: National and Individual

One of the problems in utopian scholarship has been the tendency to treat utopias from different countries as if they were part of a single tradition, which they are, rather than of multiple traditions, which they also are. In the mid-1990s, I hypothesized that colonies produce utopias, often with a concomitant dystopian experience for the colonized. Much of my recent work has been intended to test this hypothesis and tease out the national differences among the expressions of utopianism in English-speaking countries.[6] Each country will have a unique way in which national identity is created by and reflected in utopian literature. And that way will be derived from a version of the past of the originating country, suitably revised.

And, as noted here, colonies show both the positive and negative aspects of utopianism. They are positive in their creation of new beginnings and their strivings for a better life but negative in their willingness to kill, displace, and culturally emasculate indigenous populations in order to do so.

Individuals also use utopian imagery in creating themselves, often as part of a sub-group identity. The most obvious example is the way feminists used feminist utopianism as part of the definition of feminism and themselves as feminists. Other sub-groups have used utopian imagery in similar ways. For example, there are sub-sets of utopias concerned with, respectively, racial, sexual, or religious identities. In addition, contemporary utopianism is concerned with more narrowly defined political identities, such as the many works presenting a changed relationship between human beings and the natural world.

Utopian Energy

These political identities in particular represent something I have been calling *utopian energy*. That energy is sometimes displaced, or at least differently placed, into activities other than the creation of utopias. The general idea of utopian energies is that the will/willingness/ability to create new forms can be channeled in a number of different dir-

6   See, for example, Sargent, "Utopia and National Identity" and "Utopianism and the Creation of New Zealand National Identity."

ections, that there may be only a limited amount of such energy at any given time, and that if it is going elsewhere, it will not be going into actual utopias or intentional communities. This may help explain why certain countries, like Ireland, appear to have strong utopian traditions while having an erratic tradition of actual utopias. Utopia can be repressed, suppressed – including by poverty – or displaced.

Just because utopias can be in some way displaced or pushed aside, it takes a certain level of commitment, or energy, to be a utopian. Specifically, utopian energy is often displaced into other projects that have a tinge of utopianism but are not normally considered utopian, like nation building, reform, and social movements advancing the status of a sub-group in society. All of these are, I want to argue, projects into which utopian energies can be displaced. However, these very projects can then give rise to a new cycle of utopian thinking.

In the U.S., for example, little was explicitly utopian in the early years of the country when energy was directed to nation building, constitution writing, and so forth. Bernard Bailyn, one of the foremost historians of early America, refers to the period in much these terms:

> these were extraordinary flights of creative imagination – political heresies at the time, utopian fantasies – and their authors and sponsors knew that their efforts to realize these aspirations had no certain outcome. Nothing was assured; the future was unpredictable (5).

Once the institutions were created, there was a tremendous upsurge of utopianism in the United States up to the Civil War. In 1840, Ralph Waldo Emerson wrote to Thomas Carlyle, "We are all a little wild here with numberless projects of social reform. Not a reading man but has a draft of a new Community in his waistcoat pocket" (*Correspondence* 308–9). In the next century, the Great Depression initially gave rise to various utopian projects in the United States. At this time, poet Archibald MacLeish, who later became Librarian of Congress, wrote:

> the truth is that there is no substitute for Utopia and no substitute for hope and that the moment men give up their right to invent, however extravagantly, their own future and submit themselves, as the communists and capitalists tell them they must, to inevitable economic law, the life goes out of them (198).

These projects generally disappeared in the New Deal, World War II, and the anti-communism of the McCarthy era, but at the close of that period, the civil rights movement started the United States back toward utopianism, which gave rise to the explicitly utopian 1960s. But as Moylan has argued, it was a chastened utopianism, much more aware of its own limits. There also emerged what was once thought of as a contradiction in terms, a utopianism of the Right, ranging from a conservative nostalgia for a 1950s that had only existed on television to a far right agenda aimed at undoing the gains of the civil rights and feminist movements.[7]

Utopia and the Past

There is a sense in which many utopias, correctly thought of as radical and transgressive, are profoundly conservative in that they often hark back to the past for the ideals that they project onto the future. One can say, where else could they look, but it can be argued that few utopias are actually radically inventive. In a sense, this simply reflects a commonplace of scholarship in the history of political thought, that new ideas must use the intellectual tools available to the authors in creating the innovative ideas. Or, as Marx put it in the famous "Preface" to *A Contribution to the Critique of Political Economy*, the new society has to develop first within the confines of the old.

My contention is that most utopias are inevitably recreations of the past placed in the future. Much utopianism looks back at some improved version of the past to find inspiration for the future. In one sense, until very recently most utopianism looked for the simplicity of the Golden Age, a world where there is no hunger, no fear of tomorrow. Some still does. The creativity takes place in the way the past is improved when placed in the future. Classic examples of what I mean are Plato looking back to the *polis* that had broken down and recreating a better version of that *polis* in his *Republic* and *Laws* and

7   On the far Right utopias, see Fitting; and Sargent (ed.), *Extremism in America*.

More looking back to monasticism for part of his inspiration for the institutions of *Utopia*. Of course, both had other sources as well, but in each case a major source was found in the past and transformed into a eutopia.[8]

While there are many articles on literary and other sources and influences, there are few substantive studies of where the moral, social, and political ideas came from. Exceptions include the studies of the influence of Sparta on the whole utopian tradition, beginning with Plato; of monasticism on More; and the Tao and anarchism on Ursula K. Le Guin, all of which support my point.[9] But the more important point, of course, is what is done with the past when it is projected onto the future, or an isolated island. The creativity of the utopia is in how the materials are transformed, given life and moral authority; although the Golden Age and Earthly Paradise traditions locate the eutopia in the past, and, more importantly, as lost and not recoverable. Utopias clearly recognize that the past was not eutopia, so the past has to be changed and moved to someplace accessible. Morris's Middle Ages projected into the future in *News from Nowhere* has little in common with the actual period (e.g., no church, no monarchy). Eutopia is what the past would have looked like if the past had gotten it right. One can call this romanticizing the past, and sometimes this is the correct label. Sometimes it is nostalgia, but nostalgia is always for a past that did not exist, that has been made

---

8   Ireland is a particularly interesting case of the use of the past. The more I look at Irish literature, the more it seems to me that the quintessential Irish utopia is an Irish past that never existed. I have begun to wonder if the Irish students of utopianism should be reading historical novels rather than looking for more works written explicitly as utopias. For example, one book written as a eutopia reads as much like a historical novel as it does as a eutopia. *The Professor in Erin*, by Charlotte Elizabeth McManus, presents a parallel history, which is based on the assumption that the Irish defeated the English at the Battle of Kinsale in 1602. As a result, Ireland becomes a eutopia.

9   On Sparta, see, for example, Ollier; Rawson; and Tigerstedt; on monasticism in More, see, for example, Duhamel; and Gordon; on the Tao and anarchism in Le Guin, see, for example, Bain.

better in memory, with the pasts that make us uncomfortable or embarrassed conveniently forgotten.[10]

Conclusion

As human beings, we look both backwards and forwards, always moving from an ever-receding past into an always-unreachable future. Therefore, it is hardly surprising that one of our cultural artifacts, Utopia, does the same. And, always discontented but hopeful, we re-write our pasts and put the better version into the future. Utopias are repositories of our hopes and fears, both individual and collective. And some, fearful and hopeful, actively foster change to bring us closer to our dreams and farther from our nightmares. At times, such change becomes a real possibility, not just a dream, and our individual and collective energies achieve at least some of what we hoped for. Usually what we accomplish is less than we desired, and, after a rest, we dream again, achieve something, and dream again. In some places at some times, we have reached at least some approximation of past utopias. The starving peasants of More's day do not exist in the developed world, although they still exist elsewhere in the world; and there are people in the developed world living lives that make one wonder at times if we have achieved anything. But we have. And we have because we have dreamed. And, thankfully, we still dream.

10   For studies of utopianism that discuss nostalgia, see Battaglia; Lerner; Flinn; and Shklar. Baccolini and Geoghegan have explored the idea of memory in particular texts. It is clear that certain classic texts in the genre were backward looking, most notably More's *Utopia*. And Orwell's *Nineteen Eighty-Four* is well-known for its depiction of the control of the past as a way of controlling the present and the future, a mechanism in general use by governments today. See Adelson; and Blanchard.

Works Cited

Adelson, Joseph. "The Self and Memory in *1984*: In the Labyrinth of Political Deception." *American Educator* 7.3 (Fall 1983): 12–15, 40, 42.

Baccolini, Raffaella. "'It's not in the womb the damage is done': Memory, Desire and the Construction of Gender in Katharine Burdekin's *Swastika Night*." *Le trasformazioni del narrare*. Ed. E. Siciliani, A. Cecere, V. Intonti, and A. Sportelli. Fasano: Schena, 1995. 293–309.

—— "Journeying through the Dystopian Genre: Memory and Imagination in Burdekin, Orwell, Atwood, and Piercy." *Viaggi in Utopia*. Ed. Raffaella Baccolini, Vita Fortunati, and Nadia Minerva. Ravenna: Longo, 1993. 343–57.

—— "'A useful knowledge of the present is rooted in the past': Memory and Historical Reconciliation in Ursula K. Le Guin's *The Telling*." *Dark Horizons: Science Fiction and the Dystopian Imagination*. Ed. Raffaella Baccolini and Tom Moylan. New York: Routledge, 2003. 113–34.

Bailyn, Bernard. *"To Begin the World Anew": The Genius and Ambiguities of the American Founders*. New York: Knopf, 2003.

Bain, Dena C. "The *Tao Te Ching* as Background to the Novels of Ursula K. Le Guin." *Extrapolation* 21.3 (Fall 1980): 209–22.

Battaglia, Beatrice. *Nostalgia e mito nella distopia inglese: Saggi su Oliphant, Wells, Forster, Orwell, Burdekin*. Ravenna: Longo, 1998.

Blanchard, Lydia. "Memory, Authority, and Feeling in Orwell's Concept of History." *Papers in Comparative Studies* 4 (1985): 23–34.

Bloch, Ernst. *The Principle of Hope*. Trans. Neville Plaice, Stephen Plaice, and Paul Knight. 3 Vols. Oxford: Blackwell, 1986.

The Correspondence of Thomas Carlyle and Ralph Waldo Emerson 1834–1872, 2nd edn. 2 Vols. Ed. Charles E. Norton. Boston: James R. Osgood, 1883.

Cox, Harvey. "Fantasy and Utopia: A Theological Essay on Festivity and Fantasy." *The Feast of Fools*. Cambridge, Massachusetts: Harvard University Press, 1969. 82–97.

Dohrman, H.T. *California Cult: The Story of "Mankind United."* Boston: Beacon, 1958.

Duhamel, P. Albert. "Medievalism of More's *Utopia*." *Studies in Philology* 52 (1955): 99–126.

Festinger, Leon, Henry W. Riecken, and Stanley Schachter. *When Prophecy Fails*. Minneapolis: University of Minnesota Press, 1956.

Fitting, Peter. "Utopias Beyond Our Ideals: The Dilemma of the Right-Wing Utopia." *Utopian Studies* 2.1–2 (1991): 95–109.

Flinn, Caryl. *Strains of Utopia: Gender, Nostalgia, and Hollywood Film Music*. Princeton: Princeton University Press, 1992.

Geoghegan, Vincent. "The Utopian Past: Memory and History in Edward Bellamy's *Looking Backward* and William Morris's *News from Nowhere*." *Utopian Studies* 3.2 (1992): 75–90.

—— "Remembering the Future." *Utopian Studies* 1.2 (1990): 52–68.

Goodwin, Barbara. "The 'Authoritarian' Nature of Utopia." *Radical Philosophy* 32 (1982): 23–7.

—— "Utopia Defended Against the Liberals." *Political Studies* 28.3 (1980): 384–400.

Gordon, Walter M. "The Monastic Achievement and More's Utopian Dream." *Medievalia et Humanistica* 9 (1979): 199–214.

Gutiérrez, Gustavo. *A Theology of Liberation: History, Politics, Salvation*. Trans. Caridade Inda and John Eagleson. Maryknoll: Orbis, 1973.

Hartsock, Nancy C.M. *The Feminist Standpoint Revisited and Other Essays*. Boulder: Westview, 1998.

Hoffer, Eric. *The True Believer: Thoughts on the Nature of Mass Movements*. New York: Harper and Row, 1951.

Lerner, Laurence. "Arcadia and Utopia." *The Uses of Nostalgia*. New York: Schocken, 1972. 81–104.

MacLeish, Archibald. "Preface to an American Manifesto." *Forum* 91.4 (1934): 195–8.

Mannheim, Karl. *Ideology and Utopia: An Introduction to the Sociology of Knowledge*. Trans. Louis Wirth and Edward Shils. New York: Harcourt, Brace & Co., 1936.

Manuel, Frank E. (ed.). *Utopias and Utopian Thought*. Boston: Beacon, 1967.

Marx, Karl. "Introduction." *Contribution to the Critique of Hegel's Philosophy of Law*. 1844. *Karl Marx and Friedrich Engels. Collected Works*. London: Lawrence & Wishart, 1975. Vol.3: 175–87.

—— "Preface." *A Contribution to the Critique of Political Economy*. 1859. *Karl Marx and Friedrich Engels. Collected Works*. London: Lawrence & Wishart, 1987. Vol.29: 261–5.

Molnar, Thomas. *Utopia: The Perennial Heresy*. New York: Sheed & Ward, 1967.

Moylan, Tom. *Demand the Impossible: Science Fiction and the Utopian Imagination*. London: Methuen, 1986.

—— *Scraps of the Untainted Sky: Science Fiction, Utopia, Dystopia*. Boulder: Westview, 2000.

Mumford, Lewis. *The Story of Utopias*. London: Harrap, 1923.

Ollier, F. *Le mirage Spartiate; Étude sur l'idealisation de Sparte dans l'antiquité grecque de l'origine jusqu'aux Cyniques*. New York: Arno, 1973.

Polak, Fred L. *The Image of the Future: Enlightening the Past, Orientating the Present, Forecasting the Future*. Trans. Elise Boulding. 2 Vols. Leyden: A.W. Sythoff/New York: Oceana, 1961.

Popper, Karl. *The Open Society and its Enemies*. 4th edn. revised. 2 Vols. Princeton: Princeton University Press, 1962.

Rawson, Elizabeth. *The Spartan Tradition in European Thought*. Oxford: Clarendon, 1969.

Rose, Lisle A. "A Bibliographical Survey of Economic and Political Writings, 1865–1900." *American Literature* 15 (1944): 381–410.

Sandburg, Carl. "Washington Monument by Night." *Slabs of the Sunburnt West*. New York: Harcourt, Brace, 1922. 18–19.

Sargent, Lyman Tower. "Authority & Utopia: Utopianism in Political Thought." *Polity* 14.4 (1982): 565–84.

—— "Human Nature and the Radical Vision." *Nomos XVII: Human Nature in Politics. Yearbook of the American Society for Political and Legal Philosophy*. Ed. J. Roland Pennock and John W. Chapman. New York: New York University Press, 1977. 250–61.

—— "The Necessity of Utopian Thinking: A Cross-National Perspective." *Thinking Utopia*. Ed. Jorn Rüsen, Michael Fehr, and Thomas W. Rieger. New York: Berghahn, forthcoming.

—— "A Note on the Other Side of Human Nature in the Utopian Novel." *Political Theory* 3.1 (1975): 88–97.

—— "Revolution, Evolution, and Reform." *Anarchy 114* 10.8 (1970): 253–7.

—— "The Three Faces of Utopianism Revisited." *Utopian Studies* 5.1 (1994): 1–37.

—— "Utopische Literatur und die Schaffung nationaler und personaler Identitäten." Trans. Frank Born. *Die Unruhe der Kultur: Potentiale des Utopisten*. Ed. Jörn Rüsen, Michael Fehr, and Annelie Ramsbrock. Weilerswist: Velbrück Wissenschaft, 2004. 125–33.

—— "Utopianism and National Identity." *CRISPP: Critical Review of International Social and Political Philosophy* 3.2–3 (2000): 87–106.

—— "Utopianism and the Creation of New Zealand National Identity." *Utopian Studies* 12.1 (2001): 1–18.

—— "Women in Utopia." *Comparative Literature Studies* 10.4 (1973): 302–16.

—— (ed.). *Extremism in America: A Reader*. New York: New York University Press, 1995.

Shklar, Judith. "The Political Theory of Utopia: From Melancholy to Nostalgia." Manuel. 101–15.

Skinner, B.F. *Walden Two*. New York: Macmillan, 1948.

Skinner, Quentin. *Liberty Before Liberalism*. Cambridge: Cambridge University Press, 1998.

Songs of the Workers. Chicago: International Workers of the World, 1956.

Talmon, Jacob L. *Utopianism and Politics*. London: Conservative Political Centre, 1957.

Taylor, Walter Fuller. *The Economic Novel in America*. Chapel Hill: University of North Carolina Press, 1942.

Tigerstedt, E.N. *The Legend of Sparta in Classical Antiquity*. 3 Vols. Stockholm: Almquist & Wiksell, 1965–1978.

Tillich, Paul. "Critique and Justification of Utopia." Manuel. 296–309.

—— "Kairos und Utopie." *Zeitschrift für evangelische Ethik* 3 (1959): 325–31.
—— "The Political Meaning of Utopia." *Political Expectation.* Trans. William J. Crout, Walter Bense, and James L. Adams. New York: Harper & Row, 1971. 125–80.
—— *Die politische Bedeutung der Utopie im Leben der Völker.* Berlin: Weiss, 1951.

RAFFAELLA BACCOLINI AND TOM MOYLAN

Conclusion: Utopia as Vision

As we close this volume, we want to thank this immediate community of scholars for their contributions. As is usual in utopian studies, the real work grew out of this collective effort, and each of us has learned from the other as we have explored these matters of Utopia, method, and vision. And so, we end with a meditation on Utopia that grows from our reading of the ideas and words of our *UMV* colleagues.

In one way or another, we recognize that any of us working on Utopia struggles against the spirit of the time. In our opening paragraph, we reported instances of the cooptation of Utopia, but as Lucy Sargisson said, in the proposal for her essay, Utopia is also "rejected, ignored, and vilified by scholars of politics" as well as policy makers and the general public. And so, as Lyman Tower Sargent reminds us, Utopia "can be repressed, suppressed – including by poverty – or displaced" (310) or, at best, as Ken Roemer observes, it "seems to have retreated to the margins" (132).

Yet, as Peter Fitting argues, there is a place "for utopian studies or Utopia itself in these increasingly dark times" (259) There is a "need for utopian imagining, even as these visions and descriptions are not meant to be taken literally, but [...] to remind us of all that we lack and are denied" (Fitting 259). Informing such utopian need is, as Greg Claeys notes, the double motivation of fulfilling "desire" and satisfying "want" (90), or, as Raffaella Baccolini claims, a "desire for change, for a better place, and a better life," even as that desire is always best accompanied by the memory of a "slight suffering" (159, 162). However, Claeys rightly complicates the discussion of desire by pointing out three types – "the desire for power; sexual desire; and the quest for property and ostentation" – that nineteenth-century British utopias, depending on their standpoint, tried variously to control or fulfill (97). Indeed, his discussion of these utopias' efforts to manage the period's "unleashed [...] passions for wealth and power" resonates with the concerns of contemporary utopias as they confront the global system of commodified desire and rampant "corruption" and power (Claeys 90).

Utopia, therefore, is as timely as ever. This utopian need, as Ruth Levitas puts it, is continually "born out of a conviction and two questions. The conviction is 'it doesn't have to be like this.' The questions are, 'how, then should we live?' and 'how can that be?'" (48). However varied the answers to these questions, the utopian response must be, as Tom Moylan puts it, a matter of "strong thought" (215) and usually, as Vince Geoghegan adds, a matter of realism. Here Geoghegan cites Roberto Unger's claim that "we must be visionaries to become realists" (77): for "if one does not succumb to a simplistic utopianism/realism distinction, one is left with a cluster of ways of thinking about the future, each possessing different objectives, forms, contents, methods of assessment, and, let it be said, differing strengths and weaknesses" (Geoghegan 77). Indeed, Claeys demonstrates that, in the history of (at least British) utopias, there has long been a realist strand in which social needs such as "scarcity, sin, crime, and malevolence are controlled rather than wished away" (104). Thus, in Phil Wegner's words, the "no where" of Utopia "becomes reinscribed as 'now here,'" even as that present possibility pulls us into the future (124); or, as Baccolini says, "the utopian moment [...] [is] a matter of linking the 'never more' of nostalgia with the 'Not Yet' of utopian possibility" (176). Utopia therefore meets a "fundamental need in our present [...] to re-invent [itself] as much as we need to re-imagine our collective belonging to a truly global community" (Wegner 127).

This recognition of the centrality of community to the utopian project runs through all of the essays in this collection, and it resounds both at the level of method and of vision. As Fitting reminds us, in a reference to the entire field of utopian studies, the "interlocutors [in this scholarly project] have all been or become friends" (257). Thus in our method and form, as Naomi Jacobs observes, in what she calls the "Beloved Community," we "re-affirm the vitality of utopian hope and embody the practice of living this hope within a community of others" (227, 229). If this is true in the study of Utopia, it is perhaps even more true and necessary at the level of political life: by participating in an engaged movement such as WCAR, the World Social Forum, or others we are, as Hoda Zaki suggests, "inventing and fashioning a more democratic version of [civic community] to better prepare for the struggles ahead" (294).

This invocation of community or, what Fitting calls "the sense that another world [is] possible" (249), reminds us that Utopia's vocation of producing alternate visions is important because such anticipations, articulated in a "future public tense" (Jacobs 229), reach "beyond the restricted public of the already politicized and [speak] to a wider audience which often [seems] to no longer believe in the possibility of desirable or feasible alternatives to the fundamental insufficiency of the present" (Fitting 252).

In this process, Utopia gives us a new sense of space and time. Indeed, Zaki's discussion of the importance of the role of institutional space in utopian practice (citing the experience of traditional black colleges that arose in the American South after the Civil War) is an apt example of a social space within which a utopian vision and practice developed and still carries on. Zaki describes such intentional locations as "organizing space[s]" within which the process of utopian action can develop (284). A different sense of utopian space – more personal and yet political – emerges in Levitas's discussion of the layered locale of Hammersmith (in which Morris's, her parents', and her own life intersect). Here memory joins the future, as Utopia provides "a standpoint of judgement," and at least "a possibility for consideration, if not necessarily a possibility" (49). Thus, as Baccolini also argues, memory, even in its nostalgic mode, can create a connection (as in Hammersmith between "the aesthetics of the built environment, the nature of work, the quality of human relationships, the fundamental economic and political structures of the whole society") that nurtures "the process of transformation, the path from here to there" (Levitas 49).

As well, Utopia generates a new range of temporal perspectives. On the one hand, Zaki and Moylan both note the more ephemeral nature of utopian intervention, what Moylan calls the *"half-life"* of Utopia (216). As Zaki sees the temporary space of WCAR in utopian terms, she reminds us just how much a certain "temporariness" is required of all utopian practice, so that even within "already existing

utopias" (as texts or as lived communities or politics) an "open,"
"critical," and "temporary" "utopian energy" (to use Sargent's term)
must be constantly produced to keep utopian spaces themselves from
imploding into closed, ideological zones that deny the very utopianism
that produced them in the first place. To paraphrase Baccolini, an
"authentic" utopian process can be seen as a matter of "cracking the
image" of a fixed past, present, or indeed utopia (186). Yet Utopia
also has a long vision. For example, in his discussion of religion,
Geoghegan reminds us of Bloch's sense of the duration of Utopia:
"indeed one of Bloch's great contributions was that he wished to
celebrate the commanding achievements of the human imagination,
artistic and religious conceptions of the sublime, which lay far beyond
any possibility of accomplishment in the conceivable future" (77). In
this sense, Utopia carries across time, in memory, in intertextuality, in
what Bloch would call "heritage," and in political practices. Utopia
can therefore produce what Moylan sees as "temporal solidarity"
(218).

We need to remember, however, that Utopia's refunctioning of
space and time always occurs and must always be regarded in a
context of historical and cultural specificity. While all of the contributors, in one way or another recognize this, it is perhaps Roemer
who brings this to light in his discussion of reading practices and
Sargisson who does so in the account of her ethnographic practice.
Focusing on the geographical, ethnic, class, and gender diversity of
real readers, Roemer works against one-dimensional interpretations of
utopian texts that are dependent on either "theoretical constructs of
readers" or invocations of "an actual reader" when it is "often the
critic posing as the competent, ideal, or clever reader" (136, 140). This
important methodological contribution at the very least gives us a
better way to read cultural specificity, but it can also change the entire
way we work with Utopia by incorporating reception studies in all of
our approaches. Thus, "placing readers at the forefront of utopian
studies will [...] help us to understand more fully and accurately what
the noplaces of Utopia have done, do, and will do to the someplaces of
our world" (Roemer 154).

Shifting from reading to doing utopianism, Sargisson's extensive
study of more than sixty intentional communities across the U.K. and

New Zealand enables her to recognize the variety of utopian experiments and value their multiple contributions in the face of the monoculture of our global system. As she puts it, "utopias can help us to think about the world in different ways, to break old patterns and paradigms of thought and approach it anew. By showcasing new ways of being, they can inspire or catalyze change" (39). On another, creative, register, Jacobs describes the writing community that generated the path-breaking postmodern utopia of Bernadette Mayer and her New York friends and neighbors as they brought their collective imagination to bear on a playful yet committed shared narrative of a better world that grew from their everyday life experiences, struggles, and joys. And in a more directly political register, Fitting, Moylan, and Zaki detail the utopian charge of movements such as the World Social Forum, the left-wing governments of countries such as Venezuela and Bolivia, and the WCAR.

In this variety of utopian creations and practices, there is nevertheless the persistent presence of what Sargent calls a "utopian energy": i.e., "the will/willingness/ability to create new forms" (309). While he warns us that such an energy can be lost if it is diffused into the limited reform of present social reality, he recognizes that it can play an important role when channeled into "actual utopias or intentional communities" (310). In such contexts, this utopian energy, with its "textual footprints" (Zaki 288), can work in several modes: as "intermittent, a tendency or process, as opposed to Utopia as a monolithic goal" (Jacobs 225); or, as Geoghegan's attribution of Bloch's *Principle of Hope* as "a *flâneur*'s encyclopedia" (76); or, as political movements; or as Unger's visionary realism; or, as the rigorous *totalizing* (see Wegner) analysis proposed by Levitas in her IROS method.

In all these cases, whether they risk being too open or too closed, these utopian alternatives and projects are always political. Indeed, as Jacobs says in her discussion of Mayer: "why would anybody write if they did not want to change the world?" (242). And, as Zaki reminds us, "Marx was right: the aim of knowledge is to change the world and not only to understand it" (294). In short, "politics needs Utopia and Utopia needs politics" (Sargisson 44). Whatever one's definition of politics, Utopia and politics "exist in a symbiotic relationship" and this can be seen whether we consider overt political forms – such as the conceptions of politics "as an activity, a set of assumptions, institutions and/or practices," something that is tied to a particular location, a form of social criticism, or "the negotiation of differences" (Sargisson 25, 26, 33) – or creative forms such as writing, film, architecture, or other cultural practices. All these possibilities may be dangerous – with some leading to compensating and compromising temptations to reform (as cautioned by Wegner, Fitting, Moylan), or others to fundamentalism and authoritarianism (as acknowledged by Jacobs, Sargisson, Sargent) – but it need not be for Utopia may be "dangerous […] [but] it is both omnipresent and necessary," and we need to come to terms with this (Sargisson 25).

Therefore, as Fitting reminds us, "however inhospitable the present moment is to Utopia, it is essential to defend and maintain what we have accomplished in the past few decades, and to continue that scholarly and critical work" (261). We hope through these conversations that the *UMV* project has contributed to this utopian work. In carrying out this work, we have, as often happens in utopian studies, temporarily created a very utopian community and process, one that resonates with we all have written. The best conclusion this can lead us to is that of the last essay in the collection, wherein Sargent says that the only way forward in these dark times is that "we must choose Utopia. We must choose the belief that the world can be radically improved; we must dream socially; and we must allow our social dreams to affect our lives. The choice for Utopia is a choice that the world can be radically improved" (306).

Raffaella Baccolini and Tom Moylan
Limerick-Galway-Bologna-Castell'Arquato, 2003–2006

Notes on Contributors

RAFFAELLA BACCOLINI, Professor of English at the University of Bologna at Forlì, is the author of *Tradition, Identity, Desire: Revisionist Strategies in H.D.'s Late Poetry*, and articles in English and Italian on women's writing, dystopia, sf, poetry, and modernism. She has co-edited several volumes, including *Dark Horizons: Science Fiction and the Dystopian Imagination* (with Tom Moylan) and *Le prospettive di genere: Discipine, soglie, confini*. She is one of the editors of *mediAzioni*, an online journal of interdisciplinary studies on languages and cultures. She is currently working on history and memory in fiction and film.

GREGORY CLAEYS is Professor of the History of Political Thought at Royal Holloway, University of London. He is the author of *Machinery, Money and the Millennium: From Moral Economy to Socialism 1815–1860*; *Citizens and Saints: Politics and Anti-Politics in Early British Socialism*; *Thomas Paine: Social and Political Thought*, and has edited some fifty volumes of primary sources, including sixteen volumes of British utopian writings. He co-edited, with Lyman Tower Sargent, *The Utopia Reader*.

PETER FITTING is Professor Emeritus of French and Cinema Studies at the University of Toronto, and a past president of the Society for Utopian Studies. He has published more than fifty articles on sf, fantasy, and utopia – from critical analyzes of various sf and utopian writers; to theoretical examinations of the reading effect in utopian fiction, the problem of the right-wing utopia, gender and reading, and the work of Fredric Jameson; to overviews, of cyberpunk and of the turn from utopia in the 1990s, or the Golden Age and the foreclosure of utopian discourse in the 1950s; as well as articles on sf and utopian film and architecture. He is the editor of the critical anthology *Subterranean Worlds* and is at work on a collection of his writing on sf.

VINCENT GEOGHEGAN is Professor of Political Theory and Director of Research in Political Theory at Queen's University Belfast. He is the author of *Reason and Eros: The Social Theory of Herbert Marcuse*; *Utopianism and Marxism*; and *Ernst Bloch*. He has published a number of articles on topics such as Irish political thought, early Irish socialism, and writers such as Edward Carpenter and Olaf Stapledon. He is currently exploring the utopian dimensions of religious narrative, attempting to relate this to the development of post-secularism.

NAOMI JACOBS is Professor of English at the University of Maine, where she teaches courses in British and American fiction, women's literature, creative writing, and feminist theory. She is a past president of the Society for Utopian Studies (North America) and author of *The Character of Truth: Historical Figures in Contemporary Fiction*. Her utopian studies publications have included articles on William Morris, Ursula K. Le Guin, Ernest Callenbach, Octavia Butler, and Austin Tappan Wright. Current projects are a novel as well as scholarly pieces on George Orwell, the feminist poetry movement, and the monstrous body in utopia.

RUTH LEVITAS, Professor of Sociology at the University of Bristol, is the author of *The Concept of Utopia* and *The Inclusive Society? Social Exclusion and New Labour*, and editor of *The Ideology of the New Right*. She has published numerous articles on aspects of utopianism and political thought. She is co-founder and chair of the Utopian Studies Society (Europe), and vice-chair of the William Morris Society. Thinking about space, time, and Utopia, she is currently working on two books: *The River Runs Through It*, on William Morris, *News from Nowhere*, and Hammersmith; and *The Imaginary Reconstitution of Society: Utopia as Method*, on Utopia and social science.

TOM MOYLAN is Glucksman Professor of Contemporary Writing and Director of the Ralahine Center for Utopian Studies at the University of Limerick. He is the author of *Demand the Impossible: Science Fiction and the Utopian Imagination*; *Scraps of the Untainted Sky: Science Fiction, Utopia, Dystopia*; and essays on sf, utopia, cultural studies, and theology. He co-edited *Not Yet: Reconsidering Ernst*

Bloch (with Jamie Owen Daniel) and *Dark Horizons: Science Fiction and the Dystopian Imagination* (with Raffaella Baccolini). He is currently working on Irish utopianism and Irish sf.

KENNETH M. ROEMER is an Academy of Distinguished Teachers and Academy of Distinguished Scholars Professor at the University of Texas at Arlington. He has written four books: *The Obsolete Necessity: America in Utopian Writings* (which was nominated for a Pulitzer); *Build Your Own Utopia, Michibata de Deatta Nippon (A Sidewalker's Japan)*; and *Utopian Audiences: How Readers Locate Nowhere*. He has edited *America as Utopia*; *Approaches to Teaching Momaday's* The Way to Rainy Mountain; and *Native American Writers of the United States*, and co-edited *The Cambridge Companion to Native American Literature* (with Joy Porter). He is the author of numerous articles on American literature, Native American studies, and utopian studies. He is a past president of the Society for Utopian Studies.

LYMAN TOWER SARGENT, Professor Emeritus of Political Science at the University of Missouri-St. Louis; Fellow at the Stout Research Centre, Victoria University of Wellington; and Honorary Research Fellow in the Department of History at Royal Holloway and Bedford New College, University of London, is the author of numerous articles and books, including *British and American Utopian Literature, 1516–1985: An Annotated, Chronological Bibliography* and *Contemporary Political Ideologies*; editor of *Extremism in America* and *Political Thought in the United States*; co-author with Lucy Sargisson of *Living in Utopia: Intentional Communities in New Zealand*; and co-editor of *The Utopia Reader* (with G. Claeys). Co-adviser for the Bibliothèque Nationale and the New York Public Library exhibit "Utopie: La quête de la société idéale en Occident/Utopia: The Quest for the Ideal Society in the West," he is co-editor of the exhibit catalogs (with R. Schaer and G. Claeys). He is a past president of the Society for Utopian Studies and founder and former editor of *Utopian Studies*. He is the recipient of the Distinguished Scholar Award of both the Society for Utopian Studies and the Communal Studies Association.

LUCY SARGISSON is Associate Professor in Politics at the University of Nottingham and honorary secretary of the Utopian Studies Society (Europe). She is an editor of *The British Journal of Politics and International Relations*. She is the author of *Contemporary Feminist Utopianism* and *Transforming Bodies and the Politics of Transgression*; and co-author, with Lyman Tower Sargent, of *Living in Utopia: Intentional Communities in New Zealand*. She is a political theorist who has worked on utopias and utopianism, and she is currently working on a book on different manifestations of utopianism in our times, from religious fundamentalism to utopian visions of art and architecture.

PHILLIP E. WEGNER is Associate Professor of English and associate graduate coordinator at the University of Florida, where he teaches modern literatures, narrative theory, cultural studies, and critical theory. He is the author of *Imaginary Communities: Utopia, the Nation, and the Spatial Histories of Modernity* and *Life Between Two Deaths: Repetitions and Revisions in U.S. Culture, 1989–2001*. He has published a range of essays on cinema, sf, utopia, modern literature, Marxism, and critical theory.

HODA M. ZAKI, Professor of Political Science and Director of African American Studies at Hood College, Frederick, Maryland, has published articles on the intersection of sf, race, gender, and utopian thought. She is the author of *Phoenix Renewed:* The Survival and Mutation of Utopian Thought in North American Science Fiction, 1965–1982 and Civil Rights *and Politics at Hampton Institute: The Legacy of Alonzo G. Moron*. She is currently working on a book on the World Conference Against Racism.

Index

Ralahine Utopian Studies

Ralahine Utopian Studies is the publishing project of the Ralahine Centre for Utopian Studies, University of Limerick, and the Department of Intercultural Studies in Translation, Languages and Culture, University of Bologna at Forlì.

The series editors aim to publish scholarship that addresses the theory and practice of utopianism (including Anglophone, continental European, and indigenous and postcolonial traditions, and contemporary and historical periods). Publications (in English and other European languages) will include original monographs and essay collections (including theoretical, textual, and ethnographic/institutional research), English language translations of utopian scholarship in other national languages, reprints of classic scholarly works that are out of print, and annotated editions of original utopian literary and other texts (including translations).

While the editors seek work that engages with the current scholarship and debates in the field of utopian studies, they will not privilege any particular critical or theoretical orientation. They welcome submissions by established or emerging scholars working within or outside the academy. Given the multi-lingual and inter-disciplinary remit of the University of Limerick and the University of Bologna at Forlì, they especially welcome comparative studies in any disciplinary or trans-disciplinary framework.

Those interested in contributing to the series are invited to submit a detailed project outline to Professor Raffaella Baccolini at Department of Intercultural Studies in Translation, Languages and Culture, University of Bologna at Forlì, Forlì, Italy or to Professor Tom Moylan, Dr Michael J. Griffin or Dr Joachim Fischer at the Department of Languages and Cultural Studies, University of Limerick, Republic of Ireland.

E-mail queries can be sent to ireland@peterlang.com.

Series editors:
Raffaella Baccolini (University of Bologna, at Forlì)
Joachim Fischer (University of Limerick)
Michael J. Griffin (University of Limerick)
Tom Moylan (University of Limerick)

Ralahine Centre for Utopian Studies, University of Limerick
http://www.ul.ie/ralahinecentre/

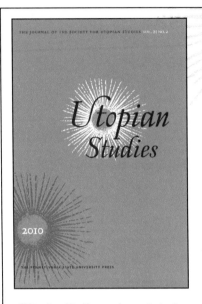